W9-AVS-437

DANGEROUS LESSONS AND GUARDIAN ANGELS

AN AIRLINE PILOT'S STORY

CAPTAIN PJ SPIVACK

P. J. Spivack

Copyright © 2012 by PJ Spivack

All rights reserved,
Including the right of reproduction in whole or in part in any form.

ISBN: 0615588204
ISBN 13: 9780615588209

Library of Congress Control Number: 2012930552
Belle Aire Aviation Press

There must be a place where old pilots go,
When their wings become heavy, when their airspeed gets low,
Where the whiskey is old, and the women are young,
And songs about flying and dying are sung.
Where you'd see all the fellows who'd 'flown west' before,
And they'd call out your name, as you came through the door,
Who would buy you a drink, if your thirst should be bad,
And relate to the others, "He was quite a good lad!"

— Captain Michael J. Larkin, TWA (Ret.),
'Air Line Pilot' magazine, February 1995

In Memoriam

*"To fly west, my friend, is a flight we must all take
for a final check." -- author unknown*

Capt. Fred Bahr- United
Capt. Tony Berko- Capitol
Capt. Robert Bioren-Northwest
Capt. Dave Clapp-ONA
Capt. Gene Duffy- Capitol
Capt. Albert Eisenhut-Atlantis
Capt. E.S. Fox- Capitol
Capt. G.F. Harman-Capitol
Capt. R. Hosford-Capitol
Capt. W. Leeman-Capitol
Capt. C. Lewis-Capitol
Capt. J.R. Lagerquist- Capitol
Capt. August Martin-Seaboard
Capt. R. McNulty-Capitol
Capt. R.L. Moon- Capitol
Capt. G.J. Musante-Capitol
F/O F.J. O'Connell-Capitol
Capt. Lucien Picket- US Airways (Germany)
Capt. W. Reid-Capitol
Capt. John Rogers-Capitol
Capt. Pete Rozday-Capitol
Capt. Johnny Sossaman-Capitol
Capt. Gerald Smallwood- ONA
Capt. Sy Weiner-ONA
Capt. Hank Wharton- Biafra
Capt. D. Wilson-Capitol
Pilot John Harpole- FAA Air Carrier inspector
Pilot Ed Golden
Instructor Pilot Harry Stacy
Pilot Athol Williams

To Laura + Phil
Fair winds + smooth seas!
P J Spevack

To Renee, Sam, and Barbara
This is how the flying was!.

Acknowledgements

Who can write a book and not think of the people along that journey who generously helped, prodded, and gave moral support whenever needed.

Sincere thanks to Dick Croy, and Arlene Usander for their expertise in editing.

My gratitude and *sympathy* to Barbara for reading and re-reading the manuscript in order to help make it the best it could be.

PJS

Contents

Preface   xv
Chapter 1. Scene of the Crash   1
Chapter 2. Beginning of an Airline Career   15
Chapter 3. The Seasoning of an Airline Pilot   31
Chapter 4. The Jet Age   45
Chapter 5. Right Place at the Right Time   59
Chapter 6. Challenge of My Career   75
Chapter 7. Flying the Line   89
Chapter 8. The Vacation   109
Chapter 9. Day at the Office   119
Chapter 10. A Setback…Then Back in the Left Seat   135
Chapter 11. Not What They Seemed to Be   153
Chapter 12. East Meets West   171
Chapter 13. Last Great Cowboys   187
Chapter 14. Approaching Retirement   201
Afterword   217
Glossary   231
Appendix   235
References   281
Bibliography   289
Index   291

Impressions of A Pilot

Flight is freedom in its purest form,
To dance with the clouds which follow a storm;

To roll and glide, to wheel and spin,
To feel the joy that swells within;

To leave the earth with its troubles and fly,
And know the warmth of a clear spring sky;

Then back to earth at the end of a day,
Released from the tensions which melted away.

Should my end come while I am in flight,
Whether brightest day or darkest night;

Spare me your pity and shrug off the pain,
Secure in the knowledge that I'd do it again;

For each of us is created to die,
And within me I know,
I was born to fly.

— G. Claude Stokor

Preface

✶

For an airline pilot, flight is one of the most exciting endeavors imaginable. When we take flight, we are transported into another dimension the moment the wheels leave the ground. Yes, there are rules and regulations to guide us, but the safe outcome of leaving and returning to Mother Earth rests with the pilot. Though largely masters of our own fate, we are often responsible for the fate of hundreds of other lives in addition to our own.

This book contains many stories, all true. Some are amusing; others are sobering, even frightening. They have been told, for the most part, in chronological order. When you read them, keep in mind that many of the airlines I flew for were so-called non-scheduled (charter) airlines. To have survived thirty-five years of piloting with non-scheduled airlines during the '60s, '70s, '80s, and '90s, one had to learn strategies for dodging bullets, both figuratively and occasionally literally, along the way.

These non-scheduled airlines typically flew older models of aircraft, often to unfamiliar airports, some with poor instrument approaches. They employed fewer ground support staff and, in many cases, performed the absolute minimum maintenance required by the FAA. Thus, in those years, non-scheduled airlines tended to experience a higher percentage of incidents or accidents than the scheduled airlines. Many of the stories in this book are a result of such issues.

Airline operations have dramatically changed since the 1960s, when the airline captain was in charge of the airplane in every way, his authority never challenged. All of that has changed now. Innovations in airplane technology, onboard computers, CRM (crew resource management), unions, and new government regulations and procedures have dramatically changed the manner in which an airline captain conducts his or her flight today. Nonetheless, having discussed these changes with many older captains, I can say that most of the older pilots, and many passengers as well, remember those early years with great fondness.

Airplanes have become more reliable. Engine failure and shutdown rates have declined dramatically with the perfection of the jet engine. Aircraft navigation has likewise improved immensely. Flying an ILS (instrument landing system) or GPS (global positioning system) approach is many times safer then flying an NDB (non-directional beacon) approach of the 1960s.

In 1975, I flew my very *first* transatlantic flight as captain of a DC-8 four-engine jet, with 250 passengers onboard. During that flight, I experienced a complete hydraulic system failure, which required an emergency landing. I made the landing with no landing flaps, hydraulic brakes, or hydraulic flight controls. It was trial by fire for a new captain—and so it seemed to go throughout my airline career. Fortunately, with each experience, or *dangerous lesson,* I seemed to become more prepared for the next. An old friend who was an experienced airline pilot, Captain "Shotgun" Hill, told me long ago, "I'd rather be lucky than good!" "Shotgun" Hill was right about being lucky, although I would add that it wouldn't hurt to have a *guardian angel* as well.

As I look back on my aviation career, I can say that it was a very satisfying, fun-filled, and adventurous experience. Perhaps far more importantly, however, I am proud to state that during my ten million miles of airline flying, I flew every one of the more than one million passengers *safely* to their destinations.

I hope this book helps to serve as inspiration for anyone considering a career in aviation. To this end, based on the author's thirty-five years of airline flying experience, the Afterword is dedicated to charting a course toward an airline career. If that's your aim, be persistent and never give up.

For the record, I have changed the names of *some* of the people in these stories to *either* protect their privacy, or as in a few cases where the story may be construed to have reflected in a less than positive way.

DANGEROUS LESSONS AND GUARDIAN ANGELS

AN AIRLINE PILOT'S STORY

CHAPTER 1

Scene of The Crash

It's a drizzly morning here in Seattle. I'm looking out the window of my den, and my mind is wandering. I think for a moment about some of the highlights of my career as an airline pilot...and then I remember an event from another rainy morning.

Jamaica, New York, 1952. I was twelve years old, lying in bed half asleep, when suddenly, with engines roaring, a huge cargo plane sounded as if it was about to come through the window of my bedroom. A few seconds later, there was an unmistakable explosion. I jumped out of bed, threw my clothes on, and ran toward a billow of black smoke and the smell of burning rubber a block away.

The scene was chaotic. Emergency vehicles were just beginning to arrive, and badly injured people were everywhere among the scattered metal parts of a large airplane. A huge radial airplane engine was sitting on top of a crushed car, with an unlucky, motionless person inside. Parts of the airplane were still burning, and a cargo of flowers and lingerie was strewn everywhere. I wandered around the scene in awe. I had never been so close to a large airplane, never mind that this one had been reduced mostly to bits and pieces.

A few feet away were the control wheel and part of the cockpit. I noticed a black glove and wondered if it had belonged to the pilot. Why wasn't he wearing it? Inching closer, I saw that part of him was, and I got sick as I never had before, or since.

For weeks, I couldn't get that awful scene out of my mind. Why did airplanes crash? What were the pilots of that one thinking in the seconds before it disintegrated? It is hard to know how much I was affected by that horrible accident; the finality of the crash seemed incomprehensible.

Gazing from the window of my cozy den in Seattle, I wondered if there was information on this crash that had occurred more than fifty-five years ago.

I Googled: "Cargo plane crashes in Jamaica, NY." There it was! The hair on the back of my neck stood up.

New York, April 6 (AP)

A low-flying cargo plane loaded with Easter flowers smashed into the heart of a residential borough of Queens today, killing five persons and turning a block-long stretch of homes into flaming terror. The twin-engine C-46 dove out of a heavy rain with a thunderous explosion. It was the fifth airplane accident of its kind in the metropolitan area in less than four months.... Killed today were the plane's two crew members, a police inspector and two occupants of houses set afire. The pilot was identified as William B. Crockett, Jr., and the police inspector identified as Thomas V. Boylan.

The plane, trying to recover from an abortive landing attempt at Idlewild International Airport, thundered low over the roofs of a half-mile stretch of buildings, then crashed with a bomb-like explosion in Jamaica.... Smoke and fire camouflaged the scene of twisted wreckage and shattered homes for hours after the crash. The center of the crash was at the intersection of 88th Avenue and 169th Street in the Jamaica section, near a busy subway terminal, and in a substantial middle-class residential section.

A moment after I read it, that news article hit me hard. For the first time, I realized that the airplane that came close to crashing into our house and killing me in 1952 was the same make and model that would not only launch my airline career fourteen years later but would also make three more attempts on my life.

I spent much of that rainy day pondering the twists and turns life takes us through: how we live hanging on a thread yet go to sleep expecting to wake up the next morning as we do every other day in our lives.

As I thought about my childhood and first aviation experiences, I remembered my mom taking me to LaGuardia Airport. After what I had seen a few weeks earlier, my mom was sure I would never want to fly on an airplane. I remember standing near a window in the airport terminal and looking down on an American Airlines Douglas DC-6. It had just taxied in, and the passengers were deplaning. When the captain of the plane walked down the steps to the tarmac below, it was apparent how much the passengers admired him. After all, he had just gotten them safely to their destination. He was quite an impressive sight in his uniform, complete with pilot's wings and four stripes. He and most of the passengers had smiles on their faces, and I began to wonder whether flying was necessarily all that bad. The uniforms and those big, sleek planes looked mighty interesting to me. Then mom took me up another wide set of stairs toward a higher terminal level, and a moment later she said, "Look, there's Charles Laughton, the famous movie actor. Why don't you ask him for his autograph?" I obediently walked up to Mr. Laughton, and in my twelve-year-old voice, I asked him if he would mind giving me his autograph. I'll never forget his response. It was, "Get away from me, kid!" I guess it comes as no surprise that I have never enjoyed watching any of his old movies.

Well, mom and I looked on as the airplanes taxied in and taxied out for takeoff that day and I must admit it took the edge off my first traumatic experience with aviation. My mom and dad were very supportive of any ideas I had about my future career choices. Becoming an airline pilot, however, was not among those early choices.

1959
You're in the Army Now!

After I graduated from high school and finished technical college, I decided to join the army rather than wait to be drafted. (The draft ended in 1973.)

The army recruiter looked as though he had stepped out of a poster, an army ranger of huge proportions. He was blond-haired with a ruddy complexion. The brass on his uniform shined like small mirrors, and his shirt was so starched that I could just imagine how uncomfortable it must be. He was so completely dedicated to his task that I was nearly certain I could believe most every word he uttered. I mentioned that I was interested in learning to fly helicopters.

The recruiter tested me to determine whether I qualified for army helicopter school. I passed the test, and he told me it was all set up for me to attend after basic training; I would be sent to OCS training and then to Ft. Rucker, Alabama, to enter flight training.

However, that is not what happened. Instead of helicopter school, I was stationed in Frankfurt, Germany, as a radio station engineer for the prestigious army unit, AFN (Armed Forces Network) Europe. As military assignments went, this turned out to be an excellent duty assignment; I lived in the Von Breuning castle in Hoechst, near Frankfurt, Germany. The castle was built in the fourteenth century, complete with a moat, tower, and beautiful gardens. We each had our own room, complete with a maid; military duty didn't get any better than that.

"The Piper Cub is the safest airplane in the world; it can just barely kill you."

–Max Stanley, Northrup test pilot

In 1960, I joined the military aero club on Sembach Airbase and was just able to afford the four dollars per hour fee for the Piper J-3, plus two dollars per hour for the instructor. My first flight was on March 26, 1961. After fifteen minutes in the air, I was so scared that I told the instructor, Harry Stacy, that I wanted him to land the Piper Cub and terminate the lesson. He said, "You paid for an hour, and I like to fly!" After an hour with Harry, I felt better and decided to continue my lessons.

Sembach Airbase Aeroclub. Piper J-3 Cub, N9829F, aircraft in background, used for first flight lesson, March 26, 1961.

Harry Stacy was a handsome man in his early thirties, of slight build and with blond hair and a very ready smile. It was so infectious that when he smiled, you just had to smile too. Had he been slovenly or morose, I am sure I never would have continued to fly. When I passed my private pilot's license test in Frankfurt, Germany, in August 1962, Harry told me he was really proud of me. He was a great guy. You know the type: you don't really know him well but you have the sense that if you did, the two of you would become great friends. We kept in touch; he was interested in knowing whether I would continue flying and earn more ratings. Sadly, Harry's ending came suddenly and unexpectedly. A little more than two years after that first lesson, in July 1963, Harry married his sweetheart and honeymooned with her in the mountainous area of Skopia, Yugoslavia, which was halfway between Belgrade and Athens. Three weeks after their wedding, Harry, his bride, and a thousand other people were killed in a devastating earthquake in Skopia. I was deeply saddened at hearing of Harry's sudden passing.

Homeward Bound

In October, my discharge orders came to ship home. I was to leave from Bremen, Germany, on a troopship. All my clothes, toilet articles, and underwear, along with every other soldier's possessions, were thrown into the cargo hold of this ugly grey ship. The next fifteen days were the most wretched of my life. It was November, and it was a toss-up as to which was rougher—the North Sea or the Atlantic. In addition, space on these boats was very limited. The bunks were stacked four high, and I drew the least desirable, with just fifteen inches of space between the top of the bunk and the ceiling. Luckily, I wasn't claustrophobic.

After five days at sea, the smell was horrific, especially as hundreds of guys unable to change their skivvies were crowded into a small space. Whenever I could, I went out on deck until a large wave would break over it, forcing everyone to run below.

The worst day of the sail occurred the day I rode the can in a row of bathroom stalls like a rodeo cowboy as the ship wallowed in forty-foot seas; the guy next to me lost his breakfast, the ship rolled, and suddenly this soup of a breakfast was all over my right foot. That was it: I lost mine, too.

Well, I became a pilot despite the army recruiter's reneged promise of helicopter school, but after those awful fifteen days at sea, I think the army may have had the last laugh after all.

When I came back home to my welcoming mom and dad, they were as happy as I was—and I was especially happy about the improvement in food. Breakfast was now onions and eggs on New York bagels; creamed beef on toast (S.O.S as it was called) was a faint memory. However, after a week, I knew I couldn't stay in my hometown. I had seen too much of the world; travel, foreign intrigue, and adrenalin had become my addiction.

I hired on with International Telephone and Telegraph (ITT) as a field radio engineer in Greenland on a Department of Defense operation called Project Dew Drop. I was based on Pingersuite Mountain. Perhaps you've heard the expression "being sent to the Thule's." Well, Thule, Greenland, was the main base, where there were people and activities. Pingersuite Mountain was a place where there was nothing! I take that back. There *were* two huge, football-field–sized parabolic antennas and large rooms full of nine-foot-tall racks of klystron-powered transmitters and super-cooled parametric amplifiers…names of things that most people never knew existed.

At the site with me were a Danish scientist, another American field engineer, and, most importantly, an old Swede from Minnesota. He was our diesel engine mechanic. Arne kept the two large diesel generators running so that we could power the communication system and the electric heaters, which were there to keep us from freezing to death in the minus-forty-degree Fahrenheit outside air temperatures. The supervisor at our site was a man named Blevan. I didn't know much about him, mainly because he never said much. He had worked year after year without a vacation. A typical contract was one year, and I learned that most people just barely lasted a year; the isolation was pretty extreme. Blevan was on his fourth contract when I arrived at Pingersuite Mountain and was introduced to him. When you said hello or asked him a question, he just stared at you. If he did bestow a response, it was usually one or two minutes later. The delay in Blevan's response and his intense stare were very odd, to say the least. I have no idea what became of Blevan. When my contract ended, I left P-mountain on the first flight out of the main base at Thule.

The one thing in short supply at P-Mountain—other than people—was laughter.

Blevan was away for a week back at headquarters in New Jersey, and a temporary replacement flew up to be the site supervisor. I was the next senior field engineer and devised a harmless little prank for the visiting supervisor. The powerful tropospheric transmitters fed their energy to the huge antennas through a pair of rectangular, gold-plated waveguides. There was a dark, cold tunnel where the waveguide ran toward the antenna.

When the supervisor showed up, we soon found out that he was another very serious fellow seemingly devoid of humor. As soon as he arrived on the communications site, he said that he wanted to have me arrange a meeting with all of the site personnel. I introduced him to the Danish scientist and then to Arne, the old Swede mechanic, but told him that the other field engineer *was somewhat antisocial* and preferred living in the barely heated, unlighted waveguide tunnel. The supervisor wanted to meet him anyway and, despite my warnings that he would get angry if he was disturbed on his time off, the supervisor insisted. We gave him a flashlight, and he went into the waveguide tunnel and started calling the engineer's name. The other engineer was a huge guy and was wearing an arctic winter hooded coat. As it turned out, he was just coming around a door opening deep inside the tunnel as the new supervisor was approaching, just like a scary scene out of the terrifying movie, *The Thing.*

Both the supervisor and the engineer yelled out in horror! The supervisor couldn't get out of the waveguide tunnel fast enough and said he had seen the other engineer and didn't need to know any more about him. He told me that he would definitely consider my advice as long as he was there. That evening after supper and a few shots of Russian vodka, the waveguide door banged open. The supervisor tensed up and was about to run out of the dining room when we all started laughing about the prank we had just pulled. He started laughing, too, and after a few more shots of Russian vodka, he turned out to be a pretty good guy after all. That was my most noteworthy experience in what was otherwise a pretty dreary place, P-mountain, Greenland. It was part of the then-secret DEW line, which required top-secret clearance. I had one because of working for AFN while I was in the military. Fortunately, due to all this deprivation, the work paid well, and I saved a lot of money.

About the only recreation at P-Mountain was operating the ham radio station that was provided for us. It was a high quality Collins KWS-1 transmitter and a Collins 75A-4 receiver. The antennas were big high gain rhombic wire antennas in addition to a huge twenty element log periodic beam. The station's on air signal was extremely strong, mainly due to the impressively large antennas. It was almost always possible, to make very long distance (DX contacts), as well as phone patches to our families, during even mediocre radio (wave) propagation conditions. Of course using the country radio call sign prefix for Greenland (OX) meant that many ham radio stations around the world would want to communicate with us, due to the rarity of ham radio stations in Greenland.

When the one-year contract ended, I could afford to begin training as a commercial pilot at Zahns Airport in Amityville, Long Island. It wasn't long before I had my commercial pilot's license as well as an instrument and multi-engine rating. Gradually, I began thinking about becoming an airline pilot.

As there was not much hiring going on with the airlines at that time, I wrote to my old boss, Frank Mortensen, who was chief engineer of the entire AFN Europe network. To my surprise, he had a job for me. The chief engineer of AFN in Verdun, France, had just announced his retirement, and Frank offered me the position. "I know your work; the job is yours," he said. I moved to France and settled in at the U.S. army base in Verdun in the bachelor officers' quarters.

Verdun is a very interesting and attractive small town on the Meuse River in northeastern France. At the time I was there, the population was twenty-five thousand. Located midway between the German border near Saarbrucken and the iconic city of Paris, it has long held significant military value; many battles have been fought there. Unlike the inhabitants of Paris, those of Verdun were friendly and welcoming. Verdun had small cafes where you could sit and read the *International Herald Tribune* and enjoy delicious hot chocolate with wonderful croissants and then stroll along the Meuse river and watch the kids fishing happily, seemingly unaware of the horrors that took place there during World War I and World War II.

In 1884, during the Franco-Prussian War, a series of forts built near Verdun were of particular use during World War I. I spent weekends exploring these dark, evil-smelling killing grounds of the underground fortifications known as Fort De Vaux and Fort Douaumont. They were attacked in 1916 by Bismarck's soldiers, and in one of the war's most dastardly acts, mustard gas was used to kill starving French soldiers trapped in Fort de Vaux.

Walking through these tunnels, flashlight in hand, the hair on the back of my neck stood up as I imagined the horrors that took place there. Verdun is like this. Battle-scarred hills, neverending white crosses in the military cemeteries, and hundreds of thousands of human bones of unidentified soldiers on display at the monument called the Ossuaire at Douaumont. All this in contrast to the sweet smell of fresh loaves of baguettes from the town's patisserie and the incredible tournedos (filet of beef) at Le Coq Hardi, one of the best restaurants in which I have ever eaten.

Expect the Unexpected

The Verdun Aero Club had a World War I Stampe biplane, (a two-winged double decker) similar to the British Tiger Moth. On a beautiful June day with a high cloud ceiling, I invited my French girlfriend, Evelynne, to go flying. Evelynne was a petite, very gentle and pretty, dark-haired young woman in her twenties who worked for the U.S. military as a secretary and translator. I wanted to show her some aerobatics. We strapped on our freshly-packed parachutes, and after a quick briefing to Evelynne as to how to deploy the parachute by pulling the D-ring, she climbed into the front open cockpit and I followed her into the rear cockpit.

We got a hand-prop start from another pilot and slowly tax-ied toward the takeoff end of the runway. After I was cleared for takeoff, the Stampe was airborne within six hundred feet, and we entered a slow climb to four thousand feet. Upon reaching altitude, I did two clearing turns and decided to demonstrate a spin to Evelynne. A little back stick pressure, and as the airspeed decreased below 40 mph, the plane entered a stall. I applied full left rudder pedal.

With the nose pointing nearly straight down, the plane started spinning very fast in a counter-clockwise rotation. A biplane spins two to three times faster than an ordinary airplane, and sometimes it takes two heart-stopping turns to stop the rotation. Even the pilot can begin to wonder if he'll come out of the spin. After four complete turns, I applied full right pedal and forward control stick. As we leveled off, I looked at Evelynne in the mirror in front of the forward cockpit, on the trailing edge of the upper wing. She seemed to be doing well enough, and I thought I could execute one more aerobatic maneuver before she would signal she'd had enough.

At four thousand feet, I did my clearing turns again to ensure that there were no other planes nearby and then entered a shallow dive. At 120 mph, I applied firm back pressure on the stick. We were pointing straight up when I increased the back pressure, and the nose of the old Stampe compliantly came over the top of the loop. The world was upside down, as it was supposed to be—but there was one major problem. When Evelynne reached reflexively for her stomach due to the sudden G-force of the loop, she'd mistakenly pressed the release button on her seat belt restraint buckle. Gravity had taken over, and she was hanging precariously from the cockpit. I knew she hadn't decided to bail out on purpose—we were having too much fun!

I slammed the control stick full left, and we rolled right-side up. Thank God, she was still in the cockpit! I had serious doubts that she'd have had the presence of mind to pull her parachute's rip cord if she suddenly found herself in free fall several thousand feet above the ground.

It was with a great sense of relief that I flew us back to that little airport. When we landed, I helped Evelynne down from the cockpit and out of her bulky parachute. The moment her arms were free, she smacked me hard across the face. "*What?*" I said, rubbing my cheek. By then, I knew a fair amount about flying, but realized I had a lot to learn about women.

A Life-changing Decision

In March 1965, I obtained my flight instructor's license and began flight instructing part time, some Americans based in Verdun, France. It's often said that a pilot truly learns how to fly when he becomes a flight instructor and tries to teach someone else. I found this to be true. Contemplating strategies to make the science and art and pure joy of flying come alive for someone else gives you new insights about flying. That year, I thought a lot about my first flight instructor, Harry Stacy. I wished he could share with me the secrets that had made him such a wonderful teacher.

One of my students was a Dr. Adams who was an army captain and a general surgeon on the base in Verdun. Adams was a good student and a fast learner. We were having drinks together in the officers' club one evening when I told him that I had always been interested in what went on in the operating room. He told me that he would be happy to have me watch a surgery. One late afternoon, I got a call from Adams; he said he had to do an emergency appendectomy, which I could observe. I drove to the army hospital, met with Doc Adams, and was soon dressed in an operating gown with a surgical head cover. I was instructed on how to scrub my arms and hands and was soon equipped with surgical gloves. A few minutes later, I was standing next to the doctor as he made a neat, straight incision in the patient's abdomen. I breathed deeply as the first wave of dizziness came over me. Then, after using retractors to hold the incision open, Adams reached in and pulled out some of the patient's upper intestine. He asked me to hold these organs for him for a moment while he arranged his operating instruments and sutures. A large wave of nausea enveloped me, which I just barely managed to keep in check. The appendix was quickly removed, the intestines were neatly replaced in the body cavity, and the abdomen was sutured. After the operation was completed, I thanked Dr. Adams for the incredible experience and excused myself to breathe some cool evening air. After numerous, deep, fresh breaths, I felt as good as new again.

Another of my students was Ed Golden, who became a close personal friend of mine. Ed had been an FBI agent and lived with his French wife, Chantal, in a lovely chateau on the edge of town. Ed was a very bright guy and a great student. Soon after Ed began taking flight lessons, his wife of six years became involved with another man and left Ed and their two kids. It was a very sad situation, but Ed carried on and managed to remarry and do a splendid job of raising his two young sons. Ed passed away at only forty-five years of age from heart failure, twelve years later. I was very saddened by Ed's untimely death, as he had become one of my best friends.

The more involved I became in flight instruction, the more I loved flying—and then one day, it dawned on me: I was absolutely certain that I wanted to become an airline pilot. I wanted to fly big, complex airplanes. I began sending out dozens of resumes; however, every application came back rejected. Either the airlines weren't hiring or I didn't have the qualifications they were looking for. *But I persisted!*

CHAPTER 2

1966

Beginning
of an Airline Career

✳

One day, when I least expected it, I received an offer of an airline job—of sorts. It was from a company called U.S. Airways, in Frankfurt, Germany. What I didn't know then was that the company was involved with transporting weapons to various groups in the Congo and Biafra. (Needless to say, this was not the scheduled American air carrier that we know today as US Airways.

The president of the company was a man named Lucien Pickett. Pickett was a tall, rather dapper-looking gentleman in his mid-forties. I was interviewed and hired by Captain Pickett on the spot. He told me we would be flying government-sponsored flights. Problem was, he declined to identify *which government*.

Within a month, I would be an airline pilot. I was given four weeks of ground school and Link Trainer (flight simulation) on the Lockheed L-1049. At the end of the training, I was a qualified co-pilot on the Lockheed Super Constellation. My airline career was finally launched.

Lockheed 1049 Super Constellation-Biafra. Photo courtesy of Pedro Aragao and Airliners.net

My first flight as co-pilot was from Frankfurt to Milan to pick up cargo, and then to Malta. I couldn't understand why the registration number in the weight-and-balance book was different from the one on the tail of the aircraft. When I asked Captain Pickett, he told me the fictitious number had been painted on the tail for anonymity, to fool the aviation authorities. If I was uncomfortable with the fake registration number, I was even less happy to learn that on the last leg of the trip, we would be flying into Port Harcourt, Nigeria. Radio silence would have to be maintained until just before landing because the Federal Nigerians were now actively engaged in shooting down cargo planes.

Although the Nigerian Civil War didn't officially begin until July 1967 when Nigerian troops marched into the country's southeastern provinces, which had proclaimed themselves the Republic of Biafra, *gun running*, the supplying of weapons for opposing factions in the region had begun in 1965. Lucien Pickett and Hank Wharton were involved in that enterprise from the beginning.

Although this was more excitement than I'd bargained for, it was fantastic to be a co-pilot in the right seat of the Super Constellation, even if all I did was read checklists, pull the gear handle up and down, and talk on the radio to ground, tower, and air traffic control. The Constellation was a sleek and complex airplane that looked, smelled, and sounded like the legendary airplane it was. I couldn't blame Captain Pickett for letting me do little hands-on flying except to fly it straight and level over Africa for a while. I was definitely unproven, and there was too much at stake on those flights to take a chance on how good or bad I was. It was my first job as an airline pilot, and I was mighty pleased.

As for the gun running, that was a distraction, from learning to be an airline pilot. I wasn't interested in getting killed delivering guns to anyone, no matter how much more the pay was or how "noble" the cause. What did I know about African politics anyway? From my naive perspective, it appeared that the Federal Nigerians had a much more sophisticated air force, including Mig 17s and L-29 Delfin jet fighters as well as considerable military capability. Though I felt sorry for the Independent Nigerians, it did not seem that they would be successful.

What *was* immediately clear was how dangerous this flying was; when an hour out of Port Harcourt, Captain Pickett turned off the navigation lights and rotating beacon so the airplane wouldn't be seen. You cannot believe how dark it is over Africa at night. There were very few lights on the ground from buildings or cars. As we began our descent, we made one quick radio call, giving the tower a coded message to notify the tower control operator that we were *a friendly* and on our way in. On the ground, during our walk-around inspection, we counted twenty-three bullet holes on the bottom and port side of the aircraft aft of the cargo door. Fortunately, no critical aircraft systems had been punctured. With the noise of the plane's four radial engines and the earphones we wore to monitor the radios, we hadn't heard a thing.

When I returned to Frankfurt after this flight, I had dinner with Julius Graber, a Swiss citizen who was secretary treasurer of U.S. Airways, with whom I became close friends. Julius was one of the most loyal individuals I have ever met. He was of slight build, a very intense man with a pale complexion who was leading a terribly hard life. I learned a few years later that Julius had co-signed a business loan for Lucien Pickett for some aircraft parts, and that Pickett had defaulted on the loan. Graber, being a Swiss citizen, was subjected to a rather harsh Swiss debtor's prison law, which resulted in Julius's wife being arrested and sentenced to prison while her husband repaid the loan. When I met Julius, he was eating only one meal per day. He would eat his meal at the Lufthansa canteen at the Frankfurt airport. To maximize his savings to get his wife out of prison, Julius's one meal a day consisted of a tea bag that he brought to the canteen, using free hot water, and a fifty-*pfennig* (twelve-cent) hard *brotchen* (hard roll) with free butter, mustard or mayonnaise on it.

Julius continued to work for Pickett, as he did not want to let him down. Now that is loyalty! Whenever I saw Julius, I would take him out for lunch or dinner. Every time I offered him some money, he told me how grateful he was but refused to take it. Julius was a very bright, hard-working guy who was intensely sad about the situation with his wife. Several years after I met Julius, his wife died in prison. Julius and I remained good friends until the mid-1990s when he seemed to vanish. All attempts to contact him led to dead ends, and I suspect he has retired from the aviation field or perhaps passed. Julius had many business dealings with Lucien Pickett and suggested that I stay away from the Biafran operation. He said these flights were being organized by the French Secret Service and a group of businessmen from Madrid, including one Otto Skorzeny, the former SS officer who had rescued Mussolini from his captors at a mountain hotel in Campo Imperatore in September 1943.

He also told me that the airplanes were being shot down with greater regularity.

On Pickett's next trip, which I wasn't scheduled for, the aircraft made an air drop of weapons into the Algerian Berber Mountains. Pickett was arrested upon landing, but after paying a fine and spending three days in jail, he was released.

When he got back to Frankfurt, he introduced me to Hank Wharton, whom the company's experienced pilots had nicknamed "Hanky Panky." Wharton's *headquarters* was in room 223 in the Hotel Tivoli in Lisbon, Portugal. I was soon to learn that he took the expression "fly by night" to a whole new level. Wharton was a very interesting character. He was a stocky man with black hair and a light complexion, born Heinrich Wartski in Graz, Austria. He was of German-Polish background and spoke English with a slight but perceptible accent. He had immigrated to the United States and eventually succeeded in earning a very colorful reputation. Wharton told me that he needed a co-pilot to help him ferry some DC-4s from Miami to Amsterdam and Frankfurt. Being young and foolish, I volunteered.

Douglas DC-4 in Africa. Photo courtesy of Steve Fitzgerald and Airliners.net.

Although it was good experience and paid very well, I was appalled at how poorly maintained the aircraft were. Most of the radios didn't work, the engines leaked oil like you wouldn't believe, and I saw more corrosion on those planes than during all of my next forty-five years of flying. (Julius Graber told me that the airplanes were eventually sold to the French Red Cross.)

Sometime after the ferry flights, I learned from Julius that Wharton had been in Amsterdam with a DC-4 Northstar that he claimed to have purchased from the King of Burundi, a central African country. Apparently, there was some question about the authenticity of the registration, but through intervention from the Burundian embassy in Paris, the aviation authorities in Amsterdam released the aircraft for a local test flight after some engine repairs had been completed.

Instead of performing the local test flight, Wharton took the DC-4 Northstar west over the Atlantic and then, without a flight plan, turned south and landed in Frankfurt. After refueling, Wharton flew the Northstar to a small airport in Albenga, Italy. It turned out that the aircraft was going to be used for arms smuggling, financed by a Baron Von Oppenheim. Wharton later claimed that he had confiscated the DC-4 in lieu of payment owed him. After repainting new registration numbers, he flew the plane back to Rotterdam, Holland, where he was met by an arms dealer by the name of Paul Favier. Wharton was given a large sum of money, and with a cargo of 1,100 Thompson .45-caliber submachine guns made in the United States and a valid British import certificate, he took off for Birmingham, England. But instead of landing there, he turned south and flew to Palma Majorca, Spain, where the DC-4 was refueled, and then departed for Algeria. The reason for this subterfuge was that while the Dutch would never have allowed Wharton to depart Holland for Nigeria with a plane load of weapons, he did have a legitimate weapons import certificate for England, which seemed to satisfy the Dutch aviation authorities. Prior to beginning his descent into Birmingham, Wharton radioed saying that he had received a company message diverting the plane to Palma,

Majorca. He landed in Hassi-Messaoud, in North Africa. After refueling, the plane took off for Chad. Unfortunately for Wharton, he ran out of fuel and crashed forty-five miles west of Garoua on a river bank in the Northern Cameroons. Wharton survived the crash and was imprisoned. A couple of months later, he escaped from the Cameroons prison with the help of his younger, very attractive, mini-skirted German girlfriend, Sigunde Harte, and returned to Europe on a French mail boat. Despite his career as an arms dealer and pilot-soldier of fortune, Wharton managed to live to his late eighties, passing away only a few years ago of natural causes!

In March of 1969, Lucien Pickett was ferrying a somewhat derelict DC-4 from Miami to Santa Maria in the Azores via Halifax, Nova Scotia. During each leg of the flight, the airplane had significant maintenance problems, and as a result, several crew members quit and had to be replaced. Finally, about three hours after leaving Halifax on the long overwater portion of the flight, Captain Pickett made an emergency **Mayday** radio call. The airplane was in a winter storm over the north Atlantic and taking on a heavy load of ice. The aircraft's de-icing boots weren't working, and the four-engine plane was losing altitude. Finally, the aircraft ditched in the rough and icy north Atlantic, and Captain Pickett, the co-pilot, and flight engineer were never heard from again. Signs of wreckage of the aircraft were never found, though most experts believe the aircraft now rests on the ocean bottom. I thanked my lucky stars I wasn't on that flight as I so easily could have been. The most bizarre part of the entire scenario was that, according to Julius Graber, the airplane was going to be converted to a restaurant and bar. At least that was the official story.

Captain Augie Martin

One of the sad aviation incidents to come out of the war in Biafra concerned Captain August Martin. Martin was one of the first black airline captains in the United States. Augie, as he was affectionately known, had worked his way up to being a Seaboard & Western Airlines captain, flying a Super Constellation and Canadair CL-44 out of New York's JFK airport. Apparently Augie felt strongly about trying to help the people of Biafra, as he took a leave of absence from Seaboard & Western to pilot one of Hank Wharton's Super Constellations, flying Red Cross supplies to Nigeria.

On June 30, 1968, Augie and his wife, Gladys, who was writing a book about Biafra, along with Flight Engineer Thomas Brown and Co-pilot Jesse Meade, departed Fernando Poo, Equatorial Guinea, for Uli, Nigeria. The airstrip at Uli was no more than a widened road with a row of inadequate runway lights on either side. The weather over Uli that night was poor: low visibility, with rain showers and thunderstorms. Captain Martin attempted to line up the Super Constellation with the dim lights on the airstrip, but on the final approach, the aircraft reportedly struck rising terrain, and all aboard were killed. The crew and Gladys Martin were buried at a nearby cemetery outside the village of Uli.

A final twist to this story is the report that although Captain Martin's body was found in the wreckage, his head was not. This fueled speculation that the disaster was no accident after all but was rather the result of a small arms attack on the airplane by hostile forces. Apparently, taking an enemy's head was a tribal custom in the region.

1967
The Curtis Commando C-46

Fortunately, after my misadventures with Hank Wharton, my friend Julius Graber was able to get me a job interview with

Capitol International Airways, an American charter airline operator with a base in Frankfurt. This was during the Cold War. Capitol Airways flew its seven C-46 cargo planes in sub-service for Lufthansa, the German flag carrier, because the Four Power Agreement on Berlin prohibited Lufthansa from flying into that city. What could be more adventurous than flying the Berlin Corridor in an old World War II cargo plane?

I was hired as a C-46 co-pilot, and after three weeks of ground school and a week of Link Trainer flight simulation, I was in the co-pilot's seat of a 1945 Curtis Commando, C-46 cargo plane. The plane was huge; the C-46 was one of the largest twin-engine, tail-wheel airplanes in the world. However, the flight instrumentation and radios were very primitive by today's standards.

A Capitol Airways C-46 in sub-service for Lufthansa circa 1966.
Photo courtesy of Giorgio Adamo-from his private collection, and Airliners.net.

Landing between apartment buildings on the final approach to Berlin's Templehof airport, with people standing on the balconies of their apartments, waving and cheering as our lumbering

American cargo airplanes brought them food and medical supplies...I was in heaven! This was the true beginning of my apprenticeship.

What I didn't know then, however, was that it had been a C-46 aircraft that almost killed me and my family fourteen years earlier in Jamaica, New York, when the plane narrowly missed crashing into our house.

In the cockpit of a Capitol Airways C-46, in Frankfurt, Germany, circa 1966.

The Berlin Air Corridor

Flying the Berlin air corridor was very challenging. There were in fact three corridors, a north corridor, a center corridor and a south corridor. Since we flew out of Frankfurt to the isolated city of Berlin, we flew the longest of the corridors, the south corridor. Each corridor was twenty miles wide. That sounds plenty wide, however given the imprecise navigational aids of the '60s, (non-directional radio beacons), twenty miles wide often seemed not enough.

Russian Mig-19 fighters, equipped with NR-30 heavy cannons, patrolled the edge of the corridors. Stray outside the boundary of the corridor and your plane would be shot down.

As if all of this was not enough to put you on the edge of your pilot seat during each and every flight up and down the corridor, the East Germans began playing deadly games with their faux navigational beacons.

Sometimes, we would be navigating the corridor when the ADF needle (radio-compass) would start pointing off the original heading that we had established. If we followed the new course heading, we would wind up over East Germany. There were two instances I experienced when this was tried, but in each case we realized early, that a phony radio-beacon had been deployed.

During fight LH-606 from Frankfurt to Berlin on January 23, 1967 with Tony Berko in command, a Mig-19 came up behind our right wing and stayed there until we passed abeam the faux radio beacon that the East Germans put on the air, that day. When the MIG-19 peeled off to the south we breathed a sigh of relief. We didn't doubt for a second that the S.O.B. would have shot us down had we followed the phony radio beacon, and wandered outside the corridor.

Some years earlier, an Air France DC-4 with the registration number F-BELI, was fired upon and hit by eighty-nine rounds of machine gun fire, after it strayed outside of the corridor. Despite the severity of the MIG's attack, the Air France captain managed to land the airplane at Templehof airport with no fatalities to the passengers and crew.

Two months before our incident, noted above, a Pan American Boeing 727, registration N-317PA crashed under very suspicious circumstances, near Dallgow, East Germany. All aboard were killed.

The Soviet authorities in East Germany returned *only half* the aircraft's wreckage minus the cockpit voice recorder and aircraft flight recorder. The American NTSB was not able to determine what caused the airplane to descend below its assigned altitude. There was *much* speculation, at that time, that the aircraft had most likely been shot down.

....

Experience Is Something You Don't Get Until Just After You Need It.

....

Every significant experience leaves some mark. Even as I became more confident in my piloting skills, I was learning not to relax too much in an airplane, especially during takeoffs and landings.

In February 1967, flight LH-605, was under the command of a great captain by the name of Dick McNulty. Dick was from New Jersey and was a tall, slim, weathered-looking, cigar-smoking pilot in his fifties who was continually wiping his right eye because of some kind of tear duct problem. He was a mean-looking, good-hearted guy, and on top of all that, he was a very good pilot. We were flying from Cologne-Bonn airport to Frankfurt; it was late, and we were both tired. I was allowed to fly the airplane on this leg. I read the before-takeoff checklist while Dick performed action items, such as positioning switches and levers. Neither of us was aware that the flaps had not been repositioned for takeoff; they were still at the full flap landing setting, which is definitely not what you want for takeoff. Unfortunately, there was no takeoff warning horn for an improperly positioned flap control, as there is in airplanes now. The lighting was so poor in the C-46 that a pilot considered himself lucky if even the map light worked, so he could read his charts without a flashlight. He definitely needed the flashlight that every pilot carries with him to see the flap lever.

Flight LH-605 was cleared for takeoff, and Dick applied full power from the two 2,000-HP engines. The tremendous wind stream developed by the large three-bladed Hamilton standard props against the big "barn door" flaps brought the tail up almost instantly, and the airplane became airborne at about seventy-five knots. This shouldn't have occurred at less than about ninety knots, but because of the full flap setting, we were going up like an elevator. It felt very strange; any lesser airplane couldn't have done this without stalling and crashing. We scrambled to lower the nose as smoothly as possible to reach normal climbing speed. This was a close call!

Afterward, of course, Dick and I tried to determine how this had occurred. Had I neglected to call for takeoff flaps, or had he inadvertently skipped that step in the preparation for takeoff? We couldn't be sure, but I vowed never to let it happen again.

At the time of this incident, I was living in Kelsterbach, Germany, a small town of about six thousand inhabitants very close to the Frankfurt, Rhein-Main Airport. There were many airport workers, ground crew members, and pilots living in this conveniently located little town. My apartment was a small studio in a pension hotel in the middle of town. It was quiet and clean, and the owner's wife—a younger woman whom the owner jealously guarded—served good quality, home-cooked meals.

For some reason, the hotel seemed to be having trouble maintaining its table staff. Waitresses appeared to come and go with surprising regularity. One morning, at about seven, I arrived back at the hotel after a cargo flight and decided to order some breakfast before going up to my room to sleep. I sat down in my pilot's uniform in the restaurant and ordered a very nice farmer's omelet with fresh-baked German rye bread and coffee. I was too tired to notice the new waitress until I saw the note she had written on the small, round coaster napkin that was placed under the coffee cup. It said "If you will permit me, I will be delighted to come to your room this evening after I finish working." Either the pilot's uniform or my fluency in German with the American accent had attracted her; I am not quite sure which. As she came back to the table, I noticed what an attractive young lady she was and thanked her for the quick delivery of my breakfast; I also commented that she had my permission, following my comment with a slightly perceptible smile and a wink.

Chicken Dinner

Late one afternoon, two other C-46 pilots, Bob Bioren, Al Bates, and I went out for dinner in Frankfurt at a place called Hanchen (chicken) Mueller's on the Kaiser Strasse. When it was time to order, a formidable-looking waitress came over and asked what we wanted to eat. Bob and I ordered chicken dinners, but Al asked for ice cream. Our waitress obviously disapproved. "Are you only ordering dessert?" she asked.

"No, I'll have a chicken dinner myself, after the ice cream."

The waitress put her hands on her hips defiantly and said, *"Das geht doch nicht in diesem restaurant."* (That's not done in this restaurant.)

Al was quick. "Okay, no problem," he said. "I'll just have the ice cream." He ate it with great relish while we finished off our chicken, potato salad, and ice cream. We had ordered on separate checks, and when the waitress came by with his bill, *then* Al ordered his chicken dinner. The waitress had a *conniption*, knowing she'd been had. Throughout the rest of our dinner, she gave Al some pretty nasty looks, and we laughed about it for weeks.

The Temper Tantrum

Captain Harry Adams was an ex U.S. military pilot and an academy graduate. He was a dark-haired, obese chap of medium height with a fairly volatile temperament, which I came to learn about. The second flight I flew with Adams was on a flight into Frankfurt on the C-46. Adams was flying the airplane (he almost never let me have the controls), and I was talking on the radio to Frankfurt air traffic control. Several transmissions went back and forth between our aircraft and air traffic control, ending with Frankfurt control saying, "If you ever come back into this control zone with your radios sounding so bad, we will ground your airplane." Adams picked up the microphone on his side of the plane and called Frankfurt for a radio check. Frankfurt came back and said that his transmission was unintelligible. Without saying a word to me, Adams took the black Bakelite microphone by the coiled cord and smashed it as hard as he could against the heavy duty aluminum ledge of the window. The microphone shattered, and pieces of Bakelite, buttons, springs, and metal microphone parts showered the cockpit. I was speechless. I have never before or since seen anything like that done to an aircraft microphone.

"If you find yourself in a hole, stop digging."
                                                                    –Will Rogers

---

On a beautiful spring day in April, I was co-pilot on LH-408; Harry Adams was the captain and was taxiing the lumbering C-46 out for takeoff for a flight to Zurich, Switzerland. Good weather was forecast both en route and at the destination airport; it was simply a perfect day to fly. We had plenty of fuel and were relaxed and looking forward to the flight. The tower cleared LH-408 for takeoff. Adams lined up with the centerline and pushed the throttle levers up, and we began the takeoff roll. As the big tail lifted off the ground, we accelerated to flying speed. Adams gently applied back pressure on the control wheel, and we began the initial climb.

As we were approaching two hundred feet, with the nose pointed up at about twelve degrees, Adams suddenly yelled out. His seat had become unlatched, and it slid back three feet on its track. He had a firm grasp on the control wheel, the only thing to grab onto, and consequently pulled the wheel so far back that we over-rotated to what *seemed* like flying with the nose of the plane pointing nearly thirty degrees up. The airplane started to buffet, and I knew that meant an impending full stall at a low altitude from which we could never have recovered. Automatically, without time to think, I pushed the wheel forward with all the strength I could muster, pulling Adams and his pilot's seat forward at the same time. I shouted, "Harry, let go of the control wheel!" The buffeting stopped, and we were still flying! It's amazing what you can do when your adrenalin is flowing. For the record, Adams was no lightweight, yet even with the nose of the plane at a steep angle, I had managed to push him and his seat forward. Captain Adams made no comment about what had taken place, though I always felt as if he was angry that it was the *co-pilot* who saved the airplane. (As if somehow we were not both in the airplane and in danger.) If the airplane had entered a full stall, I wouldn't be writing this.

CHAPTER 3

1967

The Seasoning of an Airline Pilot

✳

Captain Tony Berko was one of my best friends. In the 1950s, he'd escaped from Hungary and made his way to the United States, then worked his way through pilot training, which he paid for himself, and became a captain with Capitol Airways. He was a superb pilot and a very bright man.

One very stormy night, we were flying flight LH-713 from Frankfurt to Hamburg carrying Lufthansa cargo. The C-46 didn't have onboard radar, so we flew blindly into our share of thunderstorm cells that evening. The C-46 was an exceptionally *uncomfortable* airplane in heavy rain. Since it wasn't pressurized, it leaked badly around the windows and through the cracks in its metal skin that you didn't like to think about. Pilots actually had to wear waterproof raincoats under these conditions to prevent becoming soaked to the skivvies.

We were flying at seven thousand feet in heavy rain and severe turbulence when lightning started flashing all around us. The turbulence we were experiencing during that flight was in the extreme category, as the airplane was occasionally uncontrollable. I wasn't very experienced at this point and kept glancing over at Tony to see whether he looked worried. He didn't seem to be; all I noticed was that each time the airplane became uncontrollable and lightning illuminated the cockpit, his skin looked very pale. Despite his pallor, he seemed braver then I was, at that moment, for I was on the edge of my seat. Suddenly, Saint Elmo's fire crackled across both windshields. I knew this often preceded a lightning strike, but I wasn't prepared for what happened next. We both remember seeing a white ball streaking toward us. The ball of lightning hit the nose of the plane, and the whole aircraft shuddered violently. Then the ball came right into the cockpit between our seats and rolled through the entire length of the plane, exiting from the rear with a deafening explosion. The cockpit was laden with the smell of ozone and a burning smell, but no smoke. I looked at Tony, who was as white as a sheet—we were both badly shaken and stunned. Neither he nor I said a word for several minutes. Then we both looked at each other and agreed that we needed to land the airplane as quickly as possible.

When we landed LH-713 at Hamburg Airport, we found a large hole in the aft portion of the rudder where the ball of lightning had exited. Boy, were we happy to be safely on the ground!

Murphy Is at It Again

One of Capitol's best C-46 pilots was a husky 5'8" chap with an infectious smile and an easygoing style by the name of Jim Kugler.

Our maintenance shop had performed an inspection on the retractable tail wheel assembly on one of our C-46s, and although the paperwork was signed off in the logbook, the inspection door had not been securely reattached. Unfortunately, all the cables for the flight controls that cause an airplane to climb or descend ran directly above the inspection door.

As you may have guessed, Murphy's Law struck again. On takeoff from the Frankfurt Rhein-Main Airport, when the landing gear was retracted, the retractable tail wheel caught the loose inspection door panel and crushed it up against the elevator flight control cables, making control of the elevator surface impossible.

The instant Kugler realized he'd lost the elevator control, he went right to the elevator trim tab and throttles. With great precision, he managed to get the C-46 back on an emergency approach to the Frankfurt Airport to attempt a landing.

Emergency procedures for the C-46 specified that with the loss of the elevator control, a gear-up landing should be performed. Unfortunately, a gear-up landing does serious damage to the belly of an airplane. Kugler felt strongly that he could land the plane with the gear down, using only the elevator trim tab. He set the C-46 up for a full-stall landing and did precisely that, deftly bringing the big plane down in a perfect three-point landing—saving the airplane and becoming a company hero.

Fate

Fate: That ultimate agency that predetermines the course of events.

It is rare that at the end of a flight, after the parking checklist is complete, a pilot can say to himself that he flew a perfect flight. There are usually one or more small errors that could have been avoided during the flight—if a pilot is honest with himself. I have on a few *rare* occasions flown a perfect flight. There is so much that goes on during a flight, so many opportunities for error. Fortunately, the kind of errors we are speaking about are relatively minor and usually don't pose any danger to the flight.

Once in a while, however, an experience shakes a pilot right to his or her very core. What if both pilots of a plane conduct their flight nearly perfectly, but a factor beyond the pilot's ability to control occurs and threatens the flight? In other words the airplane is simply in the wrong place at the wrong time. Unfortunately, this type of situation does happen, on rare occasion.

On LH flight 904, which was inbound to Frankfurt from Hamburg, Germany, Captain Tony Berko was in command and I was the co-pilot. We were cleared down to five thousand feet altitude and then received clearance to fly a holding pattern (a race-track flight pattern) over the Nattenheim radio beacon. Tony was flying the airplane and entered the holding pattern, as he should have, upon passing over the radio beacon. It was snowing in Frankfurt that afternoon, and the runways were icy; traffic had to be slowed down. Two airplanes ahead of us had executed missed approaches and were beginning to run short of fuel. As a result, the two planes were being given priority handling for new approaches. We were now in the holding pattern and were in and out of heavy snow showers. We had our hands full. The air was rough, and heavy rime ice was building at a pretty fast rate, requiring careful use of the wing de-icing (pneumatic) boots. We were cleared down to four thousand feet and were inbound to the Nattenheim beacon when my heart jumped into my throat. A portion of a large wing of a transport airplane suddenly sliced through the clouds right in front of our wing. Tony banked left and climbed one hundred feet, and the wing immediately disappeared in the clouds. Due to the heavy clouds, we never saw the airplane and have no idea what type it was. I immediately called Frankfurt ATC and reported the near miss. They claimed they had no idea what had taken place and said they would look into it. Of course, they never got back to us, as they were not interested in taking any part of the blame. That was a close call. Obviously, a pilot was not at his assigned altitude and was instead at ours. If we had been flying a few knots faster or had taken off a second earlier, it would have been a fatal accident for Tony and me and for all the people on the other airplane. On that day, fate was on our side.

The Autopilot

One of the shortcomings of the C-46 Curtis Commando was its autopilot system. It was an early version of what has become a standard and vital part of all airline aircraft today, but the Commando's mechanical/hydraulic device was responsible for various unfortunate, unexpected failures. Sometime in the mid-sixties, Capitol decided to discontinue the use of the C-46 autopilot, probably in part due to one particularly troubling incident.

Captain Tony Berko told me that several years before, Capitol was flying a military charter (MAC flight) with a group of sixty ROTC cadets to an airbase to tour the facility as part of its ROTC program. Reportedly, these kids were wearing their dress uniforms and strutting around the airport like peacocks, barking out orders to everyone they encountered. When they got on the airplane, they continued their obnoxious behavior.

After takeoff and during the climb-out, the weather turned bad and the flight started to get rough. The "restroom" on the C-46 was nothing more than a six-gallon portable potty with an attached seat. The whole thing was screwed to the plywood floor, which in some planes exhibited its share of wood rot. A black curtain served as privacy.

When this C-46 reached altitude, the captain turned on the autopilot. The autopilot maintained altitude for a while, but then slowly climbed above the assigned altitude. This continued, so every few minutes, the captain had to roll in some nose-down elevator trim to maintain the correct altitude. After about an hour, he noticed he had a lot of nose-down trim but the aircraft was still trying to climb.

About the time he determined there could be a major problem developing, the autopilot disconnected with a bang. The nose of the airplane went into a sudden dive and the tail went nearly straight up, catapulting the portable potty and its contents to the front of the plane and showering every one of those bratty ROTC kids with its malodorous contents.

My understanding is that neither the airplane nor the ROTC dress uniforms were usable for the next two weeks.

....

Remember, If You Crash Because of Bad Weather,
Your Funeral Will Most Likely Be On a Sunny Day

....

The third attempt on my life by a C-46 cargo plane was *not totally* the fault of the airplane.

During the 1960s, especially in Europe, it was not that unusual for a pilot to check in for his flight with the smell of alcohol on his breath. (Fortunately, since the 1980s, drinking and flying is no longer tolerated by the airlines, the FAA, and nearly all crew members.)

Flight LH-904 began in Frankfurt at about 10:00 p.m. We cruised over the Alps at fourteen thousand feet. The C-46 was not a pressurized airplane, which meant we had to fly with oxygen masks strapped on our faces while above ten thousand feet of flight altitude. Flying with an oxygen mask on for hours was anything but fun. First, it was uncomfortable. After several hours of use, the old rubber masks would cause skin irritations or, if one was unlucky, local skin infections. Second, the oxygen would dry the membranes of a person's throat. Especially in winter, it was not uncommon to develop a dry cough or hoarseness from the use of the mask.

We landed in Milan at Malpensa Airport about three hours later to off-load cargo and await loading for the return trip. Unfortunately, I failed to notice Captain Thompson's ruddy complexion.

The captain insisted on going to the airport café for cappuccino while the plane was being reloaded. Our chat was very friendly; in fact, he told me what a good co-pilot I seemed to be. The compliment caught me so off guard that I nearly didn't notice the brandy he kept adding to his coffee. Remember, in those days, co-pilots really didn't have much say about anything. Eventually, every good co-pilot became captain and then ran the ship his way. It worked out well enough, as long as a person survived his experience as co-pilot.

About two hours and quite a few spiked coffees later, the loadmaster walked into the café and told us that the C-46 was loaded, fueled, and ready for our return trip to Frankfurt. As we stepped out of the terminal café, a feeling of serious apprehension gripped me.

The weather had turned really ugly. Snow was falling in large, heavy wet flakes. The Alpine peaks, which we were able to see on landing, were now obscured; in fact, none of the mountains surrounding the airport were visible. But visible or not, they were there and waiting.

Thompson was having a really hard time walking toward our cargo plane in any semblance of a straight line. That said, he was feeling absolutely no pain at all. It might even have seemed funny if things hadn't gone downhill from there.

The airplane was very cold now. The leather pilot seat seemed to drain all the warmth from my body; it was wickedly uncomfortable. The lighting in the cockpit was poor, and the ground power unit, which was surging because of the cold, was causing the cockpit lights to alternate from very bright to very dim. Thompson bellowed for the before-start checklist. I found myself squinting to read the words on the checklist while periodically looking at the captain, wondering whether he was capable of flying the plane.

The checklist was completed, and I was ordered to call for our departure clearance. Malpensa clearance gave it to us in staccato, broken English with a strong Italian accent. The instant I finished interpreting the broken English and recording the clearance, Thompson called for the engine-start checklist. I had barely finished reading it when the Number-Two engine rumbled, coughed, and came to life with a sound that only an eighteen-cylinder, radial engine can make. Then the Number-One engine backfired and shook the twenty-year-old airplane as it, too, started up.

I scrutinized Malpensa's complicated departure procedure, which required a climb in a holding pattern to clear the surrounding mountain peaks.

Snow was beginning to accumulate on the wings, so I asked if we were going to de-ice. Thompsons's answer came quickly: "Get the taxi clearance!" We were on our way, ready or not! I wasn't ready, but I remember telling myself that Captain Thompson had flown this trip many times, and surely knew what he was doing. *But did he?*

As we approached the departure end of the runway, the skipper said, "Let's go." I called the tower, and LH-904 was cleared for takeoff. Captain Thompson lined up with the center line and abruptly pushed the throttle levers forward for takeoff power. Halfway down the runway, we ran into a heavy wet snow storm, with visibility decreasing to near zero. A chill ran down my spine; a sixth sense was telling me that things were going very wrong.

As we climbed through 1,600 feet, I saw rime ice building up fast on the windshield. The starboard three-bladed Hamilton Standard prop slung a load of ice that slammed into the aluminum skin barely three feet behind my head with a deafening bang. Everything was happening way too fast.

I switched on the right wing light and saw freezing rain coating the leading edge of the wing. I turned to Thompson to say, "De-ice boots," but he beat me to it.

"Boots! Carburetor heat! Prop alcohol!" he commanded—faster than I'd ever heard those words spoken before. I didn't waste time activating the controls and levers to start the pneumatic expansion of the rubber boots on the leading edge of the wing into their de-ice cycle, applying heat to the inlets of both carburetors and initiating the flow of de-ice fluid to both propellers. When I was done, my eyes darted to the automatic directional finder,—just in time to see its needle swing as we passed over the radio beacon located on the ground. Now we were supposed to turn left to enter the holding pattern. But Thompson banked right! *No!* The published departure procedure was to turn left. The turn should have been left!

"*Left* turn, not right!" I shouted. "*Left! Left* turn!" At that precise moment, between the clouds that were beginning to break up as we climbed, I saw the cold, dark-grey, brutal face of a jagged, snow-covered mountain peak a hundred yards from our right wingtip. I'll never forget that sight.

The old C-46 went into a steep left bank at a roll rate it surely had never before experienced. We had just missed a horrific air disaster and certain death.

As we climbed out of the basin and finally reached our assigned altitude, we were cleared en route to the Monte Cenari radio beacon. I thought of how devastated my mother would have been had she received news that LH-904 had crashed and her son was gone. I remember wondering whether I was being too selfish and inconsiderate of my caring family to be living so recklessly. What was I doing?

The Cargo Door

Dick McNulty was a great captain to fly with. Somehow he got the nickname McNasty, but despite what one might assume, it was actually meant in an endearing way. We had a flight to

Stuttgart, Germany, one afternoon. This was a special day for Dick; it was his wife's birthday, and he was planning on taking her out for a fancy birthday dinner when he got back to Frankfurt. Everything was going as planned. The weather that afternoon was beautiful. It was a sunny spring day, with deep blue skies forecasted for the entire day and lovely, warm temperatures.

When we walked out to the C-46, which was parked rather conveniently in front of our operations office in Frankfurt, the cargo loading was just being completed. The cargo master handed me the final weight-and-balance loading data with the required information of how much weight had been loaded onto each cargo pallet and where each pallet was located in the airplane. I then began the tedious but necessary weight-and-balance calculation to ensure that we were not overweight and that the cargo was safely distributed so that we would be neither nose-heavy nor tail-heavy. Dick checked the aircraft logbook to be sure that there were no maintenance items open that would create a safety issue; once he was satisfied, he went outside and did the aircraft walk-around to determine that the aircraft appeared airworthy for the flight. These are the kinds of things that would go on prior to each and every flight.

Everything was going well, and an on-time departure seemed sure. Dick was really concerned that we arrive back to Frankfurt on time so that he wouldn't be late for his wife's birthday dinner. The weight-and-balance was completed, all doors were closed and locked, the checklists read, and start clearance was received. Before long, we were taxiing out for takeoff. After we received the air traffic control clearance, we were cleared for takeoff. Dick let me fly, so I smoothly brought the power up on the two huge 2,000-HP engines, and in less than a minute, we lifted off the runway at Frankfurt and were climbing in smooth air to our assigned 8,000-foot cruising altitude for the short forty-five minute flight to Stuttgart. It wasn't long before we were cleared to the radio beacon at Stuttgart. I flew the ILS (instrument landing system) approach to the runway, made a decent landing, and taxied to the cargo terminal. We completed the parking checklist and walked down the stairs only to be greeted by the German cargo master, complete with uniform, stripes, wings, and a hat. He walked up to Captain McNulty and, after a snappy salute, stated that his men would be unloading our cargo shortly and then would load the cargo for our return flight to Frankfurt. McNulty told him to please do his best for an on-time departure as it was his wife's birthday and he was taking her out to celebrate in Frankfurt. The cargo master saluted again and told McNulty that it would be no problem.

Captain McNulty was happy as a clam at high tide. We went to the outdoor airport café and enjoyed some freshly brewed coffee as we watched the C-46 being loaded across the airport from where we were sitting. About forty-five minutes later, we decided it was time to walk back toward the airplane. As we approached, we could see that the outbound cargo was nearly all loaded. Everything was going fine until we heard a loud metal tearing sound followed by the sound of something heavy falling to the tarmac. The cargo master came running over to us. He saluted Captain McNulty and said in a heavy German accent, "*Herr Capitan*, the airplane is loaded, *und* as you can see, we are early, but *zer ist* one minor problem. *Zer* has been a *schmall* unfortunate accident. We just *rrripped zer* cargo door *uf* your airplane, off *zer* hinges." Without a word, Dick removed his hat, threw it on the tarmac, and started stomping on it while he let out a fusillade of choice words.

We walked over to the other side of the airplane and could hardly believe our eyes. There was the large cargo door of our airplane lying on the cargo loading ramp. It was not a pretty sight. After regaining his composure, a few minutes later, Dick was speaking with a local aircraft and engine mechanic. In the interest of expediency, and so that Dick could get back to Frankfurt for his wife's birthday dinner, everyone decided that it would be okay to make an emergency repair. Rolls of tape were brought to the airplane, and while the loaders held the cargo door in place, multiple layers of duct tape were wrapped around the airplane and cargo door every twelve inches. I bet a thousand dollars' worth of duct tape was used. Then, as if that wasn't enough, heavy ropes were wrapped around the airplane fuselage and over the cargo door. Then layers of tape were placed over the ropes. It looked strong, but it surely wasn't pretty!

We took off about twenty minutes behind schedule, but considering what had happened to the airplane, it was nothing less than a miracle. The flight back to Frankfurt was pretty normal, though McNulty decided to fly a little slower than usual to avoid pushing our luck with the cargo door repair.

We landed in Frankfurt and taxied to Capitol's cargo ramp. After the completion of our parking checklist, we walked down the stairs and were greeted by three of our mechanics. The comments were Oh S—! What happened to the airplane? McNulty apologized and said he was late for a very important appointment and that the co-pilot would be happy to fill them in with all the details. I heard later that it took them far longer to get the tape off the airplane than it took us to have it put it on.

Every time I flew with McNulty after that, all I had to do was look at his crumpled captain's hat—and I would start laughing.

Pick Yourself Up and Brush Yourself Off

The next day in Frankfurt was another beautiful day. It was sunny and mild, with a nice west wind that made the smell from the IG Farben Chemical Werks noticeably absent. With this touch of springtime, what better idea was there for a twenty-six-year-old unmarried pilot than to put his uniform on, run the top down on his Austin Healy, and go for a ride? Particularly on days like this, I missed Evelynne. She'd forgiven my aerobatics, which had resulted in the slap that was a first lesson in the *right* way to impress a young French woman. We'd come close to tying the knot after seeing each other steadily for two years, but my being stationed in Frankfurt was the final straw and had put an end to our relationship.

I parked outside the airport departure terminal. As I strolled along the Lufthansa ticket counters, I couldn't help noticing Anke, a blonde, green-eyed, very pretty *fraulein*. She had been the girlfriend of another Capitol pilot who'd left her to go back to the States to upgrade on the Lockheed Super Constellation. What I didn't know was that Anke was out for *revenge*.

Walking over to her counter, I asked her if she'd like to go for a beer after work. I was startled to hear her say, without a microsecond's delay, "*Ja*, I'd luff to!" It didn't occur to me until the next day how mechanical her answer was.

A pitcher of Berliner Weise in a cute outdoor café later, and Anke suggested coffee back at her flat. One thing led to another and, finally, without too much protest on my part, she had her way with me. I can still remember that contented feeling, the smug, cat-like expression I must have had on my face. Then, without warning, Anke asked, "Are you working in the morning?"

I told her I wasn't.

"But I am! *Auf Weidersehen*." (Good-bye)

Ouch! I still remember *that* too.

CHAPTER 4

1968

The Jet Age

✳

Airline seniority is *mostly* a wonderful thing. Uproar broke out among the pilots when the telexed announcement came in to the Frankfurt dispatch office; who would be the lucky ones to be sent back to Wilmington, Delaware, to train on the Douglas DC-8 four-engine turbojet airliner? I had seniority. I had survived two years on the C-46 Curtis Commando. My reward was to fly the DC-8.

Scotty Forbes was brilliant, probably the best ground school instructor I ever had. He was a DC-8 flight engineer with a photographic memory and a thick Scottish accent that kept us entertained. In those days, it was very common to delve into the most finite detail of every aircraft system. That type of ground school is seldom given by airlines today. The four weeks training with him passed quickly.

My Seat Mate

After ground school, there was simulator training at the Braniff Airlines simulator at Dallas's Love field.

I boarded a Braniff plane at Newark Airport with a first-class ticket and spent the first hour memorizing the immediate action items on the DC-8 emergency checklist. I didn't pay any attention to the guy sitting next to me other than to notice his huge cowboy boots, which he kept buffing with his handkerchief. At breakfast, I ordered cereal. When I'd finished eating it, my seat mate placed half the steak he'd ordered on my plate and said, "Hey, little buddy, you hardly had anything to eat." I thanked him and enjoyed the addition to my breakfast.

Soon afterward, the Braniff flight engineer stepped out of the cockpit into the galley and poured himself a cup of coffee. He walked over to my seat row and asked the guy next to me what he thought of the Pete Rose deal. I was too engrossed in my studying to hear what he said. The flight engineer (F/E) returned to the cockpit, and my seat mate, having noticed my checklist, asked if I was a pilot. "Yes," I said and, as he seemed to know our flight engineer, asked him if he was an F/E as well.

The look he gave me was one I'll never forget. He squinted at me, scratched the side of his head, and said softly, "I'm Mickey Mantle."

Did I feel stupid? I guess you could say that! We chatted for the rest of the flight, and I found the Hall of Fame slugger to be very friendly and a really down-to-earth guy.

The Box (aircraft simulator)

Braniff's simulator was no simple Link Trainer (old generation aircraft simulator). It was a multimillion-dollar, computer-driven, electronic/hydraulic exact duplicate of the DC-8 cockpit. Sitting in it, one could not easily distinguish the simulator from the airplane's actual cockpit. Training scenarios were devised to simulate both dramatic emergency situations and normal day-to-day flying. Everything was done safely at less than thirty feet off the ground. No one has ever been killed in a simulator crash, although after a bad session in one, you might almost wish you had been.

Simulator training lasted a week, followed by a company check ride. Then we went back to Wilmington for training in the actual airplane. I'd received just one hour of flight training when Capitol announced that, due to a reduction in business, there would be a furlough; the DC-8 would have to wait. Welcome to the airlines!

The Classic Beech D-18/C-45

Airline hiring was at a standstill now, so I purchased a current copy of *Trade-A-Plane* magazine to see if there were any temporary jobs in the corporate aviation world.

A commuter airline, Baltimore Washington Airways, was looking for experienced captains on the Beech D-18, which was the old army C-45 twin-engine, ten-passenger, tail-wheel airplane. I figured that if I could fly the C-46, I certainly could fly the C-45.

Unfortunately, I was not an experienced D-18/C-45 captain; in fact, I'd never even been inside that airplane. I called Baltimore Washington Airways and scheduled a job interview for the following week. (A caveat: I'm not recommending that anyone reading this follow my example.) Then I went to LaGuardia Airport in New York and hung around the corporate lounge waiting for a Beech D-18 to taxi in so that I could speak to the pilot.

After two days, I finally met a D-18 captain, a very kind fellow who took me out to his plane and showed me around the cockpit. I told him I really needed the job with Baltimore Washington Airways, and he spent the next four hours with me. I took many pages of notes, copying checklists and a number of pages from the aircraft manual. After thanking the captain for his generosity (he wouldn't accept anything else), I went home to review what I'd learned and to study my notes.

The following week, I drove down to Baltimore's Friendship Airport and met the chief pilot of Baltimore Washington Airways. He was a regular kind of guy who seemed easy to get along with. Apparently he liked my enthusiasm. "Okay, let's give you a check ride."

I tensed up for a moment, and then I took a deep breath. "Sure, why not?" I said.

Half an hour later, I was in the left seat of a Beech D-18, and the chief pilot was in the right seat reading me the before-start checklist. My only problem at this point was locating the switches and controls in a manner that would make him believe I was an experienced D-18 captain. After I started the engines, we taxied out for my first takeoff in a D-18. I think the fact that I had 1,600 hours as co-pilot in the Curtis Commando C-46 aircraft, at least seven times heavier than the D-18, must have helped a lot. But on the other hand, I had no D-18 experience. There was a strong crosswind, and as anyone who has flown one will tell you, a D-18 takeoff in a crosswind is a handful. Because it has two tails, it is necessary to use lots of wind correction and differential power application (using more power on the upwind engine).

Surprisingly, however, everything went well until the chief pilot asked me to simulate lowering the landing gear with the emergency crank handle. I had absolutely no idea where it was. I had that deer-caught-in-the-headlights look, and the chief pilot's expression turned into a faint smile. "I guess you must have forgotten," he said. "It's under this cover."

He told me I would do fine; he would put a good co-pilot with me for a week until I "familiarized" myself again with the D-18. The remark had the tone of "Pretty gutsy try, kid." I guess he admired that.

A Beech D-18/C-45. Photo courtesy of Andres Luna and Airliners.net.

The following Monday, I started flying trips up and down the east coast with Baltimore Washington Airways. Now I was carrying passengers as well as cargo. It was a lot of fun but also exhausting, with as many as ten takeoffs and landings a day. I would fly from 6:00 a.m. until 3:00 p.m., and when I got back to my motel, I'd be so tired that I would often fall asleep in my clothes. I flew hundreds of hours with Baltimore Washington Airways and acquired a lot of great pilot-in-command experience.

Then one day, a family friend from New York named Marty Fishman telephoned to tell me that Overseas National Airways was hiring DC-9 turbojet co-pilots in a cargo and passenger operation.

1969

A Friend of Mine Once Said That Flying for a New Airline Is Like Getting a New Girlfriend.

Luckily, within three weeks, I was hired by Overseas National Airways (ONA) at JFK. I was to fly the DC-9 twin-engine turbojet. Things were looking up. Ground school at the company headquarters on Rockaway Boulevard in Jamaica, New York, was professional and smooth with no problems. Clearly, ONA was a fine company.

The second day of ground school, I invited a few classmates to join me for lunch at a terrific pizza restaurant I knew of, only a short drive away. We piled into my rental car, but when I turned the ignition key, the car wouldn't start. I looked under the hood to check the battery connections. The connections were fine, but the battery wasn't—someone had stolen it. The rental car agency was very understanding, sending someone to get the car and deliver another one the very next day. A few days later, my classmates asked if I'd take them to the great pizza restaurant. I agreed, and we all headed out to the car. This time, I was startled to find that all four tires were gone. The rental company wasn't so friendly when I called them the second time. For the rest of the ground school, I rode the bus. We never did get to that pizza restaurant. New York had certainly changed since I had grown up there.

Flight training was in Augusta, Georgia. The only unusual thing that happened there was that when we flew into Augusta, the instructor pilot's suitcase sprang open on the baggage carousel. Apparently, he was some kind of health nut; some five hundred vitamin pills of every size, shape, and color spilled out. The problem was, this was in the 1960s before many people knew what a vitamin pill was. An airline pilot in uniform with all those pills spilling out of his suitcase created quite a stir in the baggage area.

The airplane check ride went well, and a month later, I was a DC-9 co-pilot flying Navy Quick Trans cargo between air force and navy bases all over the United States. One unusual aspect of our DC-9-31 aircraft configuration was the installation of rocket JATO (Jet assisted takeoff) bottles under each wing. In the event that we lost an engine on takeoff, we had four rocket engines to give us up to a twenty-eight-second boost of rocket power, enabling the aircraft to clear any hills or obstacles around the airport. In 1969, the DC-9 was a fairly new airplane, and one serious problem at the time was that when taking off on runways with significant standing water, we sometimes came close to experiencing an engine flameout (engine failure). This was due to the engines ingesting large amounts of water from the "rooster tail"—water thrown back by the nose gear tires. When this near-flameout condition occurred, you could hear the engines surging and see the EPRs (engine pressure ratio gauge—measures engine power output) rapidly decrease momentarily. Fortunately, Douglas solved the problem by installing chinned nose gear tires with an elevated ridge on the outside rim to deflect the water to the side.

An ONA DC-9-33. Photo courtesy of Steve Williams and Airliners.net.

Much of what we flew was hot cargo—munitions, weapons, flammables, and explosives. Needless to say, we tried extra hard to make smooth landings to please our "passengers." Nevertheless, ONA was plagued with a series of accidents in the DC-8, DC-9, and DC-10 fleet, the majority of which resulted in no fatalities.

However, one particularly tragic ONA accident, which resulted in twenty-three fatalities, occurred on May 2, 1970, thirty miles east-northeast of St. Croix in the U.S. Virgin Islands; a DC-9 ran out of fuel and ditched in the ocean. I knew both the captain and co-pilot and had flown with both of them.

1974
The Douglas DC-8

In my opinion, Douglas Aircraft designed and built many terrific airplanes, and the DC-8 and DC-10 were among the best. It was my privilege to have flown a total of eleven thousand hours as captain in both aircraft, but the hours I logged, especially in the DC-8, were not accumulated painlessly.

In 1974, I was recalled back from furlough to Capitol International Airways and soon began flying as a DC-8 first officer (co-pilot). On my first transatlantic trip to Frankfurt, Germany, after completing my co-pilot line-checks, I was flying with a Captain Roberts, an overweight, unhealthy-looking fellow in his mid-fifties with whom I had never flown before. Roberts made the takeoff out of New York on what would be a nonstop eight-hour flight. Within fifty minutes, we had reached cruising altitude. A few minutes later, Roberts put his overcoat over his head and went to sleep.

I couldn't believe it! At the same time, I was really excited to be in control of a four-engine passenger jet with some 250 passengers aboard, flying at .82 percent of the speed of sound. We were navigating with Doppler radar and loran-C (long-range navigation that used pairs of ground-based transmitters and had serious accuracy deficiencies). There was plenty of opportunity to make navigation errors, so I triple-checked everything. I didn't want to betray Captain Roberts's trust in me, but I also didn't want to wake him up and have him take control of the flight. I navigated all the way to Ireland, then down the coast of England, across the Netherlands, and all the way to a holding pattern we were instructed to enter over Nattenheim, Germany. I glanced over at Roberts, and he was still asleep.

Now I hoped to make the landing, planning to wake him before the final approach fix, about six miles from the runway. But then it occurred to me that the old guy might be so startled that he could have a heart attack or something. I discussed this with the flight engineer, who'd been wide awake the entire trip and watching me, a newbie DC-8 co-pilot. (He had good survival instincts.) We decided to wake him.

I shook Roberts's arm a couple of times. He stirred but didn't wake up. Then we received ATC clearance direct to the *outer marker*, which was the final approach fix (ground-based transmitter locating a geographical position), and then we were cleared for the approach to Rhein-Main Airport, Frankfurt.

By now, the flight engineer was seriously trying to get the captain awake. I completed the approach checklist with him, and just outside the outer marker, I placed the gear lever in the down position. We were now about six miles from touchdown. Wow! I'd flown the aircraft and 250 passengers safely across the Atlantic and down the approach.

About two miles from touchdown, Captain Roberts suddenly threw his raincoat on the floor of the cockpit and shouted, "I have the airplane!"

I was really disappointed that I wasn't going to make the landing but managed to convince myself that this was better. What might have happened if he'd awakened from such a sound sleep just as we were landing? In retrospect, I can see how those were indeed the fairly wild days of aviation.

A Routine Flight

My next trip was to Las Vegas. The crew, consisting of the three cockpit crew and twelve flight attendants, was to airline out to Vegas (in other words, to fly to Vegas on another airline and not in uniform.)

Then on the return, we would fly a Capitol flight back to New York, JFK. I was the co-pilot, and the captain was Len Rew, with whom I would become good friends. Len was a grey-haired, very mild-mannered gentleman who was the local chairman of our union.

This trip was promising to be completely routine. As we climbed the air stairs to the airplane for our trip back, I couldn't help noticing that the captain was wearing basketball sneakers instead of black uniform shoes. It was really pretty funny looking, and I was trying to keep from laughing as I was hanging my uniform jacket up on the rear wall in the cockpit before taking the right-hand co-pilot seat. Captain Rew must have noticed the look on my face and started telling the flight engineer that it was the last time he was going to let his wife pack his bag, as she forgot to put his uniform shoes in his suitcase. Soon we were all joking a bit about it, and before long, we got back into our routine of reading the before-start checklist. We got our passengers onboard and shortly thereafter received our start clearance. With engines running, we were cleared to taxi and thus began what appeared to be a typical flight to JFK. Upon reaching the cruise altitude of thirty-one thousand feet, we completed the cruise checklist and began to enjoy the changing desert colors as the sun started its journey below the horizon behind us. First, the beautiful painted desert around Bryce Canyon passed beneath us, and then a short time later, the twinkling lights of Colorado Springs could be seen to the north. It was all so peaceful, and the air at this altitude was cool and silky smooth.

As I started sipping my coffee, the cockpit cabin interphone rang and Rew picked it up. I heard him say, "You've got to be kidding me!" As he hung up, he said, "Jay, there's a disturbance in the cabin. Go back and see what is going on, but be careful." Len told me that the senior flight attendant said that a young man was chasing an older woman up and down the aisles, and no one seemed to know exactly what it was all about. I put my jacket and pilot cap on and left the cockpit, locking the door behind me. The senior flight attendant led me to the second cabin, where pandemonium had broken out. The first question that entered my mind was—what was happening to this nice routine flight?

As I walked back to the rear cabin, I saw an elderly woman run into the bathroom, followed by a heavyset young man who was now trying to get into the bathroom the woman had run into. He was banging on the bathroom door with what turned out to be our aircraft crash axe, which was stored in one of the overhead compartments. (Since all the hijacking business and 9/11, this practice of storing the crash axe in the forward overhead has been discontinued.) By the time I got near him, he had started using the pick side of the axe and was actually chopping through the bathroom door.

I found three really big passengers who were willing to help me. The first thing I tried was to order him to put the axe down. This had no effect; he was intent on getting to the woman, who turned out to be *his mother*. Slowly, the three burly passengers edged ever closer to him, and at an opportune moment, wrestled the axe out of his hand and him to the floor. He was quickly tied up with seat belt extensions and strapped securely in his seat for the rest of the flight to New York. His poor mom was coaxed out of the bathroom and spent the rest of the flight apologizing for her son's behavior. You had to feel sorry for her. The remainder of the flight went well, and upon arrival at JFK, the airport police took the young man into custody. Luckily, no one was hurt.

A Capitol Airways Douglas DC-8- 60 series.
Photo courtesy of Udo K. Haafke and Airliners.net.

The Tax Exempt Engineer

A couple of flights later, I was co-pilot on a flight to Amsterdam, Holland, with a particularly disparaging flight engineer by the name of Bob Clater. I think you might know the type—if you said something was white, he would say it was black, and so on. We all had just entered the cockpit when Bob asked the captain how much he had paid in withholding tax in his last paycheck. Then he asked me. When I asked him why he wanted to know, he said something about being in a group of taxpayers and attorneys who were protesting paying taxes. I listened to Bob's story and concluded that he might want to reconsider the position he was taking. Bob insisted it was I who was being foolish and that I was wasting lots of money each month. I flew with Bob several more times that month, as we were both flying on the same bid line (a schedule comprised of specified trips for the month). Unfortunately, during each trip, he would ridicule both the captain and me. On the last flight of that month, Bob did not show up for his flight; another flight engineer took his place. When the captain and I asked where Bob was, the answer seemed to roll off the (replacement) flight engineer's tongue: Bob had been given a free trip *up the river* to prison for tax evasion. His tax challenge had been heard in court, and a judge had issued a verdict.

Fun and Games

Through the years, my non-flying male friends have often asked me how it was to fly with some of those sexy-looking flight attendants, and whether there was much socializing between the pilots and cabin crew. I have given it some thought over the years, and this is what I have concluded.

To begin with, it is now possible for a flight attendant to get a pilot pregnant. Yes, things have changed drastically since the 1980s. The change occurred gradually, at first, and then began to accelerate into what we have to contend with today.

In the 1970s and 1980s, pilots and flight attendants usually flew the same bid lines for an entire month. In other words the same crew were together for all of the trips flown in that month. So, during layovers, the cabin and cockpit crews most often stayed in the same hotel. It was very common for the entire crew to arrange to meet for dinner. Under these conditions, it was not uncommon for people to pair off, and eventually romances blossomed, sometimes even among married flight attendants and pilots. That did happen occasionally, and sometimes with disastrous results.

In the '90s, computers were beginning to be used to construct crew schedules. Airlines were now able to easily schedule flight attendants on trips with various cockpit crews during the month. In other words, the flight attendants were not flying with the same cockpit crew members every trip. Scheduling in this manner, with a conscious tendency on the part of airline management to break down the camaraderie between the cockpit and cabin staff, was a successful divide-and-conquer strategy, which served the airlines well during pilot or cabin work stoppages (strikes). Over the years, many pilots have stated that this strategy was the result of a deep-seated jealousy that airline management harbored toward the cockpit crews because of the fun and carefree lifestyle they were leading. Regardless of what caused the scheduling changes to take place, they did take place, and they dramatically changed the social landscape.

As if all of this were not enough, laptop computers, the Internet, and iPhones have become a nearly complete substitution for human contact for many people. Now, instead of pilots and flight attendants going down to the lobby of the hotel in a foreign country to see which other crew members might show up, they stay in their rooms and send e-mails or text messages. I would opine that it is a turn for the worse. The coup de grace is that many airlines now employ one hotel for the cockpit crew and another hotel for the cabin staff.

By the 1990s, many older pilots seriously longed for the good old days!

CHAPTER 5

1973

Right Place at the Right Time

I was co-pilot on flight CL-906 from JFK to Columbia, South Carolina, one evening. After we landed and taxied in, I went down to operations to pick up the computer flight plan and weather update. On the way out to the airplane, I noticed a lot of commotion around another Capitol DC-8 nearby.

I walked over and met Jim Obrien, an old acquaintance who had been a C-46 maintenance supervisor in Frankfurt. Jim told me that this DC-8 aircraft had recently returned from a series of hajj flights (flying pilgrims to Mecca) in Africa and that while he was in one of the cargo compartments straightening out the "Fly Away Kit" (Spares: tires, extra parts, etc. especially on a plane used for charter), he had found a heavy wooden box that wasn't part of the aircraft spares. When he opened it, he was astonished to find it full of gold bars.

The company instructed him to contact the FBI, who then contacted the Treasury Department.

A few years later, I saw Jim again, and he told me that by mid-1976, about three years later, no one had claimed the gold and it became his property. It was worth more than a million dollars, but he said it hadn't changed his life much other than that his Capitol maintenance position had become more of a hobby by that point in his life. It couldn't have happened to a nicer guy.

In-flight Turbulence

In early March of 1973, I was on flight CL-912 from New York to Amsterdam as co-pilot with a Jimmy Logers, a captain who, although essentially a nice guy, could be really feisty at times. We were cruising at altitude when the senior flight attendant came up to the cockpit with a note from a passenger in the front row, near the galley. The note was from a private pilot asking if he could come up to visit with us and see the cockpit. In 1973, this was not prohibited and, in fact, was quite commonly done. Problem was, the captain was not in the mood for a visit. He sent a message back that we were expecting turbulence and that he could not permit the visit. A few minutes later, a terse note came back from the passenger saying that he didn't believe that turbulence was really expected.

I needed to use the head (lavatory), so I left the cockpit. The forward head in the plane was inoperative on that trip, so I had to walk to the rear lavatory. When I got to the back, it was occupied. I was standing behind the rear seat row when the airplane yawed side to side fairly significantly. It didn't feel like turbulence, more like a malfunction of the autopilot. I got a good grip on the seatback just in case.

Then the plane went into an extremely strong yaw. A heavy-set woman in the rear lavatory came flying out and landed on her knees, undies down to her ankles. After helping the embarrassed passenger up, I went to the head and then quickly walked toward the cockpit. The private pilot in the front seat row got my attention when I walked past. "You can't fool me—that wasn't real turbulence," he said.

I entered the cockpit to find the captain with a big grin on his face. He said something about wondering whether the turbulence had satisfied the back seat pilot in the front seat row. I'm not *quite* sure what happened while I was in the head, but I'm glad that the only things hurt were some feelings.

Coffee, Tea, or...

Another rather dramatic passenger incident took place while I was flying as co-pilot late one night on CL-905, a New York to Frankfurt flight. It was a routine flight that had started to become boring. I went back to the galley for a cup of coffee. As I stood there drinking my coffee, a passenger in the third row held his cup up for a refill. The flight attendant began pouring but became distracted by a passenger in the fourth row. You guessed it—hot coffee in the guy's lap.

He jumped up and grabbed for the headrest on the seat in front of him. Unfortunately, he missed the headrest and grabbed its male occupant's hair—which turned out to be a toupee, which came off the wearer's head. When this man jumped up to retrieve his hairpiece, he knocked the tray and coffee pot out of the flight attendant's hands.

By this time, the first six rows of passengers were either screaming or laughing uncontrollably. I was in the latter category and retreated to the cockpit. I didn't want my name anywhere in that incident report.

The Flashlight

The flight engineer on this flight was a real character by the name of Dave Ruth. The thing about Dave was that all the flight attendants loved him. I mean *really loved him*! I didn't know exactly what it was that he had that I didn't, but whatever it was, at my thirty-four years of age, I wanted it, and I secretly studied his every move. The only thing I came up with was that he was very daring. I could never have gotten away with the things he dared to do. For example, on this one particular flight, he took his huge, four–D-cell flashlight and put it down the leg of his uniform pants. A few minutes later, a somewhat junior and less experienced flight attendant came into the cockpit and took both the captain's and my beverage orders. Then she turned around to take Dave's beverage request, but the way Dave had positioned the flight engineer's seat caused her to bump into his huge, four-cell flashlight hidden in his pants leg. The squeal she let out was quite shrill. It wasn't the sound of someone terrified but rather of unexpected surprise. Amazingly, at exactly that moment, I turned around to look at Dave and figured out his secret: the expression on his face. He had mastered the expression of complete angelic innocence.

Box Lunch

As I sat there looking out the cockpit window into the starlit, moonless night, my mind flashed back to a flight I'd had as a co-pilot with Overseas National Airways a few years before. It was a CAM (commercial air movement) flight for the military in a DC-9 in which we were flying military personnel from one airbase to another. I was flying with a captain named Tom Vitrelli. Tom was a handsome captain, very clean cut, whom the flight attendants adored. We had just been brought our lunches, which consisted of a cardboard box lunch with half a sandwich (typically tuna or chicken salad), a round mound of cottage cheese with half of a maraschino cherry on top, a Hershey bar, a small packet of two pieces of chewing gum, and an apple. When the box lunch came, Tom and I both moaned our disapproval. The flight attendant quickly assured us that we would live and that it was actually pretty good. Well, that set the wheels in motion in Tom's head! As soon as the flight attendant left the cockpit, Tom started to cut a hole in the cardboard box beneath the mound of cottage cheese. Without any apparent sense of shyness, he unzipped his pants and placed something inside the cottage cheese from bottom to top, and the maraschino cherry on top of that. Then Tom rang the flight attendant's call button. The stewardess who had brought us the box lunches earlier came up to the cockpit again and asked what we wanted. Tom said, "This box lunch is inedible." The stewardess quickly said, "I ate it, and I thought it was great." "Not mine," Tom said, where-upon the flight attendant flipped the cardboard top of the box lunch open, jumped back, and nearly fainted. I recall Tom had that same look on his face, a look of innocence. The look on my face was of wonderment. I was wondering if we would still be employed at ONA by the following week.

Bombproof

In those days, it was not uncommon for a captain helping a co-pilot upgrade to captain to allow the co-pilot to fly the aircraft from the left seat, the seat the captain normally flies from, during good weather.

The left seat has the nose-wheel steering control, so a co-pilot gets experience not only in flying the aircraft from the left seat but also in maneuvering the aircraft on the ground in close quarters. This is the best way to learn the delicate application of power control while taxiing, which is necessary to become captain. The only captain who will put a co-pilot in the left seat is one who has come to trust him and wants to help him to the next level.

At Capitol, there were three or four captains who would often let me fly from the left seat. These were great guys from my point of view, taking a certain amount of risk to help me get ahead. There was nothing I wouldn't do to help them, if I could. I'm forever grateful to them.

One such pilot was Sam Johnson, a very kind man who had overcome the disability of polio as a young boy and had gone on to become an extremely competent airline captain. Sam called me at home one night before our flight the next day to Frankfurt. He wondered, since I had an engineering background, whether I could fix a biofeedback machine that wasn't working; it was one he'd built from a kit. As we had a two-day layover in Frankfurt, he asked if I could bring a soldering iron and a multi-meter (portable volt-and-ohmmeter) with me for the repair. I told him I looked forward to the opportunity to be of help.

Our hotel in Frankfurt, the Ritters Park hotel, was several hundred years old and had been frequented by German aristocracy in a bygone era. It had two noteworthy aspects: the personnel were pretty uppity and, due to the age of the hotel, there were very few electrical receptacles in the guest rooms. We landed in Frankfurt and were promptly transported by bus to our hotel. After we checked in, I met Sam in his room, and we looked for a wall outlet for the soldering iron.

The only one we could find was behind the huge, hand-carved bed that must have been three hundred years old. We decided to push it away from the wall. Sam and I got on each side of the massive headboard and pushed with all our strength. Suddenly, we heard the sound of wood splitting. The headboard began to topple over, and the ancient mattress fell to the floor. As a dark cloud of dust rose from beneath the mattress, the footboard broke away with a loud crash.

A moment later, a *putzfrau* (cleaning lady) knocked at the door. *"Vass haben zie gemacht?"* (What have you done in there?) *"Dass geht doch nicht in diesem hotel!"* (You can't do that in this hotel!)

Sam and I froze. We didn't make another sound for the next five minutes. Thank God, the cleaning lady didn't use her key to come into the room. I'm sure we'd have been arrested for destroying this three-hundred-year-old national treasure.

As the dust settled, we planned our next move. We needed to put the bed back together before the *putzfrau* could discover the damage. But it was Sunday; the lumber yard would surely be closed. There was a small store on the corner that was open, however, with a sign in the window advertising hobby supplies. This was probably our best, maybe only, chance to find something we could use to repair the bed. But all we could find was some balsa wood and clear wood glue.

With these meager supplies in hand, we began gluing the bed's massive head and footboards back together. We used a lot of glue and balsa wood. Eventually, the glue dried, and—lo and behold—the huge bed was back together and propped against the wall. Sam decided to wait until just before our departure in the morning to replace the mattress, to give the glue twenty-four hours more to dry.

Half an hour before departure, Sam gingerly replaced the mattress and carefully made the bed. He straightened the room, got some new towels for the bath from the maid's cart, and hoped she'd think the room didn't need to be cleaned. We hadn't decided what to say to the incoming Capitol captain about the bed, as that captain would be assigned the same room.

When the crew bus arrived with the incoming crew, we waited to greet the captain. As he stepped off the bus, we knew instantly what we would say. He was not among our favorite pilots. Sam and I looked at each other without expression, greeted the captain, bid him a pleasant layover, and then boarded the bus.

Two days later, we arrived back in Frankfurt. The outgoing crew was waiting as the bus arrived. The outgoing captain had a foul look on his face, and Sam asked innocently if he'd had a good layover. I could barely contain myself as he recounted his story. He said he was already taking a lot of flak from his German girlfriend about his weight, and when they jumped into bed together, the huge three-hundred-year-old antique bed collapsed.

When we checked into the hotel, Sam was told that the captain's room was not available due to some furniture repairs that were being made in the room. As I went to my room to clean up, I noticed that the door to the captain's room was open and that three carpenters and a supervisor were working around the bed. I walked in and spoke to the supervisor. Whether it was my uniform or my fluent German that impressed him, he told me the entire story.

His company had held the contract to make all the furniture repairs to this old hotel for the past fifty years. He said that although they had no record of having performed the work themselves, apparently they must have, as it was obvious that the bed had been recently repaired. Herr Schmidt said that he was absolutely horrified that one of his men would use balsa wood and hobby glue for such an undertaking. He was sure that it must have been a disgruntled employee, to sabotage the company's reputation with the hotel. To affirm his company's excellent work, he told me it had a reputation for making each and every furniture repair *bombenfest* (bomb-proof). I guess it's a German thing.

Little Amber Annunciator Light

Captain Len Rew was another great captain I flew with in my early DC-8 co-pilot days. He would often let me fly from the left seat and gave me lots of pointers and good advice on becoming a captain. One winter night, we were on our departure from JFK Airport and climbing out in a cloudless, starry sky en route to Las Vegas. I was in the left seat. It was warm in the cockpit, and there was pleasant conversation going on among the three of us.

After a while, the senior flight attendant came up to the cockpit and asked if we wanted all our meals at the same time. Captain Rew, true to his easy-going nature, answered, "Sure why not?" A few minutes later, the three meals arrived, and before long, we were all happily chowing down.

As we continued to climb, I found myself amazed at the performance of the DC-8 that night. Instead of me having to lower the nose of the aircraft at 23,000 feet in order to maintain its 300-knot climb speed, I was actually having to increase the pitch angle (raise the nose) to avoid climbing at a higher than normal speed. A couple of minutes later, I had to pitch the nose up again, as the climb speed had increased. I figured it must be the colder air temperature that was giving us greater climb performance.

When I mentioned this to Captain Rew, he agreed that the colder ambient air must be responsible. A moment later, however, a faintly lit little amber light on the annunciator panel overhead caught three pairs of eyes at the same moment. The light said "pitot heat inop." Then, the stall warning went off, warning of an imminent aerodynamic stall!

As in a pilot's worst nightmare, trays full of food went flying as we scrambled to level the nose of the aircraft and apply maximum continuous thrust to the four big jet engines.

What had happened was that the pitot heater for the airspeed indicators malfunctioned and the residual moisture in the pitot system froze. Eventually, our actual airspeed decayed to the stall warning speed, set about 10 percent above actual stall speed. Another few seconds, and the airplane would have stalled and lost considerable altitude—in the very best case scenario.

Another lesson learned: it's probably best for the captain and co-pilot not to eat at the same time. In addition, one should realize that if something doesn't seem quite right, *it probably isn't.*

The Fashion Model

I needed to stretch my legs, so I excused myself, put on my uniform jacket, and walked into the cabin of the big DC-8. In those days, the early 1970s, airplane hijackings were not common, and 9/11 would not happen for thirty years. Thus, captains and co-pilots would sometimes take turns stretching their legs, strolling through the cabin, smiling at passengers, and pinning gold plastic airplane wings on kids. As I walked through the cabin that winter night, smiling, chatting, and answering the occasional question, I couldn't help noticing a particularly beautiful brunette who was staring at me with intense, beautiful hazel eyes. I stopped and asked her if she was enjoying the flight. She responded, in a German accent, that she was. I then asked her if she was from Germany, to which she replied that she resided in Frankfurt and was meeting her sister who lived in Vegas. I switched to German, and we conversed a few pleasant minutes. She was beautiful. She had the looks of a fashion model, with beautiful skin and high cheekbones. She asked me if I flew to Frankfurt, and of course I answered in the affirmative. She then scribbled her phone number on the paper napkin under her drink and handed it to me.

Helga was a high-spirited former fashion model who knew exactly how to bring out the best in any man she was with. We met on at least seven subsequent Frankfurt layovers. She would pick me up at my hotel in a Mercedes sports car, and we would go to Sachsenhausen for a wonderful dinner and then back to my hotel. It turned out that she was married to a well-known *and much older* German industrialist, whose interest in life was accumulating money. Helga felt left out of all of this, although she lived a lavish lifestyle that she clearly loved. We both delighted in each other's company during those months until we realized that our feelings toward each other had deepened. We agreed to call it off in the interest of all concerned. It was a very nice interlude that ended well. We never saw each other again, though I surely did think of her now and then.

Captain's Meal

My next flight to Europe was to Malaga, Spain, a great destination for a crew layover—nice beaches, sun, and great food. Captain Polson was the skipper. Polson was a tall, sandy-haired man with a prominent paunch. We all have our personality traits and quirks; Polson's was food. In particular, it was the *captain's meal*. As there are three crew members in the cockpit, one of the meals is always different from the others to prevent a case of inadvertent food poisoning incapacitating all three cockpit crew members simultaneously. Usually, the different one is designated the captain's meal, and quite often, it was either seafood or filet mignon. Most captains, upon first entering the cockpit prior to a flight, looked at the aircraft logbook to check for previous squawks, or problems, to determine whether appropriate corrective action had been completed. Captain Polson was a little different. The first thing he would do was check with the senior flight attendant regarding what the captain's meal was. This drove the flight attendants crazy. Hanna, our senior flight attendant on this particular flight, had a heck of a sense of humor. When Captain Polson asked about the captain's meal, she said that unfortunately it was a rather ordinary-looking Salisbury steak. Captain Polson grumbled something and said he had hoped the caterer in Malaga would be delivering the customary captain's seafood meal. Then he asked her if she could keep an eye open for it on the return trip, to prevent it being waylaid by one of the cabin staff. Hanna said, "Will do, captain."

Apparently, on the layover, Hanna went beach combing the morning of the return flight and gathered quite a few dead clams, crabs, and mussels that had washed onto the beach. True to form, when Captain Polson entered the aircraft, he asked her what the captain's meal was. The answer was quick and snappy: "Seafood."

We pushed back from the gate right on time. The takeoff and climb to altitude was smooth, and at eighteen thousand feet, the captain turned off the seatbelt sign. A couple of minutes later, the senior flight attendant came into the cockpit to take our beverage orders.

Captain Polson said he was getting kind of hungry and, when time permitted, he'd be ready for the seafood meal anytime. It wasn't long before a strong aroma of seafood drifted in from the galley.

Within about twenty minutes, Hanna came up to the cockpit with the captain's meal. She stood there as Polson lifted the cover off the entrée dish and looked at the seafood. His only comment before taking the first bite was that he'd never seen such a variety of clams in his life and that it sure had a seafood smell!

Fortunately, Hanna grabbed his hand before the fork got near his mouth. She made some funny comment about being careful what you wish for. Captain Polson laughed along with the rest of us and realized not only that a joke had been played on him but why. I flew with Captain Polson several times after that flight and never again heard him ask anything about his captain's meal.

....

Aarrgh, Them That Died Were the Lucky Ones!

....

I always enjoyed scuba diving, and on one of my frequent fly-fishing trips to Islamorada in the Florida Keys, I met Carl Fismer, a well-known and successful treasure diver and museum curator. Carl and I hit it off well, and soon afterward, he invited me to dive a Spanish treasure wreck with him off Sebastian Inlet, on the east coast of Florida.

The wreck was on an Admiralty claim by Mel Fisher. Mel had just discovered the *Atocha*, from which he was about to salvage $400 million worth of gold, silver, and emeralds. The 1715 Fleet galleon off Sebastian inlet was not a big wreck by *Atocha* standards, so Carl was working the site for Mel. We anchored on top of the wreck in a fairly shallow thirty-five feet of water. Unless you were a really experienced treasure diver like Carl, you'd never have known you were anchored over a shipwreck of any kind.

Carl Fismer looking over some of the coins found on the 1715 fleet galleon. .

On the back of our dive boat was a device called a "mail-box," which, when lowered into place, diverted a strong current of water from the boat's turning propeller, gently blowing sand away from the ocean floor. Then with underwater metal detectors, one could hope to uncover the secrets and treasures of the nearly three-hundred-year-old Spanish galleon.

We worked the wreck on a hookah system, in which air was pumped through a hose to our regulators. In thirty-five feet of water, there were no nitrogen problems, and you could dive all day long without getting the bends. The only problem was the large Sheepshead fish that would bite your ears, removing chunks of flesh, often causing a fair amount of bleeding. Think sharks!

One afternoon during a lunch break, a friend of Carl's came aboard. This was Robert F. Marx, author of forty books on treasure diving and archeology. Bob was a very pleasant fellow with a huge scar down his thigh caused by an encounter with a hammerhead shark off the Serranilla bank north of Colombia, in South America. Bob was a tough ex-marine, and my guess is that the hammerhead paid dearly for that encounter.

"Mail-box" on the back of the treasure salvage boat.
"Mail-box" shown in the up position while underway.

After lunch, we were down on the wreck again. Uncovering pieces of eight (Spanish silver coins) and other artifacts last touched by another person three hundred years earlier was almost as much of a thrill as learning to fly big jets. It proved to be lucrative too!

Silver and gold coins found on the 1715 galleon.

CHAPTER 6

1974

Challenge of My Career

✳

About the time I had flown five hundred hours as a DC-8 co-pilot, Capitol announced a bid based on the company's seniority list for pilots to upgrade to *captain* on the DC-8. Having the seniority required for upgrading, I found myself on the way back to Braniff's simulator in Dallas. I was about to experience one of the biggest challenges of my career.

Our check pilot, Steve Wolf, was conducting the simulator training. Wolf was a short, heavyset, round-faced man who came from a military flying background. One unmistakable feature of his personality was his very well-developed belief in himself. When he spoke, his voice resonated with the mellifluous sound reminiscent of every knowledgeable expert you had ever met in your life. He made it clear to me that he preferred upgrading pilots to captain when they either had a heavy military transport background, like his, or considerable co-pilot experience in the airplane in which he was upgrading to captain. He said that I met neither criteria and would receive a "thorough" checkout. I didn't know exactly what he meant by "thorough," but I knew it wasn't going to be easy.

Even under the best of circumstances, with the most benevolent airline and the most sympathetic check airman imaginable, the airline takes a pilot's first captaincy on a large airplane very seriously, as do the FAA and the pilot himself. True, the pilot has served an apprenticeship as a co-pilot under the tutelage of experienced captains. Still, he has not proven how he would handle a dire emergency on his own without the guidance of an experienced captain in the other seat. Considering that a big Douglas DC-8 or DC-10 jet in the '70s carried between 250 and 380 passengers, one can see the seriousness of a decision to pronounce a new first-time captain qualified to take command of a large airplane with that many people's lives dependent on him.

In the best of scenarios, it becomes a step-by-step process. First, a new pilot is in command of a light, twin-engine plane. Still later, he is in command of a medium-sized, twin-engine airplane, and then a medium-sized jet. This type of transition makes the upgrading process much easier and makes a check pilot's or FAA inspector's decision to give the final blessings much easier as well.

In other circumstances, as in my situation, the pilot has not made the transition from pilot-in-command of a medium-sized jet, though my flying experience in many different airplanes was significant. As a result, I was going to be put to the test so that everyone, including me, could feel comfortable with the decision. How a check airman goes about this training and checking varies somewhat from check airman to check airman. As I became a check airman later in my career, I personally have spent many hours and a few sleepless nights trying to devise a good training scenario that was fair to the new pilot being checked while allowing me to determine a new captain's airworthiness.

It is worth noting that this type of conundrum has occurred in many time periods in the airline industry, often during times of healthy financial growth, which propels airlines to expand rapidly. As promotion occurs in an airline based on that particular airline's seniority list, the possibility exists that a co-pilot may have the seniority to upgrade to captain on a large airplane before he has demonstrated his command ability on any airplane of significant size.

Having said all this, it must be noted that airline training programs are designed to properly and efficiently train and test pilots regularly. Modern aircraft simulators are carefully crafted to duplicate the flying characteristics of the airplane in which the pilot is being trained. The Federal Aviation Agency is tasked with ensuring that the airlines perform all their training in accordance with an approved training syllabus. The training and testing are taken very seriously, and except in extremely rare cases, there is very little benefit of doubt given where marginal performance is demonstrated.

In addition to initial aircraft and simulator training, the airlines are required to give bi-annual training or check rides in the aircraft simulator. The airline and the FAA also give annual line checks, in which a check airman may board the airplane without warning and announce that you are receiving a line check. That is, the check airman may ride along for one or more flights to determine that both pilots are flying the airplane satisfactorily and in accordance with company and FAA procedures.

Finally, the pilot in command of a large airplane receives a medical checkup by an FAA-approved doctor every six months. If any serious medical conditions are detected, the pilot is grounded until the medical condition is resolved to the FAA administrator's satisfaction. Further, periodic drug and alcohol screenings are given to the pilots at unannounced times.

I have often thought of other professions—such as the legal and medical professions—in which these types of stringent checks and tests could be useful to ensure a high level of professionalism.

Full motion modern aircraft simulator with visual display.

My Guardian Angel

Everyone should have a guardian angel. One of mine was an FAA inspector named John Harpole. I didn't know John Harpole well but knew he was a very mild-mannered, intelligent career FAA employee who was guided by a strong sense of ethics and fairness. Were it not for John Harpole, my airline career would not have turned out as well as it did.

At the end of the week, after twelve hours of captain upgrade simulator training, Captain Wolf conducted my simulator check ride. The purpose of this check ride was to determine whether I was qualified to continue my training to be pilot in command of a DC-8. The check was going very well until the last simulated emergency, another two-engine landing. Captain Wolf had told the flight engineer to program a 15-knot tailwind into the approach. This magnitude of tailwind was beyond the 10-knot tailwind limit of the DC-8, which made a smooth approach and landing nearly impossible. Somehow, I managed to land the simulator on the runway, though it wasn't particularly smooth. Captain Wolf deemed the lack of smoothness a failure, even though it was the result of his contrived scenario: a 15-knot tailwind that was beyond the landing limitations of the airplane and the DC-8 simulator.

I'm not sure how the FAA heard about this, but two weeks later, I was back in the simulator with FAA inspector John Harpole, Capitol Airways' principal operating inspector, in attendance. He was there to ensure that Capitol was giving simulator training in accordance with the FAA-approved training syllabus and within DC-8 *operating limitations*. (Gradually, I came to regard John Harpole as my Guardian Angel. On several occasions, he intervened to ensure that my training was in accordance with the FAA-approved flight-training syllabus.)

This time, it all went without any hitches, thanks to hard work, a little luck, and a guardian angel. The only one in the simulator who didn't have a big smile on his face at the end of the check ride was Captain Wolf.

Good Judgment Comes from Experience, and a Lot of That Comes from Bad Judgment
                                                          −Will Rogers

---

I guess it was no surprise to anyone that Captain Wolf would preside over each and every line check I was to receive before being signed off to fly the line as a DC-8 captain. The stakes were high for both of us. Problem was, it seemed we each wanted a different outcome.

My first line check was a flight from Cincinnati, Ohio, to Gatwick, London, and then on to Brussels, Belgium. I was in the left seat with Wolf in the right, and, of course we had a flight engineer at the flight engineer's panel behind us. FAA inspector John Harpole was sitting on the observer jump-seat. This flight was shaping up to be anything but routine, due to the antiskid system being inoperative that day. The anti-skid system allows maximum wheel braking to be applied, regardless of runway conditions such as rain, snow, or ice, while preventing wheels from locking up and skidding. There are eight large main tires on a DC-8. It is not uncommon for airplanes to be flown with certain systems inoperative as long as those systems are not *no-go* items—systems required by the airplane manufacturer or the FAA. We had checked in the aircraft *Minimum Equipment List* and determined it was allowable to fly with the anti-skid inoperative as long as sufficient runway length was available at the destination airport in accordance with the airplane's landing performance charts. To make matters worse, however, Gatwick Airport had closed the first eight hundred feet of the runway we would be landing on, due to work in progress. Further, it was forecast to be raining at the time of our arrival. This scenario was truly shaping up to be a pilot's nightmare. In accordance with the charts, there was just enough runway available, considering the inoperable anti-skid system.

The takeoff, climb, and cruise portion of the line check flight went fine. Just before beginning descent, we requested the weather and runway conditions from air traffic control, and the engineer quickly checked the runway length required, once more. Although there was steady rain at Gatwick, the aircraft performance charts indicated that we had just enough runway length available. The cockpit was very quiet during the descent and approach. Checklists were read and responded to in a very professional manner. We broke through the lower deck of clouds at four hundred feet, and the runway appeared to the right due to the heading we had to maintain because of the strong left crosswind. The runway was very wet, and you could see the reflections of the runway lights in the wind-blown water on the runway. It was not very inviting, and at that moment, I definitely wished I were somewhere else.

The flight engineer called one hundred feet above the ground, then fifty feet. I started to raise the nose of the aircraft and gradually began taking out the wind correction,"crab". We were right on speed, and the aircraft was pointing straight down the runway as we made a moderately firm touchdown to get the tires through the film of rain. I applied moderate to heavy braking and reverse thrust. The airplane decelerated nicely, and we came to a stop a couple hundred feet from the end of Gatwick's runway. We taxied to the gate, and I breathed a sigh of relief. A few minutes later, a mechanic came into the cockpit to tell us that one of the tires was flat and needed to be changed. Wolf had a fit and blamed it on excessively hard braking. Harpole, the FAA inspector, spoke up and disagreed with him, maintaining that it was due to the antiskid being inoperative. Wolf didn't say any more about it, but I could see by the expression on his face that he wasn't happy.

An hour later, we were ready to depart on our next leg to Brussels, Belgium. The weather was dry in Brussels, and the runway was more than two miles long. It was a short, thirty-minute flight, and we would be landing at a light weight. We broke out of the weather at three thousand feet, and the runway was straight ahead. On touchdown, I applied reverse thrust and decided to use the entire runway length to stop. Upon landing, Wolf told me to get off the brakes. Harpole, the FAA inspector (and my guardian angel), who had been watching quite closely, told him that until that point, the brakes hadn't been used. I was getting the feeling that the FAA inspector was starting to pay as much attention to Captain Wolf as he was to me. As we taxied to the gate, Wolf said that I put the landing gear down too early in the approach. Harpole said that he was more concerned that it was put down prior to the final approach fix and that he was quite happy with how the approach was flown. It seemed to me that Wolf was having a really hard time coming to terms with my being a captain on the DC-8, and I was surely hoping that this would settle down.

The remaining flights on that series of line checks went well, and upon our return to JFK Airport, Inspector Harpole told me that I had done a good job and that he would probably be flying with me again.

The next line check I received was on a flight from JFK, New York, to Rome, Italy. I was in the left seat, and Captain Wolf was in the co-pilot's seat to conduct the line check. The FAA inspector was *not* onboard. In the cabins behind us were 250 people. The tailwinds were light, and the passenger load and baggage were heavy, so an intermediate fuel stop was scheduled in Gander, Newfoundland.

The flight was going fine until I requested the Gander weather, about two hundred miles out from Gander Airport. The news was not good: the weather was below *landing minimums*, with low ceilings and ground fog. Our alternate, St. John, Newfoundland, had good weather, so it was a no-brainer. Or so I thought.

I told Captain Wolf that we needed to divert to St. John and that we would refuel there. With an odd look in his eyes, he stated that we would be landing in Gander. I voiced my protest. Wolf disagreed, insisting that since he was the check airman, we would begin an approach to Gander and see what the weather looked like as we approached the final approach fix.

All checklists completed, we were inbound to the final approach fix for a straight-in approach. We obtained an update on the weather one mile outside the fix. It was still *below minimums*. In the landing briefing (that's the briefing by the flying pilot to the non-flying pilot and engineer), I stated that we would execute a missed approach at the final approach fix and divert to St. John. Wolf said, "Absolutely not," and placed his hand over mine on the four power levers. "Just fly the approach," he said.

The Sperry flight director (the artificial horizon with instrument landing system [ILS] signals integrated with computer commands) on this DC-8-63 Stretch aircraft was big and accurate, but it wasn't designed for what we were about to do.

At 250 feet above the ground, we were in solid clouds and fog. I stated that we should execute a *missed approach* at our company minimum of two hundred feet if the airport was not in sight. Wolf tightened his hand over mine, which was on top of the four power levers. "Keep flying, and when I call fifty feet altitude above the ground, raise the aircraft pitch angle one needle width (about one degree)," he said.

I had a huge problem with what was happening, but this was not the time to get into an argument. I had to fly a perfect ILS (instrument approach). There could be no excuses; this could be life or death.

Captain Wolf announced, "One hundred feet above the ground." It was very tense in the cockpit; we were below minimums, and no lights were in sight. Then Wolf said, "Fifty feet above the ground." I raised the nose one needle width on the Sperry Flight Director. Two seconds later, the main gear touched down. We were traveling at over 160 miles an hour, and we could see nothing through the cockpit windows, not even the runway lights. I pulled the power levers of all engines into reverse and applied maximum continuous thrust (MCT) and very firm braking: 100 knots, 80 knots, 60 knots, then thrust reversers out, and I eased off on the brakes. We were safely stopped. But we still couldn't see a thing. We had no idea where we were on the runway. Only that we were on the runway, *safe*, and the airplane was in one piece!

The yellow follow-me vehicle had difficulty finding us in the thick fog, but when it finally did, it led us to the airport terminal. I was not happy about what had taken place. It was the worst aeronautical decision making I had ever seen, and it was done by the airline's check airman.

Did Captain Wolf do this to test my nerve? Did he do it as part of my training? Did he do it just to save time, to avoid backtracking to St. John? No matter what his misguided reasoning was, it was really the wrong thing to do. It had placed the airplane, passengers, and crew at risk. Having said all that, the experience I obtained that day was responsible for saving my life, the lives of the other two cockpit crew members, and an airplane one night many years later. For that, *I will always be grateful to Captain Wolf.* The check rides weren't over. I was scheduled to fly to Amsterdam via London. But on this trip, I *had* my guardian angel riding along. FAA Inspector John Harpole was sitting in the cockpit jump seat. Most pilots worry when an FAA inspector is onboard, but I didn't because I knew he would also be watching Captain Wolf.

The trip to Amsterdam went smoothly. On the trip back, the destination weather was not too good at JFK. In addition, we got cleared for the infamous Canarsie approach—a visual approach in which the pilot has to visually find and identify the meandering white strobe lights that lead to one of the two southeast-facing runways, 13L and 13R. When flying in to JFK at night and being cleared for the Canarsie approach over the Belt Parkway, there are thousands of lights: car lights, street lights, house lights, and parkway lights. The trick is to find and identify the *lead-in lights*. Not as easy as it might sound.

Fortunately, it all went well. We landed softly, and I taxied in. FAA inspector Harpole stood up and said, "Congratulations, Captain Spivack. I don't need to see any more." Boy, did I feel great!

Captain Wolf, however, was not a happy camper. "Meet me at the KLM lounge after we clear customs," he snapped in a stern voice. Forty minutes later, we were sitting in the KLM lounge. Wolf proceeded to chew me up one side and down the other for half an hour or more. He wasn't saying anything specific, just a lot of hyperbole. But he concluded with, "You are not going to fly as a captain with this company as long as I am check pilot." I was beginning to get the idea that we would never be best friends. (I never found out why he had it in for me.)

Our one-sided conversation must have been unsettling for passengers hearing it in the KLM lounge. I'll bet when they boarded their plane that night, they glanced in the cockpit to see who their pilots were—and I'm sure they were glad to see that it wasn't us.

Most Exciting Flight of My Life

Two weeks went by, and no calls from Capitol. Then I got a call from crew scheduling. I was set up with Captain Wolf for a ferry flight from JFK to Boston, where the plane was to be used for a charter flight.

When I arrived at flight operations, I met the flight engineer (F/E), Dick Stillwood. Dick LaPlata, who was a DC-8 co-pilot, was also there, presumably to fly in the right seat while Captain Wolf gave me a line check from the jump seat.

I ordered fuel for the trip, and Dick Stillwood, our F/E, went out to preflight the airplane and monitor the fueling. Dick

LaPlata and I walked out to the big stretched DC-8-63, sat down in the cockpit, and did our checklists and cockpit set-ups.

About thirty minutes later, the ramp mechanic called on the interphone and asked how much longer it would be until we pushed back. I told him I would let him know in a minute. I called operations and asked where Captain Wolf was. They said they hadn't seen him and he hadn't called.

I looked over at my fellow crew members. "Look," I said, "I'm not sure what the hell's going on here, but maybe the company is testing my ability to make a decision. What would you think about me flying the plane up to Boston without Wolf?" It was a risky gamble, but if successful, it might very well end the check rides. Dick LaPlata jokingly said, "No problem. I might pick up a seniority number tonight when the company fires you." I thought about it for a couple more minutes, then decided it was a risk worth taking.

I told Dick to call for push-back clearance. I heard the big Caterpillar diesel engine of the aircraft tug start-up, and a moment later, I received the request for my brake release. I confirmed brake release, and the push-back from the gate began. Clearance came to start all four engines, and a few minutes later began the taxi for a flight I will never forget.

We were cleared to line up on 31R, and as I did so, it struck me what a brilliantly beautiful night it was. The lit-up skyline of New York stood out like diamonds on a bracelet. My legs trembled slightly as I held the brakes. I was a bit anxious about what might happen if I was misjudging this situation; it could mean the end of my career.

The big plane was empty because it was a ferry flight, and the engines, even in idle, pushed hard against the brakes. It would have been okay, as far as I was concerned, to just sit there a while longer; I wished this incredible feeling could last for the rest of my life. I couldn't believe that this was my first flight as a jet captain in a big, heavy, four-engine jet. There was a possibility, however, that it would be my *last*.

Suddenly, the radio broke the silence. "Capitol 907, cleared for takeoff."

I pushed the power levers forward, and the empty airplane, accelerating at an incredible rate, jumped into the air like a scalded rabbit. It was all I could do to hold that raw power back and keep the plane from exceeding the maximum allowable speed of 250 knots until we reached 10,000 feet.

At 10,000 feet, I pushed the power levers up to climb power, and within fifteen seconds, we were doing 320 knots. For those fifteen seconds, I was like a kid with a new toy. We had barely completed the climb checklist when I had to call for the descent and approach checklist. Now I was slowing down again to 250 knots for flight below 10,000 feet. A short, twenty-minute flight in an empty DC-8-63 proceeds awfully fast; you never stop doing checklists, crew briefings, or setting radios.

I felt an uneasiness creep over me as I began to think about what consequences I might be facing if I'd made a mistake; what if Captain Wolf had arrived late at JFK and demanded to know where in the hell the airplane was and who was flying it? Too late now! I was on approach to Boston Logan Airport, and life was still great, at least for the moment.

The approach and landing were by the book, and I started to come back to earth mentally as I guided the plane onto the high-speed turnoff. I taxied to the gate. The station agent met us on the Jet-way, and there were no Port Authority police in sight. We opened the cabin door, and the agent asked, "How was the flight, Captain?"

"Wonderful," I said, looking around for the airport police. Yes, wonderful! It had been the most exciting flight of my life.

Looking back on it, I realize now more than ever what a profound decision I had to make that night. Years later, I asked several executives at Capitol what went on that evening. I never received an answer, just a few faint smiles. To this day, it remains a mystery to me. However, it might be worth noting that a short time later, Captain Wolf resigned.

CHAPTER 7

1975

Flying the Line

✳

I had the good life of a thirty-five-year-old captain piloting a 250-passenger, four-engine DC-8 jet airliner to international destinations, and I was getting great experience flying nearly one thousand hours per year. My career, my dreams, had all come true.

My first transatlantic trip occurred soon after I became captain. I was flying flight CL-907 out of JFK to Frankfurt, Germany, and it was a typical evening departure out of New York. The weather en route was good, and the destination weather in Frankfurt was excellent. As a new captain, my level of enthusiasm was very high and somewhat contagious to my two cockpit colleagues; before long, we were all enjoying the particularly upbeat cockpit camaraderie. We had a two-day layover in Frankfurt at a nice hotel, the Ritters Park, and had enjoyed a couple of superb meals consisting of bratwurst, schnitzels, and beer in the little town of Bad Homburg.

Two days later, we were on our way back to JFK. We were about halfway across the ocean at about thirty-five degrees west longitude when the yellow master caution light illuminated on the glare shield in front of me. I turned to the engineer and asked him what was going on. He broke the news in quiet tones. We were losing hydraulic fluid, and he was going to see what he could do to stop the leak. About fifteen minutes later, the engineer said he could not stop the leak, and that at the current rate of hydraulic fluid loss, we would lose all hydraulic pressure by the time we approached Halifax, Nova Scotia. As I studied the navigation charts, I concluded that we would plan an emergency landing in Bangor, Maine. The Bangor runway was long, and the weather was good. The main problem was that we would be landing with no flaps and slats (the lift devices on the leading and trailing edge of each wing), and no hydraulic brakes. We would be able to use only a few applications of emergency air brakes.

I instructed my co-pilot to contact aeronautical radio and was able to get a phone patch into our company headquarters. The company agreed that Bangor was the best choice and was standing by in case we needed their help. We declared an emergency with Gander air traffic control and received priority handling all the way to Bangor approach control. The first order of business was to have the Bangor, Maine, emergency rescue trucks and equipment standing by in case we overran the runway or the emergency landing went badly. We then reviewed all of the emergency procedures regarding a landing with zero flaps and slats and prepared for the approach. It was essentially a visual daytime landing, as the weather was good. In most respects, what we were planning to do was similar to the zero-flaps landings we practiced during training in the DC-8 aircraft simulator. The main difference, of course, was that this time we were playing for keeps with the lives of 250 passengers and crew. The flight attendants had been briefed early in the emergency, and they had prepared the cabin and briefed the passengers as to why we were landing in Bangor, Maine. They also informed the passengers that the landing would be without flaps and slats and that, as a result, we were going to land at a very fast speed, and the braking might feel rougher than normal.

Because we could not lower the flaps and slats, we were going to be touching down at a speed of over 217 miles per hour. The aircraft tires were rated for 225-mph maximum speed. At this speed, we would eat up the runway length at an incredibly fast pace. The touch-down had to be near the beginning of the runway, and the engine reversers had to be immediately deployed. Then the airbrake usage needed to be very carefully applied and not released until the aircraft stopped. If we applied the airbrakes several times and released the pressure each time, we would deplete the emergency air and run out of air brakes, which could have very disastrous results.

We set up for a long final approach some fifteen miles out. This enabled me to fly a stable but shallow descent path with the touchdown as close to the beginning of the runway as possible. The aircraft flight controls were extremely sensitive at the high speed we were flying. The touchdown would occur with nearly no perceptible flare (level off).

I touched down right on our selected (bug) speed, which was 195 knots, or close to 218 miles per hour. We were screaming down the runway when I applied maximum continuous reverse thrust. I gingerly rotated the emergency air brake handle until the brakes began to respond. They were very sensitive but extremely effective. The idea was to bring the airplane safely to a stop without flattening eight main tires. We used nearly 10,000 feet of the 11,400-foot runway that day. It was an exhilarating emergency landing, and the three of us in the cockpit as well as the 250 passengers were pleased with the safe, happy ending.

The local aircraft and engine repair shop did the troubleshooting; the problem turned out to be a leaking hydraulic line. A few hours later, with the line repaired and the aircraft logbook signed off, we were on our way back to New York.

The flight back to JFK was uneventful, and except for arriving several hours past the scheduled arrival time, there was no harm done, other than to the passenger's serenity. It was an exciting flight and another experience that seasoned me as a captain and helped to prepare me for what was to come.

New captain in the Douglas DC-8- 63 four engine jet circa 1975.

In and Out of Africa

In December 1975, I was sent to Accra in Ghana, Africa, to fly the pilgrimage flights from Accra to Jeddah. These trips were known as the hajj flights.

I found the people of Ghana amazing. They didn't seem to worry about what might happen the next day; they simply lived their lives minute by minute. They lived in the here and now.

One afternoon, the first officer, flight engineer, ten flight attendants, and I were walking from our hotel to a restaurant two miles down the road. The temperature was about 102 degrees Fahrenheit. A Ghanian man and his young son stopped their car and asked if they could give us a lift. Abdul was in his late thirties, of medium height, and somewhat on the thin side. His son was about seven years old, thin, and very shy. The man took us to the restaurant, four at a time. When he arrived at the restaurant with the last load of crew members, I asked him to join us. He agreed but said he just wanted to listen to our conversations; neither he nor his son would order anything. I asked him to order food and told him it was our treat, but he declined again.

After we finished eating, he asked me if he could eat the leftovers on our plates. We were all shocked by the request. He was a very proud man, who would not allow us to repay his kindness, yet he was very hungry. Eventually, he allowed us to order food for him and his son. We acquired another perception of the people of Ghana that day.

I continually witnessed many examples of kindness toward our crew members while we were based there. I often wonder if the people of Ghana are still so kind and innocent today.

The 2¾-Engine Ferry Flight

Captain Lagerquist, Capitol's director of flight operations, telexed me that they needed a captain who could perform a three-engine takeoff and fly from Accra to Madrid to have the Number-Two (inboard, left side) engine replaced. Apparently, it had ingested some FOD (foreign objects, probably sand), had lost inlet turbine blades, and was inoperative.

I was chosen for the flight. The fact that I had never trained in this delicate takeoff procedure didn't worry the director of operations. He told me he had all the confidence in the world in my flying skills. All I needed to do was to study the Douglas aircraft flight manual (AFM) on the plane, in which there was a chapter dedicated to the method of performing this risky maneuver.

There is something to be said for the term "impetuous youth." The director of operations stroked my ego, and I fell for it. After studying the procedure in the flight manual, I assembled a crew. I chose Jim Luster as co-pilot and John Respass as the flight engineer. Jim was a tall, well-built fellow in his early forties and had been an F-86 fighter pilot in the Korean War. He was a good pilot and proved to be an indispensable asset on this flight. John Respass was nearly sixty and was an absolute delight to fly with. He was a slightly rotund man of medium height who was full of laughter and could recite an endless stream of jokes when the time was right. John was one of the best flight engineers in the business.

We reckoned that a 7:00 a.m. departure would yield the coolest ground temperature, giving us optimal aircraft performance. The next morning, John Respass did the takeoff performance calculation and determined that we were safe to go. We all wanted to get home to the United States for a while, so we were in a "go" mode.

The three-engine takeoff procedure requires that symmetrical, or evenly distributed, power be applied before brake release; then, to compensate for the differential thrust, that thrust on the remaining good asymmetrical engine must be gradually increased as the airplane's speed increases and the rudder gains effectiveness and directional control. The bottom line is that you have to be able to keep the airplane on the runway during the takeoff roll while simultaneously meeting takeoff performance requirements: not running out of runway and clearing obstacles in the flight path. This is all much easier said than done, and many airplanes and crew have been lost in years past attempting a three-engine takeoff in a four-engine airplane.

We taxied out to the run-up position adjacent to the runway. Since this was a ferry flight, we had only the three cockpit crew members—no passengers, flight attendants, or cargo—and only the minimum fuel required for the flight. We were as light as we could be. The three of us were the only people at risk. Some consolation!

With all checklists and briefings complete, I started up and checked each of the three working engines. Unfortunately, the Number-Three engine (inner right side) was indicating only about 75 percent of maximum power. This was unexpected and needed to be factored into our calculations.

John Respass went back to the takeoff performance charts and after checking and rechecking, finally determined that we could still manage a takeoff with the amount of runway available, considering the blistering temperature.

That settled, we called for takeoff clearance. Clearance received, I lined up with the runway. Holding the brakes, power was brought up on engines Numbers-One and Four to equal power. When power was set, I released the brakes. Getting the power up on Number-Three was critical.

We weren't accelerating fast. At seventy knots, I started to bring in the Number-Three engine. I found myself holding full right rudder, but as our speed increased, I could bring in more and more power from Number-Three and still keep the airplane close to the runway centerline. At ninety knots, Number-Three was producing 75 percent of full thrust. The crew hotel, which was about a mile from the end of the runway, was beginning to appear much larger now. *We were running out of runway.*

Jim Luster called "*V1*, (decision speed) *Rotate!*" The main gear continued to roll along the runway for an unbearably long time. I was focused on the end of the runway coming up—how slow everything was happening—when I heard John Respass shout, "*Positive rate!*" (We were climbing.) I responded, "*Gear up!*"

I could see that we could not continue flying straight ahead; the hotel was less than a half-mile in front of us. I banked gently toward the good inboard engine, and a moment later, the hotel roof just slid by. John called, "*V2!*" (takeoff safety speed). We were safely airborne, *but it wasn't over yet.*

It is important to note that once you departed from an airport in Africa, the terrain became completely inhospitable. If you were not flying over dense jungle, you were flying over desert sands. Sand storms were common, and visibility in those storms was nearly always zero.

We clawed our way up to nineteen thousand feet. The airplane, an older DC-8-33 model, would climb no higher because of the Number-Two engine being shut down, the Number-Three engine being sick, and the high outside temperature at nineteen thousand feet.

In 1975, there was little, if any, air traffic control over most parts of Africa. Collision avoidance was a matter of listening to other aircraft when they made their progress reports on the airways and then calculating where they were relative to your airplane's position.

Also, a sharp visual lookout was mandatory.

Our flight was about thirty-eight minutes north of Accra when the **fire bell** went off and the **bright-red master warning light illuminated** on the glare shield in front of me. "*Fire in Number-One engine!*" John shouted. God, what now? I thought.

A couple of seconds later, there was a loud bang and then a tremendous vibration. "*Number-One engine power lever idle, Number-One engine fuel shutoff lever off, Number-One engine fire shutoff lever full forward! Fire agent discharge! Check if the fire is out! Checklist!*" I commanded. The words slid out effortlessly. This was what we'd learned to memorize. But now, there was a completely unfamiliar crisis to deal with. My brain felt numbed by the magnitude of what we were facing. We had two engines out on the left wing, and the inboard engine on the right wing was sick, putting out only 75 percent of maximum power. With maximum continuous thrust (MCT) available only on Number-Four engine and only 75 percent of max power On Number-Three engine, it was impossible to maintain altitude. The outside air temperature over French Equatorial Africa that day at nineteen thousand feet was ninety degrees Fahrenheit. Number-Three engine was now showing a high exhaust gas temperature (EGT) well into the red range of the instrument, and I wasn't sure how long the engine would survive at this power setting.

The DC-8 was descending at nine hundred feet per minute. We could remain airborne for less than twenty minutes more. Within sixteen minutes, we would be setting up for either an approach to an airport or an approach to our grave in the desert; it was as simple as that.

The airport at Accra from which we'd departed was out of the question; it was too far. I asked Jim to quickly locate an airport that was within fifteen minutes flying time from our present position. Within one minute, Jim gave me the name of an airport: Niamey, Niger, and he said it would be on a heading of 160 degrees magnetic, would be fifteen minutes away, and it was the only airport we could reach. That was the way it was in the cockpit of an airliner, especially when things were going very wrong. You had to be willing to trust your fellow crew member with your life; a one-man show would not work. Each of us was nearly overwhelmed with just doing our own specific job. If Jim was mistaken and the airport was twenty-one minutes away, we would probably not make it down alive.

Niamey in Niger was a French Foreign Legion airbase. I asked Jim to call them on their approach and tower frequencies. We needed them to have their emergency equipment standing by in case we crash-landed.

There was no response from Niamey approach or tower after repeated calls. We then switched to the international emergency frequency of 121.5 Mhz and kept calling a MAYDAY as we continued a downward drift while maintaining airspeed in our descent toward Niamey Airport. It was clear; they were not going to answer us.

I was strangely calm. I had experienced this in myself once before: when I was forced to make the approach and landing in total fog with Captain Wolf. When the situation became life or death, I was sanguine. It was almost as though I were outside of my body watching what I was doing. In less dire circumstances, I have found myself in much more turmoil.

We located the airport visually while passing through six thousand feet. I was on a down-wind leg at two thousand feet, parallel to the landing runway, and called, *"Gear down!"* At nine hundred feet, I turned base leg about one-half mile past the approach end of the runway. Then I rolled out over the extended center line of the runway at five hundred feet above the ground just as the landing gear lights flashed three green, indicating that the landing gear was down and locked. I briefed John Respass to roll out the rudder and aileron trim when I retarded the power levers to engines Numbers-Three and Number-Four, on short final, once I estimated I could glide to the runway.

There could be no mistakes on this approach and landing. A do-over was not possible; we couldn't execute a missed approach on two engines. History had shown that any time a missed approach was attempted with two engines out on the same wing, with landing gear down, the results were the same. The airliner would roll upside down, and everyone would be lost in a fiery crash.

As soon as we were over the centerline of the runway, Niamey tower finally came to life. They shot a continuous stream of red flares, signifying that we were not allowed to land. *C'est dommage* (too bad)! We were landing, and no one could stop us now.

When I could see that we were going to make it to the runway, I had Jim set twelve degrees of flaps so we could obtain full rudder control. At one hundred feet, I began retarding the power levers. With only twelve degrees of flaps, our approach speed was very fast; stopping was going to be a problem. We had only one engine reverser that we could use.

We touched down on the centerline about six hundred feet past the beginning of the runway at 175 miles per hour. I pulled Engine-Three into reverse and applied maximum braking, my eyes glued to the end of the runway. The airplane finally came to a stop just two hundred feet from the runway end.

We all breathed a deep sigh of relief, we were lucky to be alive, but I had one more concern: I knew the brakes would be smoking. I just hoped we wouldn't have a wheel fire, given that the outside air temperature was hot as Hades. I could bet that our French friends might be reluctant to extinguish the fire, as we obviously were not welcome.

We couldn't taxi the airplane with two engines inoperative on the same side, so, to add insult to injury, we were now blocking the only runway at Niamey.

As we opened the forward passenger door, a wicked blast of hot air hit us in the face. It was hot in a way that I had never before experienced—over 105 degrees Fahrenheit.

A group of well-armed French legionnaires, commanded by a crusty-looking colonel with the name-tag Pelletier, marched out to greet us. The only thing warm about their greeting was the desert air.

Fortunately, I spoke conversational French well enough to communicate our situation; otherwise, I'm sure we'd have wound up in a French Foreign Legion jail eating rat soup for dinner. The colonel was a stocky man in his early fifties who had a scar on his face from his right eye to just behind the front of his chin. He was sweating heavily and, because of his annoyance with us, did not exhibit any sense of humor at all.

It took forty of the French troops, twenty on each main gear, to push the big DC-8 off the runway and into the parking area. (Luckily, there wasn't a cliff nearby.)

The first few nights, our crew's sleeping quarters were tents, complete with the occasional scorpion. After that initiation, we were invited to stay in the permanent officers' barracks, a fairly significant improvement—although they displayed no Michelin stars on their entrance either.

Although we were initially the target of French jokes and innuendos, our hosts seemed to warm up to us within a few days and were offering us Gauloises cigarettes and cognac in return for American underarm deodorant and aftershave lotion. Given the desert heat and scarcity of water, we were the beneficiaries of that trade.

Within a week, Union Transport Arienne, a French charter airline company, arrived with a new DC-8 engine, other spare parts, and a bunch of mechanics. Those poor guys worked every day without a break in 100–108-degree heat to change the engine and get us on our way. By the end of the second week, we were ready to go. Our French Legionnaire buddies seemed genuinely sorry to see us leave. To be honest, we were getting to like them, too. The French Foreign Legion soldiers were some very tough men who lived under extremely harsh conditions and did not seem to have much, if any, material things. Many of them showed us a kind side that we hadn't expected.

When the time came to leave, we had to do serious engine run-up checks on the new engine to be sure it was working well and that it had been installed properly. John Respass, our flight engineer, did a wonderful job checking out the replacement engine and our sick Number-Three engine to ensure that we would have the necessary takeoff performance for our second three-engine takeoff.

The three-engine takeoff went smoothly, devoid of further drama, and we flew on to Madrid without a problem—after having learned a few more *dangerous lessons*.

Hat emblem, wings and ID Capitol Airways. (Chapter 3)

Hat emblem, wings, and ID card Fine Air,
parent company of Aerolineas Latinas. (chapter10)

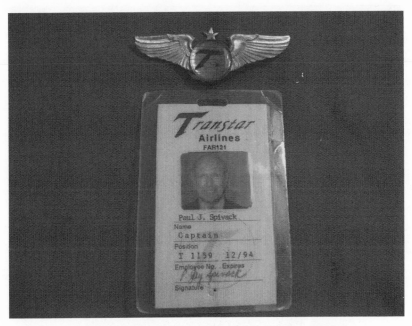

Wings and ID Card Transtar Airlines (chapter 11)

Hat emblem, wings and ID card, Southern Air Transport. (chapter 11)

Leisure Air wings and ID card. (chapter 11)

Korean Airlines hat emblem, wings and ID card. (chapter 12)

Great American Airways hat emblem, wings and ID Card. (chapter 13)

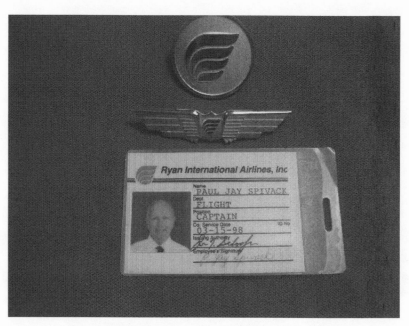

Ryan Airlines hat emblem, wings and ID card. (chapter 13)

CHAPTER 8

1976

The Vacation

✴

By the time February came around, I was ready for my thirty-day vacation. We decided to stand by for a flight to Auckland, New Zealand. I'd heard the fly-fishing was superb, and it was now summer south of the equator. Several days went by, and I wasn't having much luck finding standby seats on any airline; the flights were completely full.

Then a good friend of mine, Fred Egan, who grew up in Argentina, suggested I try to catch a flight to Buenos Aires and then fly to San Carlos de Bariloche, where he'd heard the fishing was excellent. Sure enough, my wife, Elke, and I were able to acquire standby seats on an Aerolineas Argentina flight to Buenos Aires. Elke who was a pretty, blue-eyed blonde, and I, had met in Germany in the mid-60s and married in 1968. We shared a nice life together until our divorce in 1982.

The flight arrived in Buenos Aires at 10:00 a.m., and next on our list was finding a hotel. The first thing I discovered about Argentina was that things were not as well-organized there, as they were in the United States. We couldn't help noticing that the airport was a completely chaotic scene. Trying to book a hotel in Buenos Aires from the airport wouldn't be successful in our wildest dreams; it surely was different south of the border.

At that time, during the seventies, you exchanged foreign money on the black market, in doorways, in alleyways, or at best, with the hotel concierge. As a result, everything was cheap. We ate in the finest restaurants, stayed at five-star hotels, and drank the finest Argentine wines for a small fraction of the cost at comparable venues in the States. We spent several fun days in Buenos Aires, but after a while, we knew it was time to fly to San Carlos de Bariloche and experience fly-fishing in Patagonia.

Our Austral Airlines DC-9 arrived in San Carlos de Bariloche in the evening after a very turbulent flight. The Patagonian winds were howling at more than fifty miles per hour on the ground. We hired a taxi, which took us from the airport to town and dropped us near the small city center. The driver didn't think we would have a problem finding a hotel. We walked, struggling against buffeting winds about a block, and came upon a really charming-looking restaurant and hotel.

At this point, we were sure this hotel would be fine, no matter what. We walked in and were greeted by a rather portly chap, who was of light complexion with deep blue eyes and black hair that seemed strangely out of place. He spoke Spanish with a strong German accent. "Guten tag," I said. He was surprised and asked, "You speak German?" So we got into quite a conversation and eventually were given a beautiful room for the night. After freshening up, we went down to the restaurant and had a great schnitzel dinner, every bit as good as we ever had in Germany.

After a while, the proprietor came over and offered us a bottle of his favorite white wine. I asked him if he'd care to drink a glass with us. He sat down and, several glasses later, introduced himself as Herman—Herman the terrible, he said with a wink that seemed more like a twitch. Then, with a smile, he added something about a big "misunderstanding" regarding what had really happened in Germany. Anyway, he told us how nice it was to speak to an American who spoke German and then said that he needed to get back to work. We heard a few years later that Herman was deported to Italy to resolve some "misunderstandings" that had occurred in the early 1940s.

The next day, we rented a small French Citroen (the one that looks like a Cinzano can) that the car rental agency thought we needed to navigate the unpaved mountainous roads to the Mecca of Argentine fly-fishing: the town of Junin de Los Andes. The name Junin de Los Andes means people of the Andes in the Mapuche Indian language.

The three-hour ride took us through rivers that had flooded, roads we shared with sheep, and thousands of large rocks and ditches waiting for maintenance crews to clean and repair them. It was quite a rough trip, but I knew one thing for sure: there would not be a lot of other anglers to compete with.

About ten miles from Junin, our destination, I pulled off the road and stopped. There in front of us was a beautiful picturesque river that I just couldn't resist. I rigged up my fly rod with a floating line and a #6 Muddler Minnow fly and cast it out about thirty feet, to where the fly drifted into a deep, dark pool near a large tree. Wham! A big, beautiful, speckled brown trout weighing more than six pounds slammed the Muddler fly, and the fight was on. I had never seen a brown trout go acrobatic, but this guy obviously hadn't read his trout operations manual. He stood on his tail, then flipped head over tail and jumped again. What a fish! He took all the fly line and one hundred yards of Dacron line backing. My first cast—I couldn't believe it. I landed the big trout and then carefully released it to the cold Chimehuin River.

First cast in Argentina landed this beautiful trout on the
Chimehuin River near Junin de los Andes.

There was no question in my mind that this was going to be a spectacular fishing vacation. Well, it was time to continue to Junin and the famous refuge of the fly fisherman, the Hosteria Chimehuin. Less than twenty minutes later, the sign on the side of the road said Junín, but it wasn't what we were expecting. This was a high desert town with dusty dirt roads—quaint to say the least.

At the end of one of the dirt roads near the south side of town was the Hosteria Chimehuin. We drove in through the gate between the tall poplar trees to a gravel parking area. As we got out of the car, we were greeted by an elderly Spanish-speaking lady who welcomed us and asked if she could help. We told her we would like to see if we could find accommodations for a week or two. Doña Elena was an icon in the region. She masterfully managed the Hosteria, which, it turned out, was world renown.

We unpacked our bags and rested for an hour, then thought we'd go downstairs for a drink before dinner. There was a nice lounge outside our room, and as we walked in, we were greeted with "good evening" by a pleasant-looking, well-dressed gentleman and his wife. We exchanged greetings and chatted for a few minutes. Then he introduced himself and his wife as Prince Charles and Princess Radziwill; without hesitation, he asked if we'd try a special pear schnapps he had brought from Paris. It was delicious. These wonderful people spoke to us as though we were friends.

In Argentina, it was customary to eat very late, from 10:00 to 11:00 p.m. was common, which took some getting used to. Dinners in the Hosteria were delicious home-cooked, multi-course meals. There was locally raised meat, wild freshly-caught trout and salmon, home-grown vegetables, Chateau Montchenot and other fine Argentine wines, plus homemade desserts. One never left the table hungry or unsatisfied. The problem was how to sleep after eating such a meal so late.

The next day, we went fishing on the Chimehuin River a few miles downstream from the Hosteria. Just upriver from me were Prince Charles Radziwill and Charles Ritz, the very dapper hotelier from Paris. The fishing was excellent, and everyone was catching rainbows of four to five pounds.

Without any warning, Charles Radziwill lost his footing on the gravelly bottom and went completely into the river, waders and all. I threw my rod onto the river bank, tightened my wading belt, and started swimming out to get him. Luckily, I was able to grab his wading suspenders, and I swam to shore with him.

Charles Radziwill said I saved his life that morning, though I doubt that. He was just being the gracious person that he was. That evening, Prince Radziwill offered me a toast at dinner; it would be hard to forget that moment. I reveled in the respect and admiration I felt that night from the fishermen in the Hosteria, resulting in my lifelong adoration of Patagonia and the people who inhabit it.

The next day, we decided to fish at the Boca Chimehuin. This is a place about twenty-two miles north of Junin, where the Chimehuin River begins its journey out of Lago (Lake) Huechulaufquen. Huge trout inhabited this quarter-mile stretch of river; twenty to thirty-pound rainbow trout were regularly caught there.

We arrived at the Boca (the mouth of the river), in the late afternoon. As every fly fisherman knows, a well-practiced routine is common when preparing to fly-fish. First you put on your waders, socks, and boots. Then you stock your fly jacket with the flies you expect to use. After that, you select your fly line and set up your rod and reel. Then you kind of center yourself in a state of well-being, in tune with nature. I was very busy and at first didn't notice the large chauffeured car that pulled up next to us.

A man and his wife stepped out; before long, they had poured themselves some tall, cool drinks. I couldn't help glancing at them as I continued my ceremony to get ready. The man looked at me and with a strong Southern accent said, "It's too early! Wait an hour; the fishing will be better."

"Sounds like you've fished here before," I said.

"Oh yeah—what are you drinking?" he asked. I walked over to the trunk of his car and there was a big cooler full of ice, another cooler full of jumbo Gulf shrimp, and a dozen or so bottles of liquor.

"I'd like whatever you're drinking," I said.

"Bourbon." We toasted each other. "Billy Pate's my name," he said.

"Jay. Jay Spivack, and my wife, Elke. Cheers!"

Billy Pate—one of the greatest big-game fly fishermen in the world; world record-holder of a 188-pound tarpon on a fly rod; member of the Fly-Fishing Hall of Fame—and I have been close friends from that day on.

That evening, I caught and landed a fifteen-pound brown trout that was one of the prettiest fish I caught and released that year.

Pescado Grande (big fish)

The next morning, we drove from Junin de Los Andes up to the south bank of the Boca at the outlet of Lake Huechulaufquen. I wanted to walk out as far as I could into the lake, to where it began to flow into the Chimehuin River. Note that walking in the early morning into the lake where the river begins is more than a little perilous. The lake bed in that area is lava outflow and has large holes into which you can fall, and then, if you are particularly unlucky, you can be swept into the river and may wind up many miles downstream while swimming for your life.

Elke and I made it out to the mouth of the river in the dark, quite far into the lake. The sun had not yet risen over the hill behind us, and the temperature was so cold that the rod ferrules had ice on them. Two hours later, it would be eighty degrees Fahrenheit.

It was still dark when I began to false cast. I made my first cast, and the fly drifted into the mouth of the river, drag free, when it got slammed by a huge fish. After twenty minutes of heart-stopping action, I landed a beautiful, twenty-four-pound rainbow. Dan Bailey of Montana had tied that fly for me, a fly that imitated the local crab (cangrejo) that inhabited the Huechulaufquen Lake and the Chimehuin River. After releasing this fish, I decided to wait a few minutes before casting again. After about ten minutes more, I made another long cast and mended the line so the fly would head straight downstream without any drag. The fly drifted no more than fifteen feet when a fifteen-pound brown came out of the water to smash the fly. After a fifteen-minute battle, the fish surrendered, and I released him, too.

Fish after fish pounded my artificial flies for the next hour and a half. Two of the fish were so big that I hadn't landed them. One straightened out my heavy-duty size 1/0 hook, and the other snapped my ten-pound tippet. I don't know how big *those* fish were, but they must have been tremendous, judging from the fight they put on.

Casting at the "Boca" Chimeuin, Lago Heuchelaufquen, for pescado grande.

Starry, Starry Night

Throughout my airline career, I have often been asked one question: Did you ever see anything strange while cruising along at thirty-five thousand feet on those clear, starry nights with no other planes in sight? My answer was always the same: No, not really. Sometimes a star will catch your eye and, because of atmospheric particulates, some light refraction would take place, and the star would seem to change colors. Soon you imagine it's not a star but rather a light from another craft. But then after a while, you draw the same conclusion: it was just a star after all.

In forty years of flying, I never saw a UFO—until early one morning in Argentina in 1976, when all of that changed.

My wife and I were driving to the Boca Chimehuin to arrive before first light, before the most cautious trout would have the chance to spot us. I would hopefully cast my *cangrejo* (crab) fly to a huge, unsuspecting trout in the dark. I was on a mission.

It was 4:30 a.m. The road to the Boca wasn't paved in those days, and there were no street lights.

In fact, along about fifteen of the twenty-two miles of road, there were only large rocks and big jackrabbits. It was a particularly dark night with no moon. The Southern Cross was clear and well-defined; it was striking. What a beautiful, peaceful place!

Suddenly, a blinding white light appeared through the passenger window. I jammed on the brakes, and we skidded to a stop. The light, as bright as the light from an arc welding torch, was moving perfectly horizontally over a small local mountain range about twenty miles north of us. It was a round, saucer-shaped, disc-like object. As the lighted disc moved, it brilliantly lit up the tops of the mountains beneath it. I could not see a beam of light beneath the disc, so I couldn't understand how it was that the mountains beneath it were illuminated so brightly. Based on the distance to the mountains, I estimated the disc-shaped object to be moving at 400–600 mph.

The disc continued west until it was over the Andes Mountains, about twenty-five miles west of us; then, without a microsecond's pause, it made a sharp, ninety-degree left turn and followed the Andes range south for about two minutes. Then all at once, again without slowing, turned right ninety degrees and climbed steeply while accelerating to a phenomenal speed... and disappeared.

It was like the instantaneous acceleration of a spacecraft to the speed of light in a science fiction movie—but my wife and I had seen it with our own eyes, in real life. For several minutes, we just sat there in the car, stunned. Elke said she didn't believe what she had just seen.

In my forty-plus years of flying, I have never seen anything like what I saw early that morning. I have no doubt that it was a controlled craft and that it made turns and accelerated at speeds that would have created bone-crushing g-forces. This was the first and only UFO I have ever seen in my life, but I was instantly converted to a believer.

That afternoon, the local newspaper had a front page headline about flying discs witnessed the previous night and that morning by hundreds of people all over Neuquen Province, Argentina.

During the following week, I spoke with no fewer than ten Argentines about what we had seen. None of the people I spoke with expressed any surprise. UFOs, which are called OVNI in Argentina, are commonly seen in Neuquen Province. Most everyone I spoke to had seen a UFO at one time or another. What is very interesting is that some of the sightings were of discs, while others were of cigar-shaped objects. Most of the people I spoke with believed that the UFOs had some connection to the large, deep lakes in the region.

In any case, I can assure you that UFOs *do exist*!

CHAPTER 9

1978

Another Day at the Office

✴

Business for Capitol was booming and got even better after airline deregulation. We began flying scheduled transcontinental and transatlantic flights, and flying as a DC-8 captain continued to enhance my resume.

The more hours you acquire in an aircraft, the more you uncover any quirks or idiosyncrasies it may have. But, other than a stiff landing gear, the DC-8 didn't have many issues, in my experience. A technique called "rolling the aircraft on" was helpful in making really smooth landings. Just before main gear contact, you gently relax a little back pressure on the control yoke. If timed just right, this results in an ultra-smooth touchdown; if not timed properly, however, it could have the opposite effect—which is why real mastery was required.

On the ramp in Acapulco, Mexico, circa 1978.

Life became even more interesting when I was elected chairman of the Capitol Airways Pilot Negotiating Committee and also became a member of the board of directors of ALPA (the Airline Pilots Association). I was a busy guy and loving the life of an airline pilot.

Happy Birthday

One flight in February of 1979 remains especially fresh in my memory. It was a ferry flight (no passengers) from New York to Los Angeles, and we were positioning the plane for a return flight to New York after a twenty-four-hour crew layover. In addition to myself, there were twelve flight attendants, the co-pilot, and our flight engineer onboard. Capitol flight attendants had their own version of the pilot seniority list, and there were all kinds of ratings for each pilot, some not suitable for PG audiences. Our flight attendants were some of the prettiest ladies in the industry. About half of them were American young women, and due to our European trips, the other half were German, Dutch, French, and Swedish. In those days, attractiveness, age, and charm were an acknowledged part of the criteria used in hiring new flight attendants.

It was my birthday, and the flight attendants apparently knew it. When I walked into the galley for a cup of coffee, I was surrounded by eight lovely flight attendants who wrestled me to the cabin floor. By this time, I was laughing hysterically. Then two of the stewardesses unbuckled my belt and pulled my pants down while the rest held me to the floor.

A flight attendant by the name of Annaliese had a razor in her hand and kneeled between my legs. I stopped laughing— until she said, "This is going to be your birthday shave!" By the time they had finished, we were all laughing hard. But what the hell was I going to tell my wife?

I got home from the trip and was greeted at the door. Elke and I had a nice dinner, chatted a while, sipped some wine, and went to our bedroom. When I came out of the shower, I said, "Honey, we're going to try something different tonight." With a flare, I removed the towel I was hiding behind. We both broke into hysterical laughter as I revealed my birthday shave.

Can you imagine if this were to happen today? The entire crew probably would have been fired. It was innocent fun among adults. Regrettably, this kind of attitude doesn't exist today. Everybody would have ended up suing everyone else.

The Commute

Elke and I lived in Connecticut in a cute little custom rambler a block from the Long Island Sound. It was nice to have my Bristol-30 sailboat so close by. I kept my boat at the private dock of Kay Williams, a friend of mine who was a well-known lobster fisherman.

As I was based at John F. Kennedy Airport, New York, the commute from Connecticut was reasonably short as far as miles were concerned. JFK was about fifty miles away from my home. In fact, many airline pilots who flew out of Kennedy Airport lived in Connecticut. Theoretically, the commute should have been about forty-five minutes of driving time, but in practice, it was an hour and three-quarters, and I always allowed three hours. It wouldn't do for the pilot to be late for the flight, and I never wanted to take that chance. One early afternoon, I was driving to the airport for a flight to Zurich, Switzerland. I was going to be flying there as a passenger with my crew. We would be staying at a hotel for a day in Zurich until our airplane arrived for the flight, which we would then operate back to JFK. I was in regular clothes, and my uniform was packed in my suitcase. It was a typical summer day commute, which gradually turned worse as the traffic slowed down to stop-and-go along the congested Van Wyck expressway in Jamaica, New York. I was born not far from that spot about thirty-nine years earlier, and as I drove, I thought about how much the area I'd grown up in had changed. It had been a tidy middle-class neighborhood until the 1960s, when it seemed that all hell broke loose. How I longed for the *good old days*.

The traffic crept along until the Belt Parkway turn-off; then the pace picked up, and I finally pulled into the long-term employee parking lot at JFK. I stopped next to the employee bus stop and dropped my suitcase and flight bag off, and then I started looking for an empty parking space. As I drove, I kept my bags in sight in the rear view mirror. After all, this was no longer the New York I grew up in. As I pulled into a vacant parking space, I took one more glance toward my bags in time to see the worst case scenario taking place. My suitcase was gone, and my flight bag was being thrown into the open trunk of a beat-up, dented, Oldsmobile sedan. Damn! I had to get my suitcases back. I was about to leave on a flight.

I was driving my old Dodge Ram four-wheel-drive pickup, and I wasn't sure I could catch these bastards, but I was sure going to try. They saw me giving chase and smashed through the wooden barrier gate at the entrance to the parking lot, as though it wasn't there. At this point, I was about five hundred feet behind them and gaining. Within two minutes, we were racing down the service road of the Van Wyck Expressway; suddenly, they decided to make a move to get me off their tail. They jumped the concrete curb, and in the process, blew out one of their rear tires. They were intent on getting on the expressway by going across the grass and dirt between the service road and the highway. My three-quarter-ton Dodge truck jumped the curb with ease, and after I put it into four-wheel drive, I tore across the grass as though I were on dry pavement. By now, the Oldsmobile was starting to lose traction due to the blown tire, and I was catching up fast. I had no sooner stopped my pickup truck behind them when the two guys bailed out of their beater car like the couple of cockroaches that they were. They ran right across the highway, nearly causing accidents as cars slammed on their brakes to avoid hitting the thieves. I was thinking, what a waste of good brakes!

Now there was another problem, which was how to get my bags out of the locked trunk. I checked for the car keys, but as expected, there weren't any. The car's ignition had been jimmied; it was a stolen car. I grabbed my tire iron and began to pry the trunk of the car open to get to my bags. A moment later, a police car pulled up behind me and two New York cops with plenty of attitude demanded to know what I was doing trying to break into the trunk of the Oldsmobile. I went through the entire story and then showed them my pilot identification badge. They both looked at each other and then stuck their hands out and said "Good for you; put it there," as they both shook my hand. They went into their trunk and pulled out a pry bar, and within a minute, they had the trunk of the Oldsmobile open. I thanked them for their help and mentioned that I was really late for my flight.

They told me to follow them to the on-ramp of the Van Wyck. We went, sirens blasting and lights flashing, through several red lights and on to the Van Wyck Expressway. New York's finest peeled off as we passed the Belt Parkway turn-off, and I continued straight ahead into the airport.

I pulled into the employee parking lot again, but this time I did not—nor did I ever again—drop off my suitcase or flight bag at the employee bus stop!

"Perfect" Co-Pilot

In April 1980, I met the near-perfect co-pilot on a trip to London, where we had a wonderful two-day layover in Brighton. Brighton is a great little seaside town with friendly pubs and fantastic antique shops. My co-pilot on the trip was most impressive. His dad was an American Airlines captain and had imparted some wonderful traits on his son. The young fellow just *looked* like a captain. His demeanor and bearing were West Point or Annapolis; he was polite and very bright. But then true perfection, after all, is elusive.

When we arrived back at the airport for the return trip, we were late. The crew bus had been delayed in traffic, so there was minimal chance of an on-time departure.

The co-pilot seemed so competent that I delegated to him the tedious, time-consuming task of programming the three inertial guidance navigation units and stipulated that the flight engineer double-check his work. This would save me time while I filed the flight plan, checked the weather, and ordered our fuel load.

I arrived in the cockpit just as passengers had finished boarding. I looked at the aircraft logbook, checked that the landing gear safety pins were onboard, and received assurance from the engineer and co-pilot that their checks were complete and that the inertial guidance units were properly programmed.

My quick check of the first eight programmed waypoints (programmed geographical positions.) seemed to confirm this; they were all correct. We completed the before-start checklist and requested ATC airways clearance (for the published route we would be cleared to fly) and then received pushback clearance from the gate. We were on time, thanks in part to my *perfect co-pilot*.

Take-off and climb-out were by the book, and we began navigating the short, twisting segments of airways that exist between England and Ireland. (In Europe, published airways are often relatively short segments with significant changes of heading. This is due not only to the countries' small size and irregular borders but also to the different national aviation authorities exercising their sovereign rights.) Our *coast out* (geographical position where the aircraft begins the overwater portion of the flight) was Cork, Ireland, where we would begin our assigned North Atlantic track to Gander, Newfoundland.

As we completed the checklists and reached our intermediate cruising altitude, I began to check the three independent inertial navigation systems (INS) to see how the INS was tracking. Immediately, I saw that they were *not* tracking the airways. This was a big problem—we needed inertial navigation to fly across the ocean. They were our only source of overwater long-range navigation. What was wrong?

I rechecked the waypoints loaded into each unit, and they were exactly right. Then I looked at the initial position that had been loaded into the INS on the ramp in Gatwick, England. Ouch—here was the problem! The latitude and longitude numbers were correct except that because London is *east* of the Greenwich meridian, the longitude should have been designated *east*. But out of habit—because most American pilots are used to flying in the United States, where longitudes are all west of the Greenwich meridian—the co-pilot had designated the position as *west* of the Greenwich meridian. Neither I nor the flight engineer had caught the mistake. Now what to do?

We hurriedly tried to update the INS units, but they would accept no more than a thirty-mile update of position. I tried updating our sixty-mile error by inputting three incremental twenty-mile updates, but the computer logic wouldn't accept these, either. Nor would it accept two thirty-mile updates for the sixty-mile total error.

Then the perfect co-pilot spoke up. He had neatly written a complex trigonometric formula that, by adding a certain number of degrees and minutes to each waypoint, would keep us precisely on track. I quickly plugged in the numbers for the next few waypoints, and sure enough, as we flew over each ground radio navigation facility, the INS was spot on! We programmed the rest of the waypoints with the co-pilot's mathematical solution and we were navigating perfectly.

We coasted out right over Cork and accurately tracked the VOR radial (radio transmitter) out 190 miles until reaching our assigned North Atlantic track. All three inertial units were now working perfectly, and four hours later, we arrived right overhead the geographical fix near Gander, Newfoundland, just as we were supposed to do. I had indeed met the *nearly* perfect co-pilot!

1981
Upgrading to the DC-10

Capitol had lots of business in the early eighties and needed larger aircraft. So, to increase capacity, the company began purchasing DC-10s, and in 1981, I was sent back to school to upgrade to captain on the Douglas DC-10 jumbo jet.

Ground school was in Los Angeles with Western Airlines in charge of the training, which was very professional; the instructors were good, knowledgeable teachers. Aircraft simulator training was at the Douglas manufacturing facility in Long Beach. Ground school and simulator training combined lasted about six weeks.

The first time I sat in the captain's seat of a DC-10 was after my simulator training was complete. This was a regular revenue flight with passengers, at night, from Sacramento to Chicago. There was a Western Airlines check airman in the co-pilot's seat. I think that was probably the second most exciting flight of my life.

I'm not sure whether one should say that the simulator flew just like the airplane or that the airplane flew just like the simulator, but I could detect no difference. If you flew the simulator well, you could fly the airplane. I flew about ten flights with a check pilot and then was released to fly the line as pilot in command. I was soon having the time of my life piloting DC-10s on scheduled flights from JFK to cities in Europe, across the United States, and into Hawaii. The DC-10 had worldwide capabilities. Capitol's DC-10s were equipped with high-quality inertial navigation systems (INS). There were just a couple of important requirements that had to be fulfilled when navigating with the INS units. First, the pilot had to enter the accurate latitude and longitude of the location of the airplane on the airport ramp before it was moved or taxied. Second, the waypoints (geographical positions along the route) had to be accurately entered. The INS units, in most cases, did the rest. As there were three redundant units, they could be checked against each other. If one was inaccurate or failed, one would simply rely on the other two. Experience proved the units to be extremely reliable, and a failure of even a single unit was rare. The DC-10-30 series had a gross takeoff weight of more than half a million pounds. With moderate passenger loads, the DC-10-30 would have a range of 8,500 miles and could cruise for about fourteen hours. That was definitely long-range capability.

Capitol Airways Douglas DC-10-30 series, circa 1981.
Photo courtesy of Howard Chaloner and Airliners.net.

I loved the DC-10, as did almost every DC-10 pilot with whom I have ever spoken. The airplane was powerful with very large engines, yet very quiet in the cockpit. With numerous large cockpit windows, the visibility was truly wonderful. Add to this the spacious cockpit with very comfortable pilot seats, and you had an airplane that was a pleasure to fly.

The DC-10s that Capitol ordered had three autopilots that were constantly comparing data signals for accuracy and integrity. With that system, the aircraft had complete auto-land capability. The airplanes were capable of landing in zero visibility and zero ceiling weather conditions, although Capitol's operating certificate did not authorize such operations. I used to train new co-pilots in landings by having them watch how the auto land system landed the airplane and then instructing them to simply copy the autopilot's technique. If you began to flare (level off) the airplane at the same height that the auto land system began to level the airplane and then moved the control wheel aft at the same rate and distance that the auto land moved it (it was identical at each landing), then a pilot could make a nearly perfect landing every time.

The DC-10 didn't seem to have any notable idiosyncrasies from a pilot's point of view. The only in-flight emergency I experienced was on a non-stop flight over the North Pole from Frankfurt to San Francisco. When we started our descent, the Number-Two engine power lever was frozen; it wouldn't move—probably due to the flight's having been at a prolonged extremely cold temperature near the North Pole. I had to shut down the engine during the approach when it became apparent that it couldn't be controlled and was putting out far too much power to allow a landing. The two-engine approach and landing was uneventful, however, and the passengers were unaware that we had made a two-engine approach and landing in the three-engine airplane.

Scrabble Game

I remember another trip, CL-917, in 1982 from JFK to Prestwick, Scotland, a short time after Elke and I had divorced. It was winter, and the weather at Prestwick was miserable. The surface winds were gusting forty to fifty knots and about thirty degrees off the runway heading. The runways were covered with ice and snow, with braking action reported as poor. I know I wouldn't have been happy to do this approach in a DC-8. We touched down about eight hundred feet from the approach end and in the center of the runway. When I brought the reversers in, the airplane tracked smoothly down the runway and immediately began to decelerate. The use of the control wheel into the wind was important and very effective, as was judicious application of the plane's big rudder, which was used to keep us going straight down the runway. The only thing unusual was the constant automatic releasing and reapplication of the brakes, which the antiskid was doing each time the wheels started to lock and skid. It should be noted that the maximum braking occurs just prior to the skid, so the anti-skid keeps applying and then releasing the brakes in extremely fast cycles, to obtain maximum braking. We stopped just fine, with quite a bit of runway to spare. The only problem after that was that the parking ramp was so icy it was like slippery, oil-covered glass. When we stopped, the idle thrust of the three big engines was enough to cause us to slide *with the brakes set*. I couldn't shut the engines down fast enough to get the sliding to stop. Once we finally stopped, we got a ground tug with chains on its wheels to safely pull us into our parking space.

That trip to Prestwick was memorable for another reason, too. The hotel the crew stayed at was typical of many hotels in Scotland in those days. They had a huge wood fireplace on the main floor close to the front desk where you could relax and get warm. During the day, the rooms were freezing cold and damp in the winter. Room heat, if there was any, wasn't turned on until the evening. That was pretty standard in Scotland, and it definitely took some getting used to. One thing I will give Scottish folks credit for is the down feather comforters. They were the thickest and warmest comforters I ever slept under, and believe me, they were needed.

After a very satisfying English-style breakfast, I walked into the fireplace lounge area to sit in front of the fireplace and read my newspaper. A few minutes later, Erika, one of our flight attendants, walked in and sat down on the other end of the couch. She was a very pretty, blonde, green-eyed Swedish gal who was very slim and curvy. She said hello, and we engaged in polite conversation. We talked a little about the trip we were on, then a bit about our company, and then just a little about ourselves and where we lived, and so forth. Somehow, the subject of the weather came up, and we both remarked how bitterly cold and damp it was in Scotland on this trip. We both agreed that we hadn't been prepared with sufficiently warm clothes. The subject of what we would do for the rest of the day came up, and finally, Erika asked if I played Scrabble. I told her I did, and she suggested I come up to her room and play Scrabble. I really hadn't anything better to do, so I agreed, and off we went to Erika's room. Her room was about the size of mine, but it smelled a lot nicer. There was a faint but noticeable, pleasant perfume scent that really made it delightful to be there with Erika. We played three Scrabble games on the round wooden table in the corner of the room. The chairs were straight-backed and left a bit to be desired as far as comfort, but they worked out well enough. Erika was a good scrabble player and had a wonderful, fresh sense of humor, which caused us both to laugh quite a bit.

The morning passed quickly, and we both agreed it was time for lunch and that we would take a walk and find a place to enjoy a meal. Erika and I found a cute little restaurant about a half-kilometer from the hotel. We ordered a bottle of German Rhein wine and a lunch of broiled prawns over fresh salmon with double-broiled potatoes and green beans. It was a lovely lunch filled with good cheer and laughter. We walked back to the hotel with the remainder of the bottle of wine. Then Erika asked if I wanted to play a few more Scrabble games, and as before, I agreed, as there really wasn't much else to do.

We played two more Scrabble games and then discussed the idea of sharing the rest of the wine. I was agreeable, and I must admit the wine really tasted especially good. Erika asked if we should spice up the Scrabble game a bit by betting a little on each game. We joked about how much to bet, and then Erika asked if I wanted to play *strip Scrabble*. I admitted that I didn't know how to play that game; however, Erika assured me that it was commonly played in Sweden and that she was quite competent to guide me through the rules. She told me that it was better played on the bed due to the room temperature being on the cold side and that neither of us would want to catch a cold if we got on a *losing streak*. Three games later, we were both under the down comforter. After a while, Erika began to become a little flirty with her pretty green eyes and beautiful, pouty lips. The last thing I can relate was that the Scrabble game fell to the floor and Erika commented that I was like a little boy playing in a big playground. That must have been a Swedish expression, as I had never heard that one before.

It turned out to be a wonderful layover in Scotland. I had never expected such an outcome!

I hadn't seen Erika for quite a few months after that trip. She was married, and we respected each other's private lives, as one would expect. I had learned long ago that some of those brief, unexpected, unplanned interludes had great potential for destroying marriages and families. I had observed just that kind of destruction among a few captains and their families when I was co-pilot on the DC-8.

Several months later, while on a layover in Brussels, Belgium, I was out with my crew eating at a wonderful little restaurant called the Hole In The Wall. This was a cozy restaurant owned by Margaux, a plump Belgium woman in her sixties who was an excellent gourmet cook. Margaux prepared the best pepper steak I had ever eaten. She would cut a slab of filet steak from a side of beef that was hanging in her meat locker. The meat had a green mold on its surface, which might sound terrible, but it was, in fact, very common in Europe and served to age and tenderize the meat. What a terrific steak! We all finished our meal about the same time. We were discussing dessert when my Scrabble buddy, Erika, walked into the restaurant with one of her flight attendant friends, another Swedish lady. They sat down at the table in front of us, and Erika was facing me. I nodded hello to her, and she acknowledged me with a faint smile.

I started to think about the wonderful time we had in Prestwick, Scotland, months before. I admit that I wondered whether we might wind up playing Scrabble that evening. I got up and walked to their table and asked them *both,* if they wanted to join us for dessert or wine. Erika looked up and very politely said that although they would love to, they had an early flight in the morning and therefore couldn't. I am convinced that this was Erika's subtle way of saying, "That was then, and this is now, *alskling*" (darling).

Our trip back to JFK was another typical, good trip. I loved the European trips because one could enjoy exploring European cities on the layovers. I loved the good food and wine, and for that, Europe was incomparable.

During the next few years, I flew the DC-10 on regularly scheduled trips to most all of the major cities in Europe as well as to Los Angeles, which enabled me to see my mom and dad frequently.

CHAPTER 10

1985

A Setback…Then
Back in the Left Seat

As we all know too well, life is seldom perfect. In 1985, I suffered a head injury from a fall that sidelined me as far as piloting was concerned for the next several years. The FAA takes a serious view of head injuries and unconsciousness suffered by pilots, especially when a post-traumatic seizure (PTS) occurs due to head trauma. I had reapplied for my first-class medical certificate two years after my accident, but it was another five years before the FAA approved the application. It was a life-changing experience, but I never lost hope that I would return to flying. It was a challenge to get back in the left seat after not flying for seven years. However, I *was* eventually able to resume the flying career that I loved.

A very well-regarded physician told me that the quickest way to heal was to do the next best thing I loved to do, so I decided to follow his advice.

Since the early seventies, I had spent many vacations chartering sailboats and diving in the beautiful area between St. Thomas in the U.S. Virgin Islands and the island of Anegada in the British Virgin Islands. In 1986, while recuperating from my injury, I purchased a Gulfstar 50 sailing sloop. For the next five years, I spent winters in the Caribbean aboard my sailing yacht. The year-round temperature in the Virgin Islands hovers around eighty-three degrees Fahrenheit, and the water temperature is usually about eighty-two degrees. What could have been nicer? Waking up in the morning and diving in for a refreshing swim before breakfast was a perfect place to regain one's health; one's endorphins can go wild in such a paradise.

After a while, I decided to charter my sailboat, so I joined the Virgin Islands Charter League. It was through them that I would book my charters; I would be the captain and host. The V.I. Charter League had crew available, so you could always find a first mate and cook for any charter you would book.

On charter with the Gulfstar 50 sloop and anchored off the beach in a peaceful Caribbean anchorage, circa 1986.

A typical charter would go like this: one or two couples would charter your boat for a week. They'd travel to St. Thomas and meet you at your boat slip, and then they would come aboard for refreshing drinks, and you'd get to know one another. You would discuss the week's itinerary, and within a few minutes, it was usually easy to confirm that the week was likely to go well. This was everyone's chance to bail out in the event of any major personality conflicts.

In five seasons of chartering, I never had a problem with a guest. Considering that I was living in fairly close quarters with strangers for a week, this was somewhat remarkable. I know a few other charter captains who did not have the same good experiences. My secret, if there was any, was to avoid discussing politics, religion, and any polarizing social issues. Also, I always gave my guests the option to change the itinerary; after all, they were paying for the charter. The only line I would not allow to be crossed was one that might entail putting the vessel, crew, or passengers in harm's way.

Among all of the charters, a few stand out as particularly memorable.

The Wine Tasters

One couple onboard for a week, in their sixties, was absolutely delightful to be with. I had very nice German white wines, and Italian and French reds onboard, and they loved wine—I mean *really* loved wine. They asked me to set the itinerary so that wherever we ended up anchoring for the night would be only a short dingy ride from a restaurant and bar.

This didn't present any problem at all. We would have dinner aboard, during which time the couple would usually drink *three* bottles of wine between them. At first, I was somewhat apprehensive that they might become unsteady and have a mishap aboard. That wasn't the case, at all; I couldn't see any change in their demeanor. Then I would take them ashore where they would drink more wine. At a pre-arranged time several hours later, I would pick them up and we'd go back to the yacht, where they would drink another *three* bottles in the open-air cockpit before bidding the crew goodnight.

I'd never seen anything like this. They drank *six* bottles of wine on my boat and probably a bottle or *two* ashore each evening and behaved and conversed as though they hadn't had a drink. The week's charter passed quickly and *painlessly* for all of us. They could not have been nicer guests!

Honeymooners

A honeymooning couple who chartered my yacht was from Argentina. They were also a pleasure to have onboard—when we saw them! They were in their stateroom all seven days, though they did come on deck for dinner and an occasional snorkel. They used record levels of freshwater—the shower pump ran seven times a day—and our water-maker, which converted seawater to freshwater, had to be run twice a day to keep up with their showers. The only other funny thing was their "baby talk." Sound travels pretty well on a boat, and either they weren't aware of that or just didn't care. Argentine "baby talk" sounds pretty funny and provided lots of laughs for the crew. But it was a great charter. They were having the time of their lives, and the crew and I enjoyed watching them have a great time aboard the boat.

Gourmets

The last charter I'll relate was a couple from the Northeast. I don't believe they were married, at least not to each other. She was quite pretty, and he was a very successful businessman who owned a chain of stores across the United States. As soon as they came aboard, I knew it would be an unusual charter.

I couldn't help noticing the numerous scars this otherwise attractive woman had on her face, arms, and legs. What I learned later was that she was prone to the most dramatic accidents, such as falling off ladders, car accidents, cycling accidents, and so on.

The week went nicely, although as the gentleman became more at home aboard the yacht, some habits began to surface that I would have preferred be left ashore. The cook aboard for this trip hailed from Canada, was well-bred, and had a great sense of humor. Anchored by ourselves one night in a beautiful small bay, we were having cocktails on deck with crackers and several cheese selections. The conversation was light and cheerful.

Unfortunately, the gentleman had the habit of picking his nose. The cook and I could not avoid noticing this, and every time he did, the cook would nudge me under the table. She was intentionally trying to get me to laugh, which I refused to do. Then suddenly, the guy picked his nose again and, without a second's delay, cut a piece of Swiss cheese, placed it on a Trisket—with his fingers of course—and offered it to me.

The cook, who never missed a trick, squinted her eyes at me with a serious look on her face. I could barely contain myself, and she knew it. I accepted the offering and said, "Look, over there! A porpoise!" When he looked in that direction, I tossed the cracker and cheese overboard behind me.

The cook lost it in a fit of hysterical laughter and ran downstairs to the galley, claiming that a pot was boiling over.

The girlfriend, who saw what I did, looked straight ahead and didn't blink. She was in a no-win situation but handled it perfectly.

Everyone had a great charter, and the cook and I laughed about that week, many times.

Back in the Saddle Again
1991

By 1991, I'd fully recovered from my accident, and the FAA had finally given me the clearance to reapply for my first-class medical certificate. I took the flight physical with an FAA flight surgeon and passed with *flying* colors. Medical certificate in hand, it was time to begin looking for a piloting position. I had a great many flying hours as captain in four-engine DC-8s and DC-10 jumbo jets to all corners of the world. The question was, what was my flying proficiency after not flying for seven years? We would soon find out.

An old friend of mine, Bob Savacool, a former flight engineer for Airlift International Airlines, was giving a ground school on the DC-8. I signed up for the class. Four weeks later, I had my DC-8 Part 121 ground school requirement up-to-date. Next, I needed the simulator. I signed up with a simulator training company in Miami to get my simulator currency up-to-date. After fifteen hours of simulator training, given in a two-week period, I easily passed a Part 121 FAA simulator check. Now, I was current in the DC-8 and just needed to find an airline to hire me.

A pilot friend introduced me to the chief pilot of Aerolineas Latinas, a foreign cargo air carrier, based in Miami. As a foreign carrier, Aerolineas Latinas was operating under Part 129 of the Federal Air Regulations. Training and maintenance requirements were much less stringent under Part 129 than under Part 121 of the Federal Air Regulations, with which American air carriers had to comply. (The term *Part* refers to a specific *section of the Federal Air Regulations.*)

The chief pilot told me they urgently needed another captain and asked if I wanted to take a simulator check with him. I was ready! The next day, I had a four-hour check ride in the DC-8 simulator. It went very well, so he set me up for an observation ride on a cargo flight to San Juan, Puerto Rico, during which I sat in the jump seat. As we were about to fly back to Miami, the chief pilot asked me if I wanted to fly the aircraft back to Miami from the captain's seat.

I slid into the left seat and was amazed by the feeling that everything was starting to come together. I got start-up clearance and started all four engines. We pushed back, got an all-clear from the ground crew, and taxied to runway 10 for departure out of San Juan. This was clearly going to be a very exciting flight.

The airplane takeoff, the first in seven years, was exhilarating. Still, even though I felt great, I was also feeling a little behind the airplane for the first 1½ hours of flight. The descent and approach went well. However, as I flared for the landing, I could tell I had lost a bit of the feel for how far the wheels of the landing gear were above the runway. Please bear in mind that you sit about sixteen feet above the runway when sitting in the captain's seat of a DC-8. It must have felt worse to me than it looked to the chief pilot, because two days later, the chief pilot gave me a Part 129 captain's line check evaluation. It went smoothly; I was signed off as pilot in command of the Douglas DC-8.

I had an excellent co-pilot for the next few trips, Jorge Hernandez, and I let him fly two legs to my one as I continued to get back into my comfort zone. Fortunately, all the procedures and routines came back very quickly, and after six or seven trips, I got my groove back and was as comfortable as ever.

My airline pilot career had been resurrected in about twelve weeks. This was incredibly lucky and more or less an anomaly—due in part to Aerolineas Latinas being a foreign air carrier. I was *back in the saddle* flying flights as a DC-8 captain from Miami to destinations all over South America after not having flown for seven years.

Aerolineas Latinas DC-8, on the ramp in Miami, about to load
Cargo for a trip to Bogata, Columbia, circa 1991.

I heard from a mutual friend that John Harpole, the former FAA principle operating inspector from Capitol Airways (my guardian angel), had retired. My friend gave me his phone number, and I thought this was a great occasion to call him and say hello. When I called, his wife told me the sad news: John had passed away. I had called a just few weeks too late. I was terribly saddened by this news, as John was a wonderful person and had been such a positive influence in my life.

The Supersonic DC-8

Early one evening, I checked into Aerolineas Latinas operations in Miami for a cargo flight to Lima, Peru. It was customary to obtain a clearance number for overflying Colombia and Ecuador en route to Lima. The over-flight numbers are required by some

South American countries as a condition for foreign carriers to fly over their country. For some reason, operations personnel claimed they were unable to get an over-flight number for Ecuador. Instead, they gave me a name: Pablo Escobar. I looked at the flight dispatcher and said, "You've got to be kidding. The same name as *the* Pablo Escobar, the drug lord?"

The dispatcher said, "Yep, *this* Escobar is head of Ecuador's federal aviation department. He was just on the phone with dispatch and told us to have the flight crew inform Ecuadorian air traffic control that over-flight permission was granted by Mr. Pablo Escobar."

I asked the dispatcher again if this was on the level. He assured me it was. I decided to take his word for it, though I must admit I had some doubts. We got push-back clearance right on schedule. After engine start and a short taxi, we were cleared for takeoff on runway 9L. We climbed out into a dark starlit night.

Three hours later, we were one hundred miles north of Quito, Ecuador, at thirty-three thousand feet. It had been a very smooth flight so far. We were thousands of feet above the weather, and except for the occasional flash of lightning from some storms a few hundred miles to the east, bad weather was of no concern. Just before we crossed the Ecuadorian border, the HF radio crackled with a request from air traffic control (ATC). Radio reception was poor; the thunderstorms east of us were creating loud, static crashes in our headphones, which made it nearly impossible to hear Ecuadorian air traffic control. We could barely make out the request by air traffic control for our over-flight number. When I replied with the name Pablo Escobar, there was a long pause at Quito air traffic control. After we repeated Escobar's name several times at air traffic control's request, we were told to stand by.

We were more than halfway across Ecuador when the HF radio came alive again. ATC ordered us to descend to fifteen thousand feet in preparation for a landing in Quito. I immediately responded that we could not comply, as our aircraft weighed too much for a landing at such a high altitude. Then ATC demanded that we land at Guayaquil. Guayaquil was a low-altitude airport on Ecuador's coast. My mind quickly sorted through the few options open to me. It seemed obvious that I'd been misled by our company dispatcher; landing in Ecuador wouldn't lead to a positive outcome.

I told ATC that we couldn't comply as we didn't have the approach plates with the charts and procedures for Guayaquil onboard.

By this time, we had less than one hundred miles to fly before we would be out of Ecuadorian airspace. ATC stated that they would force us to land and that they were sending jet fighter aircraft up to intercept us.

It was my responsibility to do whatever was necessary to ensure the safety of the airplane and persons onboard. (This was a cargo flight, and there were only three crew members onboard.) I pushed the four power levers up to max power. As the mach speed indicator (percentage of the speed of sound) needle touched the barber pole, or high-speed limit, the over-speed warning went off. It was indicating about .94 mach (94 percent of the speed of sound, or a little over 690 mph), and I could feel the shock wave building on the wing in the form of a very heavy vibrating rumble. We were nearly supersonic! This was as fast as I dared to go and still be able to read the shaking instruments in this thirty-plus-year-old DC-8 that was not designed to fly at almost supersonic speeds. We were now in a serious race to get to the Peruvian border as quickly as possible.

The miles were ticking off at about twelve miles per minute as we crossed the border into Peru. If jet fighters had scrambled-they hadn't caught us. My guess is that in the early '90s, Ecuador didn't have many supersonic fighters. Lucky for us!

On the way back to Miami, I filed a flight plan that enabled us to fly a *big* circle to the east around Ecuador (we flew over Columbia) in case the Ecuadorians put two and two together and were waiting for us on our return trip. When I landed in Miami, I was kind of ticked off and was looking forward to going into dispatch and having it out with the dispatcher.

The next day, I had a very heated discussion with the company dispatcher about the incident. He insisted that this Pablo Escobar *was* the head of ATC there and had given permission for the flight. I was sure there was more to the story that he wasn't revealing. I ended the conversation by stating, "*That* was my last flight over Ecuador *without* a telexed over-flight number onboard the aircraft."

"There Are Only Two Emotions in an Airplane:
Boredom and Terror"

–Orson Wells

It was an unusually beautiful, cloudless morning in Miami, and we were scheduled for a cargo flight to Maracaibo, Venezuela. The airplane we were flying was purchased from Airlift International Airlines and had been sitting on the ramp in Miami, not having been flown for quite some time. Aerolineas Latinas bought the plane, test flew it, and did a service check. Prior to the flight, I looked through the squawks (inoperative items or problems noted) in the logbook. All squawked items, including a problem with the elevator trim motor, were signed off by the company mechanic as having been repaired.

After starting the four jet engines, we were cleared to the departure end of runway 9R. Upon receiving takeoff clearance, I advanced the power levers, and the big DC-8 began the takeoff roll. V1...Rotate...Positive rate...Gear up...V2...V2+10. We were climbing out normally and starting our turn to the south.

After reaching 10,000 feet, I began reducing the pitch angle to gradually increase our climb speed to 290 knots, then switched on the autopilot and watched as Key Largo and Marathon in the

Florida Keys slid by to the west of us. As we climbed through 16,000 feet, I began putting the Jeppesen charts containing the departure procedures for Miami back into my flight bag. Suddenly, I noticed that the *pitch trim compensator* indicator was not where it should have been. At 290 knots, it normally would have been only about 10 percent extended, but instead, it was fully extended, about two and a half inches. The PTC was trying to raise the nose of the aircraft. Something was wrong, but it was impossible to tell what it was at this point. I told the co-pilot and engineer, both very competent Cuban pilots, that there was a malfunction in the elevator control system.

A second later, I noticed that the elevator trim indicator was starting to indicate more and more aft trim. This meant that the hydraulic motor in the tail was attempting to drive the stabilizer screw jack to raise the nose of the aircraft. (The stabilizer screw jack positions the stabilizer control surface on the aircraft tail, which trims the aircraft to climb or descend.) With a loud cracking sound, the autopilot, unable to handle the extreme elevator control force, disconnected. This caused the aircraft to pitch down abruptly, putting us into a steep, life-threatening dive.

The co-pilot immediately got on the VHF radio with air traffic control and declared an emergency. I started pulling back on the control wheel to raise the nose, but the control wheel wouldn't move. The airspeed needle hit the over-speed limit (barber pole) so I had no choice but to retard all four power levers to idle to prevent the plane from exceeding the speed of sound, as this would likely be quickly followed by the disintegration of the aircraft.

I tried trimming the horizontal stabilizer back, but the control switches had no effect. My mouth went completely dry. Both the co-pilot and I tried applying back pressure on the control wheel again but couldn't move it. We were now descending through ten thousand feet. Miami air traffic control was in full panic mode, diverting airplanes in every direction from our flight path.

The deep blue ocean was below us and looking larger and closer with each passing second. Our airspeed was way too fast; the over-speed warning annunciator went off again with a loud clacking sound. I put Number-Two and Number-Three engines in reverse. This slowed us to below the barber pole. (The barber pole instrument shows the maximum allowable speed) With the two inboard engines in reverse, at maximum continuous thrust, the Douglas DC-8 was now shaking and bucking like a bronco.

Then it struck me! The *stabilizer screw jack* motor or screw jack *assembly* had failed in the nose-down position. I quickly remembered reading about an Eastern Airlines DC-8 that had crashed in the Everglades with a similar problem. I recalled reading some speculation that if the pilot had pushed forward on the controls, *opposite* to what one would normally do, that might have *reduced air loads* on the stabilizer and elevator, allowing the stabilizer trim motor to turn and the screw jack to function properly, repositioning the stabilizer.

I shouted to the co-pilot, *"Push forward!"* He looked at me as though I'd just gone completely mad. But then, somehow, he must have seen in my expression; the *insightful moment* I had just experienced, because he started pushing forward on the controls. As I held the trim switches back, I could feel the air load easing off the control wheel. *The stabilizer was moving!* The nose started coming up, slowly at first, then faster. As the aircraft descended through 5,000 feet and the speed began slowing below 280 knots, I eased the thrust reversers out. We leveled off at 3,000 feet and I began adding power to maintain 250 knots. *We had been less than a minute away from death.* No one would have ever known for sure what caused the fatal crash.

We climbed to 8,000 feet, and I hand-flew the DC-8 back to Miami at 230 knots. The approach and landing were normal. When I left the cockpit, both the co-pilot and flight engineer were still sitting in their seats with dazed expressions on their faces, one of them reciting his prayers. I headed right to the chief pilot's office.

I was angry! I entered his office and, without saying a word, threw my flight bag at the wall next to his desk as hard as I could. *"Are you people out of your minds?"* I yelled.

He was caught completely by surprise. After he heard my story, he shook his head and said, "I am really sorry, and I'm sure glad you guys are safe." I think he was sincere. Hearing later that the mechanic was dismissed seemed to confirm it. I wished instead that the mechanic had been onboard with us; *I'm sure he'd have quit on his own.* He might have even realized how much he had put the crew and the airplane at risk by signing off an item that still had a problem.

Had I not read that Everglades accident report and the speculation about what might have prevented it, our own incident almost certainly would have had a tragic outcome. My only question was the following: How was my mind able to remember, at that precise moment—when I was ready to resign myself to a fatal outcome—the accident report that I'd read so many years ago? I don't honestly know the answer to that question, but I do know that I have since become a more spiritual person. *Was there a guardian angel involved?* In any case, it was not my time to go.

(The horizontal stabilizer functions much like the elevator, which determines whether the nose of the aircraft goes up or down. The Douglas DC-8 and Douglas DC-9/MD-83 share similarity in their design. Both aircraft have similar screw jack assemblies attached to the horizontal stabilizer. In the appendix, at the back of the book, I have provided the **unedited** National Transportation Safety Board accident summary of Alaska flight 261, which crashed on January 31, 2000, off the California coast. There are some similarities between my *near* accident east of the Florida Keys and the Alaska Airlines fatal accident.)

The months flew by, and the flights to South America were enjoyable, for the most part. Though I do recall sitting in the cockpit of a DC-8 on the ground in Miami when the landing gear on another DC-8 *that was being refueled*...suddenly collapsed.

I'd never heard of anything like that happening before, and I couldn't believe it! Imagine if it had occurred on landing, with a touchdown speed of 150 mph. What a disaster that would have been!

"Corrosion Corner" was the name given to the area (SW 36th Street in Miami) from which six charter airlines were operating. Gradually, it occurred to me that the name had a great deal of merit. I was starting to wonder how much longer I wanted to fly for these companies and was beginning to understand why I had gotten that job so easily.

Thank You, Captain Wolf

I flew routine flights for many months until one day, on a balmy summer evening, I signed in at operations for my cargo flight to Bogota, Colombia. It was going to be about a three-hour and fifty-minute flight. Reasonably good weather was forecast, with the possibility of some ground fog in Bogota. Cali, Colombia, our alternate airport, was supposed to have good weather with no fog.

Given the forecast of the possibility of fog for Bogota, I ordered an extra fifteen thousand pounds of fuel—"Granny" fuel as it's sometimes called—just in case Bogota weather went down in fog.

A major discussion with the dispatcher escalated into an argument when I stood my ground. Apparently, the company CEO had just issued orders that extra fuel would no longer be carried. An hour into the standoff, another forecast for Bogota came out. This one indicated that the weather trend was toward improvement, so I relented and took the minimum required fuel. Big mistake!

We departed Miami on schedule, and two hours later, picked up the weather at Maracaibo, Venezuela. Weather at Maracaibo was good, but Bogota was now forecasting ground fog. The forecast for Cali, however, was good weather the remainder of the evening. Since our alternate, Cali was still forecasting good weather, I decided to continue towards Bogota.

An hour and thirty minutes later, we were speaking with approach control at Bogota and received terrible news. Bogota had a thick fog bank off the approach end of the runway that was moving quickly toward the runway itself. I checked the weather at Cali our alternate. Cali was now *below minimums*, in heavy ground fog. This was now a *very* serious situation.

We were about to begin our descent to Bogota, with sixteen thousand pounds of fuel—enough for a few approaches to the Bogota Airport plus the required fuel to fly to the alternate, Cali, which was now enveloped in dense ground fog.

There was no other suitable airport within flying range of the fuel remaining. In other words, *we had nowhere to go*. Our minimums were two-hundred-feet decision height and one-half-mile visibility. (If upon reaching this altitude, the airport environment is not seen, a missed approach must be executed.) At two hundred feet, we would just be entering the fog bank at either Bogota or Cali. This was a nightmare about to happen.

I briefed the co-pilot and engineer. I told them I would fly the ILS, and when the engineer called fifty feet on the radio altimeter, I would increase the pitch angle one degree and hope for a reasonable touchdown. Then the co-pilot and engineer would try to spot the runway lights to guide me in staying on the runway centerline—*provided they were able to see the lights.*

This is pretty much what Captain Wolf had made me do as a young co-pilot going into Gander, Newfoundland. Although I surely disagreed with him then, *I was thankful to him now for that experience, seventeen years earlier! My knowledge from that experience was my only hope!*

We began the descent, completed the descent and approach checklists, and set up for the approach.

I had three major doubts:

- This was not a DC-8-63 aircraft; it was a DC-8-55. I wasn't sure whether a one-degree pitch increase would work as it had with the stretch DC-8-63 aircraft.
- Although this aircraft had a flight director (artificial horizon with integrated computer commands), it didn't work as well as the newer and much larger ones in the DC-8-63s.
- The flight director instrument and artificial horizon were about one-third the size of the ones in the DC-8-63, so it would be harder to discern a one-degree pitch change.

I began the ILS approach. The situation was very tense. The first one-third of the runway was now enshrouded in thick fog; I needed to fly the best ILS of my life.

At five hundred feet above the ground, the fog bank and *possibly eternity* were now directly beneath us. As the co-pilot called two hundred feet above the ground, we entered the fog. If we had not been perfectly established on the ILS at this moment, I would have executed the *published missed approach procedure*. The needles were dead-centered. Other than the instruments in the cockpit, no lights were visible inside or outside the airplane. The co-pilot reported calmly, "No runway lights in sight."

After two seconds, maybe three, the co-pilot called out, "One hundred feet, no airport lights!" in a strained-sounding tone of voice.

Then, simultaneously, the flight engineer and co-pilot shouted, "Fifty-feet above the ground!"

I rotated one degree, and a second later, the main gear slammed into the runway. I glanced out the window, and it was just solid grey. My eyes darted back into the cockpit to focus on the heading indicator. Fortunately, it was still showing runway heading. I was determined not to let the indicator move; I had to maintain runway heading, or we'd run off the edge of the runway.

I was relying on both the co-pilot and flight engineer to warn me if I got too close to the runway lights on either side. As soon as I felt the nose gear touch down, I applied max braking and max reverse thrust. I had no idea how far down the runway we were; we had to stop as quickly as possible.

Suddenly, the co-pilot shouted, "You're near the right-hand runway lights!" I immediately applied slight left rudder pressure for a split second, returning at once to the runway heading on the heading indicator. Five or six seconds later, we came to an abrupt stop.

We were on the runway at Bogota. *We were alive!* The airplane was in one piece, and we all breathed a deep sigh of relief.

We taxied behind the "follow me" vehicle, when it finally found us, which led us slowly through fog to the freight terminal. After completing the aircraft parking checklist, my co-pilot, who had been born in Cuba and seemed like a nice young man, asked me if he could make a comment. "Sure," I told him. He said that, given the same circumstances, he would have done the same things I had done and made the approach in zero-zero weather conditions.

Well, he was talking to a guy who'd just been put through the ringer; I was too mentally exhausted to appreciate the compliment. My sense at the moment was that he really had no conception of all that had gone into our successful landing: my years of flying experience; the dangerous lesson from Captain Wolf seventeen years earlier; the delicate maneuver with an uncertain outcome at the very end of the approach and perhaps, a helping hand from my guardian angel.

I looked at him with what must have been a very dour expression, which was meant to convey, "Don't allow yourself to get into such a predicament in the first place." But still numbed by what had just taken place, all I said, very slowly and deliberately, was, *"Don't...try...it!"*

CHAPTER 11

1993

Not What They Seem to Be

✳

E very pilot I ever knew who flew the DC-10 loved the airplane. The flying characteristics of the DC-10 could be described in one word: gentle.

Mac, who ran Aircrews International, Inc., a pilot employment agency in Los Angeles, called and asked me if I was interested in a Douglas DC-10 captain position for Transtar Airlines, a new startup airline. I hesitated just three seconds before saying yes.

This was in February 1993. I had just bought a mobile home park a year earlier, and it was running smoothly. My on-site manager was fully capable of managing normal day-to-day operations, so there was no reason not to continue doing what I loved.

Ground school and simulator were at the United Airlines training facility in Denver, and flight training was in Orlando. Seven weeks later, I was back flying my favorite airplane. Flights were from Los Angeles and San Francisco to Maui and Honolulu. The schedules were great, but Transtar was having serious maintenance issues with one of the DC-10s and began losing business. About eight months after I started flying for them, Transtar filed for bankruptcy, in September 1993.

Transtar Airlines Douglas DC-10-30 on the ramp in Maui, circa 1994.

In the cockpit aboard Transtar DC-10-30 en-route to
Hawaii with visiting flight attendant, circa 1994.

Southern Air Transport

The following month, I was contacted and hired by Southern Air Transport, the successor to Air America. To quote Wikipedia, "Southern Air Transport, based in Miami, Florida, is best known as a front company for the Central Intelligence Agency." These are Wikipedia's words, not mine. Flying for Southern Air Transport was interesting, to say the least. I was based in Istanbul and flying mostly to Moscow and airports in northern China.

I was captain of a DC-8-73, affectionately known as the "cave with a microwave in it." It was the venerable stretch DC-8 (the cave) with the newer, bigger CFM56 turbofan engines (the microwave). This DC-8-73 was a different breed of cat. It had a tremendous amount of power, and you could pretty much climb to any altitude within the plane's operational envelope regardless of your gross take-off weight. The only tricky thing about the DC-8-73 was that because the Commercial Fan Jet engines were larger than the original Pratt and Whitney engines, the inboard engines were very close to the ground—about nine inches away! That is very, very close. As a result, when you landed in a cross wind, it was extremely important that your wings be perfectly level. Land in a five-degree bank, and you will be grinding off the bottom of an inboard engine. In fact, our airplanes had a sensitive micro-switch installed on the oil drip stack of the inboard engines, which were in turn wired to the red master warning light on the glare shield in front of each pilot. If a pilot landed the airplane with a bank angle greater than three degrees, the red master warning and audible alarm would activate, alerting the pilots….hopefully preventing damage to the bottom of the two-million-dollar engine.

On the ramp in Istanbul and about to depart for
Moscow aboard Southern Air Transport DC-8-73, circa 1993.

Southern Air Transport was bringing cargo into Russia and taking cargo out that our government wanted, and I will leave it at that.

During the winter, the weather around Moscow was horrendous. Blizzards were commonplace; you've never experienced a bad snowstorm until you've been in one in Russia. This alone, presented challenges to flight in that country. Additionally, the English spoken by Russian air traffic controllers was sometimes difficult to understand. I've flown about 5,500 hours in Europe, and I am used to the many different ways of pronouncing English—the language used in air traffic control. But in the 1990s, the Russians combined a massacre of the English language with the incessant use of non-standard air traffic control (ATC) phraseology.

They also insisted on referencing altitude in meters instead of feet, which caused problems, as most (non-glass cockpit) aircraft manufactured in the United States had altimeters calibrated in feet.

Thus, every time Russian ATC issued an altitude request, we had to convert meters to feet on a chart, which caused a significant delay.

Moscow Airport terminal as photographed from the cockpit, circa 1993.

Another example of ATC safety issues was that whenever my aircraft arrived in Moscow for an ILS approach, we were given radar vectors to the outer marker that put our arriving aircraft *adjacent* to the marker, **not** over it. This required significant maneuvering while inbound from the outer marker at a time when the aircraft should have already been flying a well-established, stabilized approach *on the glide slope and localizer* (instrument landing system). Note: To be flying inbound from the outer marker and **not** being well-established and stabilized on the ILS would be considered an *unsafe* operation in the United States.

One of the most noteworthy experiences in Moscow occurred when we were having our aircraft de-iced. The equipment the Moscow airport used at that time was hilarious. A tractor would pull a de-icing wagon up to the aircraft, and a man would climb onto it to operate a glycol water cannon that was pressurized with a hand pump. Unfortunately, the stream of de-icing fluid was so feeble that it took three to four hours to de-ice the airplane. This was a problem if it started snowing hard; in this case, de-icing would stop until the storm subsided and then start all over again from the beginning.

On one occasion, the operator gave me a thumbs-up, signifying that de-icing was complete and that the aircraft was good to go. I sent our flight engineer out to inspect the wings and tail surfaces. When he came back to the cockpit, he said he couldn't believe it: the aileron controls were frozen solid to the wing. Had we taken off like that, the airplane would have been uncontrollable.

With Russian security police – Moscow Russia, circa 1993.

On another flight into Moscow, we had the aft cargo pallet full of wide-band communication monitoring and recording equipment, *which were in operation*, and supposed to remain on the aircraft until it arrived back at Dover Air Force Base in Delaware. We had loaded just two pallets of the return cargo back on the aircraft when a Russian security policeman realized that the rear pallet had not been off-loaded. He came up to the cockpit and demanded to know why. I told him the last pallet was just ballast: weights placed in the cargo compartment to compensate for the plane's forward center of gravity. He obviously wasn't buying my story. I went back to the cockpit and pulled my satellite phone out of my flight bag and using a suction cup attached to the portable antenna, stuck it on the side cockpit window. I turned toward the co-pilot and flight engineer who had a look of surprise on their faces. I asked if I could have a moment of privacy so I could call my "wife". Neither crewmember had a clue what was going on. They were not briefed on the *aft pallet* as they had **no** need to know. (That was often normal procedure.) I dialed the sat phone and got the message, "The number you have dialed is out of service at this time." Just great! I reached into my flight bag and found the envelope with a thick stack of new one-hundred dollar bills. I took ten out, and put nine in my pocket (in case I needed more).

I had to distract the security cop and get him off the *topic*. "Say, I'm a collector. I wonder if I could purchase the Russian security service pin on your hat?" I pointed to the white and red pin with the hammer and sickle embossed on it, that was attached to the front of his hat. I had a crisp one hundred dollar bill in my hand, which for him represented about two months' pay. A big smile came over his face, and I could feel the look of relief on mine. Needless to say, he couldn't get the pin off his hat fast enough. "*Da, Da, Da,*" he said. I still have the pin, to remind me of an incident that could have ended with a lot of drama.

Istanbul, a city divided in half by the Bosporus, is half European and half Asian, creating an exotic mixture I haven't seen equaled anywhere else. You couldn't find a city with better nightlife or finer seafood restaurants than those of the Kumkapi, Istanbul's famous seafood restaurant district.

I was browsing in the Grand Bazaar late one afternoon, looking for a little present for someone, when I literally bumped into Hannalore, an extremely attractive, slim, blonde, blue-eyed gal. As we made small talk about the little treasures all around us, she asked if I was a tourist. When I told her I was an airline pilot, her eyes lit up. She said she had always wanted to take flying lessons and asked if I could meet her at the Swiss Hotel that evening for a drink. She walked into the hotel bar at the appointed time, and it was hard for me and every other guy in the bar not to notice how strikingly pretty she was. We made small talk for a while, and then she asked me about flying and what she would need to do to become a pilot. She told me she worked for the German Trade Commission and had been living in Istanbul for years. After a few drinks that evening, she said that she was living on her own and that she led a rather dull and lonely life. The conversation was pretty lively, and it was clear to me that she certainly had good social skills. That, together with her looks, didn't quite square with her "lonely life" story. However, I went along with it, and we met a number of times over the next few months. Eventually, she told me a convoluted story about an on-again off-again marriage, which I gradually began to have even more doubts about. Our relationship warmed quite a bit, although I thought that she was just too smooth and her stories too doubtful to be trustworthy. After a while, my suspicions were confirmed. As we became more comfortable with each other, Hannalore became very focused on learning for whom I flew and what we flew. Soon it became more and more difficult to come up with evasive answers that satisfied her questions, and I realized the relationship needed to end at once.

About a week later, I was sitting in the lounge at the Swiss Hotel reading the *International Herald Tribune* when an American chap whom I didn't know sat down at a table next to me. He struck up a conversation about the spell of hot weather, then said, "I haven't seen you with Renate lately."

"Who?"

"You know—the blonde."

"Oh, Hannalore."

"No, Renate. By the way, she works for the GDR (German Democratic Republic) you know. Have a good one." Then he got up and walked out to the street.

Hannalore, or rather Renate, was a "honey trap" in *tradecraft* lingo.

Istanbul has long been known as a crossroads for spies and agents of every nationality and cause. Bordering on eight countries, Turkey boasts one of the most efficient spy organizations in the world, called the *Emniyet*. With more than fifteen different spy agencies operating in Istanbul, the competition for obtaining useful, secret, or sensitive information was at a high level. In fact, there was even a bar in Istanbul known as the *Snake Pit* where spies of all nationalities would frequently drink side by side while attempting to outsmart each other. Old Constantinople (Istanbul) was replete with stories that appeared so farfetched that they almost couldn't have been made up. I heard from several credible sources that the head of the American spy station in Istanbul had a song composed about him with the lyrics that began "Boo boo, baby, I am a spy." Every time he walked into the *Snake Pit* or the lounge at the Park Hotel, the piano player would start playing that song. There is no other city quite like Istanbul.

Istanbul, Sultan Ahmed Mosque, "Blue Mosque", circa 1993.

Leisure Air

In mid-1994, I had a difficult choice to make. Leisure Air, a charter airline that specialized in flights for tour operators, offered me a captain's position on the DC-10. I was enjoying flying with Southern Air Transport and they paid extremely well, but Maui and the idea of flying my favorite airplane were more inviting than Istanbul, Moscow, or destinations in China with the DC-8-73. Although I must admit I was getting addicted to the excitement and the nature of the flying we were doing, I wanted to spend more time at home on the West Coast.

When I gave notice, Southern Air Transport made it clear that they really wanted me to stay, making it as difficult as they could for me to quit. It was a battle of will-power for a while, concluding with someone saying, "You just can't quit flying for us like that." It wasn't the last time I heard from Southern Air Transport or the bureaucrats associated with them. It appears that once you start working in USAP (Unacknowledged Special Access Programs), they want to keep you close to the reservation. However, quit I did.

Leisure Air's four-week ground school was at American Airlines in Dallas. We had twenty-hours of DC-10 simulator in American's simulator Number-Two over a one-week period and then were given a proficiency check. It all went like clockwork. In fact, after the FAA did my route check in the airplane, the FAA inspector asked me if I would agree to become an FAA-designated check airman. I've always looked back on that as one of the high points in my flying career. Other than going into airline management, becoming an FAA-designated check airmen is, in my opinion, the most responsible position an airline captain can hold.

On the ramp with a Leisure Air Douglas DC-10-30 in Honolulu, circa 1995.

Flying the Pacific in the DC-10-30 was terrific. Our route was San Francisco to Maui and Honolulu. Additionally, I gave line checks and training to both captains and co-pilots.

On one flight, Leisure Air had asked me to give a captain's line check to a recently hired captain. The new captain and I were to meet for lunch at a hotel restaurant in San Francisco prior to the next day's line check, which would take place on a flight from San Francisco to Maui, then Honolulu, and finally back to San Francisco.

I walked into the dining room and looked around, hoping to see someone who fit the new captain's description. But the only guy who did was in the process of polishing off his second bottle of wine. This was at one o'clock in the afternoon. Sure enough, he set his glass down and beckoned me over to the table. Captain Driscoll was a man in his late fifties who had flown more than twenty years for a major air carrier that had gone bankrupt. During lunch, I tried hard not to stare at the empty bottles of wine as the fellow told me in detail what an extraordinarily smooth pilot he was.

At San Francisco's International Airport the next morning, I gave Driscoll and the flight engineer a full briefing. We sat down in the cockpit with the new captain in the left seat; I would line check him as captain while sitting in the co-pilot's seat. After checklists were completed, we called for ATC clearance and then pushback. Captain Driscoll began to taxi the big DC-10.

The first right-hand taxi turn was a humdinger. Its nature was such that my coffee cup jumped out of its cup holder and coated one leg of my uniform pants with coffee. The day was off to a grand start. Shortly thereafter, the senior flight attendant called the cockpit to inquire whether the aircraft had hit something. When I looked over at the new captain, he asked me if any problems with the nose wheel steering system had been reported in the aircraft logbook. As I stared out the window into the early morning sky, I began to wonder about Driscoll, and about how the rest of the day would go.

The takeoff and climb out went reasonably well. I could tell Driscoll had not been flying for quite a while, as he was pretty far *behind* the airplane. A well-qualified and current pilot is thinking eight miles *ahead* of the airplane: a magnification of the distance safe drivers focus on in front of the car they're driving. The experienced pilot is always planning for the next minute or so.

The next problem I discovered was that Captain Driscoll did not know, or had forgotten, how to make the mandatory (geographical) position report, required on the oceanic portions of all Pacific flight tracks. Though I did them myself on this flight, I advised him that when he became captain, he would be responsible for their being performed correctly. Then about two hundred miles east of Maui, I asked Captain Driscoll to give me his landing briefing. After he'd finished, I pointed out that the runway at Maui was short and that he had to touch down in the first thousand feet of runway and apply moderate braking and moderate thrust reverse to stop on the remaining stretch of runway, especially because we were landing at maximum landing weight.

The descent and approach were normal, but as soon as we lined up with the final to runway 6, the problems began.

On Maui's runway 6, there is almost always a strong right cross wind, requiring that a pilot establish a crab angle to keep the aircraft on centerline. Then, just prior to touchdown, the pilot uses the rudder to align the axis of the aircraft with the centerline. Driscoll was having a difficult time of it. I adjusted my seat into position so that I could take over if necessary. (One needs to give the pilot being checked the opportunity to demonstrate his capability while being ready to take command of the airplane before it is too late if a situation becomes critical.)

Somehow, it worked out, and Driscoll got the airplane on the runway with a reasonable touchdown. He was pretty much on the centerline and about a thousand feet past the beginning of the runway. He applied moderate braking as the nose wheel touched down—but neglected to apply the required reverse thrust.

I waited about three seconds and then said, "Reverse." No response. I repeated: "Apply reverse thrust," but again got no response.

At this point, I lifted the power levers into reverse myself. We were just able to exit onto the taxiway at the runway's last intersection. Another few hundred feet was the end of the runway, and beyond that, the *Pacific Ocean.*

We taxied to the terminal. The only comment from Driscoll was that he was about to apply reverse thrust and that I was simply a bit faster. I thought to myself, *"Not so good."*

After the passengers deplaned, an FAA air carrier inspector came onboard. He said he would be doing a routine line check. I introduced myself and told him I was doing a line check of a new captain. The inspector did the usual things, such as checking our licenses and medical certificates. I started performing the weight-and-balance—a mathematical calculation and record to determine that the aircraft is within weight and center of gravity limits—for the next flight, as I was acting as co-pilot during the line check.

The FAA inspector stopped me and asked to have Driscoll do the weight-and-balance. Boy, did this guy have good instincts! Half an hour later, it was clear that Driscoll did not know how to do the weight-and-balance. The inspector told me to do it so that we wouldn't have a late departure. That's when I noticed the inspector getting his notebook out.

The takeoff and departure climb-out went pretty well, and I didn't notice the inspector taking any more notes at that point. On the descent into San Francisco, we were given an arrival restriction that required us to be at 250 knots of airspeed twenty-five miles west of the Woodside radio beacon at ten thousand feet. Now this requires some thinking and some mathematical skills.

We were at thirty-three thousand feet with a 50-knot tailwind. We had a little time, but Driscoll needed to be seriously close to requesting a descent if we were to make the ATC restrictions. I could see the FAA inspector becoming more and more concerned as he leaned forward to watch the pilot's activities. Finally, I said to Driscoll, "Let me know when you want me to ask for descent." No response from Driscoll. Then two minutes later, I asked, "Are you ready for descent?"

"In a few minutes," he said.

But we were out of time. I pressed the transmit button and requested descent from ATC. We were cleared to ten thousand feet. ATC asked us if we would be able to get down in time. I told them we would. Driscoll realized he had made a grave error. He pulled the power all the way back. I asked him if he wanted speed brakes. He answered, "No." I replied that we needed them if we were going to make the restriction. I extended the speed brakes. By now, the FAA inspector was writing furiously. We just made the restriction, with perhaps fifteen seconds to spare.

The approach and landing were normal, and we taxied to the gate. After the parking checklist was completed, the FAA inspector thanked me and asked Driscoll to meet him in the passenger cabin for debriefing.

After Driscoll left the plane, the inspector told me that Driscoll was not ready to be a captain. I agreed with his findings and submitted a similar report to the airline, recommending additional training. Driscoll resigned, which may have been best. I felt bad for him, but as a check pilot, if you can't say that you would feel safe putting your wife and kids on the plane with the pilot to whom you're giving a check ride, he or she shouldn't get a passing grade.

A Co-pilot's Error

A few months later, I received a letter from Leisure Air asking me to attend the A-320 Airbus training at Northwest Airlines in

Minneapolis. The company was thinking about buying some Airbus A-320s and wanted to send its check airmen for Airbus training. I had always been curious about the A-320. Once, while riding the jump seat in another air carrier's A-320, I saw the entire pilot flight display (PFD), all of his instruments, go blank during taxi. The captain told me that it happened from time to time due to the hot outside air temperature in Las Vegas in the summer. *What's that all about?* I had wondered?

Anyway, off we went, to Minneapolis during a bitterly cold winter. The ground school at Northwest was good. The Airbus is an almost totally computer-controlled airplane. The Airbus engineers had designed an airplane that didn't require a pilot with good stick and rudder skills but rather one who could operate a computer. A complaint I've often heard from pilots on the Airbus A-320 is that their piloting skills would get rusty when they flew the Airbus for many years.

One day during training, we were on a lunch break in the Northwest cafeteria. Everyone, including the ground school instructor, was standing around the coffee machines when a tall, buxom blonde came walking across the room, dressed to the nines. All eyes in the cafeteria were on her. Then, one of the eager, handsome young co-pilots in our class casually walked up and started flirting with her. Within a few minutes, they were exchanging phone numbers.

On the way back to class, the co-pilot was bragging about what an operator he was and that he might even consider sharing some of his dating secrets with us. This went on until the ground instructor began the afternoon class by saying, "Cindy, the blond, is, in fact, a guy." We didn't hear another word from the eager young co-pilot for the rest of the Airbus A-320 program.

The simulator program was pretty interesting, but just as training finished, Leisure Air changed its mind and decided against buying the A-320 Airbus. I don't think any of the pilots were particularly disappointed.

Temperature Malfunction

I went back to flying as captain and check airman on the DC-10. Flights were still out of San Francisco to Maui and Honolulu. I liked the DC-10 much better than the Airbus A-320, and I was thrilled that Leisure Air had changed its mind about buying the computer-controlled A-320s.

In the cockpit of a Leisure Air DC-10-30 en-route to Hawaii, circa 1995.

The flights tended to be uneventful, although sometimes when you least expected it, something would happen that required some quick and thoughtful analysis. On a flight out of Honolulu to San Francisco one afternoon, I was flying with a female flight engineer. It was on flight LA-826, and I had just taxied away from the gate and was on the taxi-way that was parallel to the long reef runway in Honolulu. I started noticing that it was getting kind of warm in the cockpit. A couple of minutes later, our flight engineer, Susan, exclaimed that she was unable to keep the air conditioning duct temperature below maximum temperature and that we needed to go back to the ramp. I requested permission from ground control to hold our position. Then I set the parking brake and told the co-pilot to guard the brakes and make sure the aircraft didn't move while I went back to the engineer's panel to see what was going on. A gut feeling was telling me that this was a problem that could be resolved without going back to the ramp. (Funny when you get that kind of feeling.) Susan told me that she had the three cabin temperature controls at the minimum temperature setting, but we were still running extremely high air conditioning temperatures. I instructed the co-pilot to open his sliding window, as it was now hot as hell in the cockpit. When the outside air coming through the open cockpit window feels refreshing in the afternoon in Honolulu, then you know the cockpit is really hot. I studied the three temperature controls for a moment and then realized what Susan had done. She had turned the temperature controls all the way clockwise and put the temperature control valves into the manual mode, at full hot. I was a bit surprised that our flight engineer had made that mistake, but mistakes do happen. No real harm or foul. We selected auto mode and got the temperature back down to normal, and within a few minutes, we departed for San Francisco. The rest of the flight went just fine, as it should have, and with the nice tail-wind from the jet stream, we got back home to San Francisco and into the gate right on schedule.

I continued to fly as DC-10 captain and check airman for Leisure Air. It was a really good company but, unfortunately, was significantly plagued with maintenance delays, which eventually led to its demise. The travel agencies booking Leisure Air were getting so much bad press and publicity that they finally cancelled our contracts. Leisure Air eventually filed bankruptcy and ceased operations.

There is an old expression in the airline industry. How do you make a small fortune in the airlines? Start with a large one!

CHAPTER 12

1995
East Meets West

My old pilot employment agency friend, Mac, in Los Angeles called to tell me that Korean Airlines wanted to hire some highly experienced DC-10 captains. I applied, and KAL hired me as a DC-10 captain based in Seoul, Korea. Apparently, Korean Airlines had experienced some accidents with their pilots flying the DC-10s and had decided to find the most experienced American DC-10 captains available. Ground school was four weeks in Seoul; simulator was with Canadian Airlines in Vancouver, Canada, and lasted two weeks.

Korean Customs

During ground school in Seoul, Korean Air introduced the American pilots to Korean customs and etiquette in addition to teaching us some basic Korean phrases. I thought this was a wonderful idea, and it proved very useful.

I was quite experienced at living overseas. I had lived a total of seven years in Germany and about four years in France. Although I assimilated quite easily into German and French culture, I could quickly see that Korea would present a greater challenge. For one thing, the Korean language is a difficult, though not impossible, language to learn. I sensed that Koreans were somewhat flattered when an American attempted to use Korean phrases. Thus, I tried hard to learn as many phrases as I could.

The Korean culture is five thousand years old. Korea has historically had a number of unfortunate experiences with foreign countries, so it isn't surprising that Korea became more isolated than some other Asian countries and somewhat resistant to westernization. Koreans have some interesting cultural differences with westerners. Here are some examples:

In public, Koreans rarely smile. Although they are friendly people, they do not display that side in public.

If you visit a Korean home, you are expected to take your shoes off. Not doing so is close to an insult. (This is similar to Japanese customs.)

Eating in Korea is an experience. First, if you are invited to eat in someone's home, be sure to smack your lips and make a bit of noise while eating. This shows that you are enjoying the food, and it is expected. If you are eating rice with chopsticks, never ever, stick your chopsticks into the rice so that they stand up. This is something that is done only at funerals, not in normal dining. Whether you love kimchi or not, say you love it. Kimchi is a national obsession, and it would be almost an insult to tell a Korean person that you do not care for kimchi. Try not to blow your nose in a handkerchief at the table while eating. This is sometimes a challenge, given the spicy nature of Korean food. It is common to see and hear some Korean people sniffling constantly through a meal. Apparently, this is far more acceptable than using a hanky.

Urinating on an alley wall is not uncommon; in fact, it is accepted.

Spitting in the street is commonly done. I have even seen some women do it, too. It was very hard for me to get used to that, but when you spend time in Korea, it is one custom you have to ignore.

Family is very important in Korean life. In accordance with Confucianism, the head of the family is the father. The eldest son's responsibilities are ordered as follows: (1) his parents, (2) his brothers, (3) his sons, (4) his wife and, finally, (5) his daughters. Sisters must be considered unimportant in Confucianism, as I have never seen them mentioned in this connection.

A typical KAL DC-10 crew consisted of an American captain, a Korean co-pilot, a Korean flight engineer, and thirteen Korean flight attendants. These folks were not fluent in English for the most part; however, their knowledge of English aviation terminology was reasonably good. Communication in the cockpit between the Korean crew and the American captain was generally adequate, at least to the level necessary for a safe flight.

Unfortunately, from my point of view, the flights tended to be rather dull, as there was almost no casual conversation in the cockpit. Here I was in an Asian country, where it would have been most interesting to find out what my Asian flying counterparts were thinking in regard to aviation or, for that matter, domestic or world events. The lack of communication didn't seem to be due only to a lack of fluency in English; there was very little indication from the Korean crew of any desire to communicate.

I did work on my Korean language skills; in fact, I found that Korean is a lot easier to learn and pronounce than Chinese. While working for Korean Air, I learned many Korean expressions that I could use daily when out and about in Seoul, and almost everyone I encountered understood and responded to them. Chinese was a completely different story. The Chinese language, with twenty-six intonations, or variations in pitch, requires a far greater mastery of pronunciation, to be understood—even such simple expressions as hello, good-bye, and thank you. After many hours attempting to learn even the rudiments of Chinese, I decided that anything approaching proficiency will be in my next lifetime.

I love food, but there is one Korean food I couldn't learn to even tolerate, and that was kimchi. Kimchi is a spicy pickled or fermented combination of cabbage, onions, and sometimes fish, variously seasoned with garlic, horseradish, red peppers, or ginger. Westerners fall into two categories: those who love it and those who can't stand it. Even the smell of it was something I could never get used to. It would waft into my room at the Seoul Hilton and either encourage the beginning of a nightmare or awaken me well before it was time for me to get up.

Most mornings, I would go to the airport and check in at operations in preparation for my flight. After filling out the paperwork and checking the weather for the trip, I would go downstairs and board the large diesel bus that took the forty to fifty crew members (most of whom were Korean and had breakfasted on kimchi) to our respective airplanes. Every flight, I would pray that my airplane was close by so that I'd be one of the first off the bus. The smell of kimchi in the morning in the confines of the bus was indescribable.

Korean Pilots

South Koreans were incredible at memorizing. Most of the Korean co-pilots had memorized all of the checklist challenges, the numbered items on the checklists that the non-flying pilot reads and the flying pilot answers. The challenges usually pertain to the positions of switches and levers that need to be set in accordance with the mode of flight, such as before takeoff, after takeoff, climb, cruise, descent, approach, or before landing. I have never known an American pilot who was able to memorize all of the challenges on a checklist and in their exact order. I know I can't.

If Korean pilots had any difficulty flying airplanes, it pertained to their ability to improvise. (It should be noted that the government of South Korea has begun taking steps to change school curricula to encourage innovation and improvisation.) The following incident on a flight from Seoul to Guam one night illustrates this point.

Fukuoka, Japan with a Korean Air DC-10-30, circa 1995.

The Fuel Burn Chart

After takeoff from Kimpo Airport, Seoul, on flight KAL-7317 to Guam, we began our climb to cruising altitude. Due to a heavy passenger load, we carried just enough fuel for the trip plus the alternate fuel and extra reserves required. About fifteen minutes later, ATC told us that we could not fly at thirty-three thousand feet due to other traffic; the highest altitude we could have was twenty-nine thousand feet. My flight engineer went to the fuel burn charts and quickly determined that we didn't have enough fuel for the trip if we didn't climb to thirty-three thousand feet. He said he thought we should return to Seoul for more fuel. Yes, he actually said that!

I instructed the co-pilot to ask ATC how long we would have to hold over the next VOR (radio beacon) until thirty-three thousand feet was available.

ATC replied, "Six minutes." So we simply did a six-minute holding pattern over Fukuoka VOR and then climbed to thirty-three thousand feet, with plenty of fuel available for the flight. Both the co-pilot and engineer were astonished that I thought of this.

Keeping a Sharp Lookout

I experienced two *near* mid-air collisions in Korea, both in the Pusan Area. In one case, I had to take abrupt evasive action to avoid a group of Korean F-4 Phantom jets that were on an intercepting heading at my altitude. About a month later, an Airbus A-300-600 climbed above the altitude he was cleared to, into my altitude and directly in front of us, again forcing me to take immediate evasive action. The first near-miss was due to air traffic control not paying close enough attention to the flight path of the F-4s; the second was due to the Airbus A-300-600 pilot not leveling off at his assigned altitude.

Cockpit of a Korean Air DC-10 en-route to Guam, circa 1995.

Cabin of Korean Airlines DC-10, with crew, circa 1995.

Open Your Mind

Two other experienced DC-10 captains hired by Korean Air were friends of mine with whom I flew at Leisure Air. As I had been chairman of the negotiating committee for the Capitol Airways pilot group, my colleagues asked me to be the spokesman for the three of us should issues come up regarding the terms of our contract with Korean Air.

Issues did come up, and I spent many days in the Seoul office of Mr. Won, the head of the department in charge of foreign pilots. Korean Airlines wanted us to accept fewer than the ten days per month in the United States that our contracts stipulated. I learned quickly that I had to be just as stubborn as Mr. Won was; there was no give-and-take in these negotiations—nothing like negotiations in the United States, in which each side gives a little on something. You had to be just as unbending as they were. Negotiating with them was a grueling endurance contest, requiring the patience of a clockmaker. Each session lasted up to six hours at a time, with no progress to show for it. When the Koreans became frustrated, they would say, "Captain Spivack, open your mind."

Their biggest compliment was that I was the toughest American negotiator they had ever dealt with. I never gained any additional benefits, but I didn't lose any either. In retrospect, that was the most realistic outcome.

Noodle Soup

One sunny mid-morning, we were departing out of Kimpo Airport in Seoul, Korea, for Guam. It was a warm day, with calm winds and a heavy passenger load of 380 passengers. My flight engineer, Luan, was unusually tall for a Korean and spoke better-than-average English. I had flown with him a few times before, and he impressed me as being not only a competent flight engineer but also a very nice guy. Weather was good at Kimpo and along the route to Guam. I was looking forward to the trip, although I was thinking to myself that I wished I could coax the Korean crew to eat out at some restaurant in Guam other than the Korean one. It didn't matter where we were; even if we were in Paris, the Korean crew would eat only Korean food. I wondered whether they had ever tried other food—German, Italian, even Chinese? I think, unfortunately, that I knew the answer to that question.

We began preparing for the departure. Checklists were read, radios and instruments were set, performance data and clearances were received, doors were closed, and engines were started. I was now starting our taxi toward the takeoff runway. We left the gate on time, and the trip to Guam was starting off smoothly. There were several airplanes ahead of us for takeoff, so it would be a few more minutes before we would be cleared onto the runway. We switched over to tower frequency, and a moment later, we were cleared into position on the departure runway. About ten seconds later, we were *cleared for takeoff*, and I released the parking brakes and brought the three power levers of the DC-10-30 jumbo jet up to the takeoff power setting. We weighed nearly half a million pounds; the plane started moving slowly at first but then quickly began to pick up speed. The co-pilot called eighty knots speed, and I confirmed eighty knots on my air speed indicator. The airspeed was accelerating toward V-1; our decision speed, which was 161 knots, or about 191 miles per hour. At this speed or below, we had enough runway remaining to stop. At a speed greater than this, we would not be able to stop on the runway we had remaining. At 160 knots, *the red master warning light illuminated*, indicating a potentially serious malfunction. I commanded, *"Abort!"* I quickly brought the power levers to idle thrust, applied maximum braking, went immediately into reverse thrust, and ensured that the automatic spoilers (similar to speed brakes) had deployed, while simultaneously staying on the runway centerline, using smooth and careful application of the rudder. This was a high-energy stop. A half-million pounds moving at nearly two hundred miles per hour is a lot of mass to stop in a limited distance. Korean Air did have excellent maintenance, and I was sure the braking system and tires were up to the task. I brought the plane to a stop with about 1,500 feet of runway remaining. I got on the radio with the tower and asked them to have the emergency fire trucks report whether we had a wheel fire, which would have necessitated a passenger evacuation. There was no fire, so I requested to taxi to a safe area to allow the brakes and wheels to cool before taxiing back to our gate for maintenance. When we finally arrived back at the gate, Luan, our flight engineer, stuck his hand out to shake my hand. He said, "Captain Spivack, this is first DC-10 abort I was on when we stay on runway. I buy you noodle soup lunchee." I was happy to accept!

Expect the Unexpected

One rainy day, I was flying KAL flight 7315 from Seoul to Pusan. We were on the back course localizer approach to Pusan Airport. The back course approach is flown until the pilot has visual contact with the runway. Then the pilot enters the traffic pattern on the downwind leg and turns base leg over the hilly terrain off the approach end of the runway, completing the landing visually into the prevailing winds. As I visually located the runway, I transitioned to the downwind leg. It was an unpleasant day for flying, and the air was very rough due to strong winds and rain showers. A heavy rain shower was developing, and I was watching it move over the hill in front of us. There was no doubt we would be flying right into it and would most likely lose visual contact with the runway. I told the co-pilot that it appeared we would have to make a missed approach due to the rain shower. The co-pilot had no idea what I was talking about. I pointed to the heavy black rain shower about a half-mile dead ahead and commanded, *"Missed approach, max power, flaps fifteen, gear up!"* Instead of selecting flaps fifteen, the co-pilot selected flaps zero, and then he retracted the slats. I slammed the power levers forward just as the *stall warning went off.* The slats auto-extended, and the stall warning stopped. Immediately, the co-pilot (mistakenly) pressed the auto-extend light, and the slats retracted again, and the *stall warning went off again.* I extended the flaps and slats myself and told the engineer to guard the flap lever and tell the co-pilot not to touch any controls unless I told him otherwise. We executed the missed approach procedure in the heavy rain shower, and within one or two minutes, we flew out of it into smooth air. What the hell was this co-pilot thinking? We were given radar vectors back to the back course localizer approach. Once again, we broke out of the weather at about 1,200 feet above the ground and transitioned to a visual approach. This time, the path in front of us was free of rain showers. As I turned base leg, we completed the final landing checklist and landed at Pusan.

When we got on the ground, the co-pilot was very apologetic, bowing constantly. I spoke with him about what he did, and the best I could understand was that somehow, he was concentrating on his duties and procedures and hadn't seen the rain showers. This did not explain why he retracted the flaps and slats and then retracted the slats again when they auto-extended—with the stall warning going off all the while. I don't have any idea what could have caused him to make such serious errors. He kept saying that he had made a bad mistake. He was certainly right about that! But we were fortunate in two ways. First, the DC-10 is a gentle giant and took it in stride. Second, I was carrying extra airspeed because of the turbulence. A full stall in a DC-10 at 1,500 feet would have been a disaster.

Korean Aviation Law

Most South Korean aviation law parallels either the United States Federal Air Regulations or ICAO (International Civil Aviation Organization) regulations. However, one area that is quite different is how the government of South Korea handles aviation accidents.

I was friends with a Canadian pilot who worked as a captain for Korean Airlines on the A300-600 aircraft and was the captain in the article that follows:

August 12, 1994, from *Times Wire Services—LA Times*

The pilot and co-pilot blamed each other Thursday for a crash that destroyed a Korean Jet Airliner. Both were jailed on suspicion that they caused the accident by quarrelling during landing. An officer investigating the crash said the Canadian pilot and the South Korean co-pilot disagreed over what to do when the plane touched the runway after the flight from Seoul.

"The co-pilot wanted to take off again in view of the short length left on the runway, while the pilot believed he had enough distance to bring the plane to a halt in time," the police officer said. In the struggle to control the plane, the Airbus A-300 skidded and rammed a safety barricade. But instead of disaster, the crash on the resort Island of Cheju turned into a miracle story. All 152 passengers and eight crew members survived by sliding down an escape chute moments before the plane exploded in flames. Police say the landing should have been aborted because there was not enough runway remaining after the winds of an approaching typhoon gave the airplane an extra push. In custody were the pilot Barry Edwards Woods, 52, of Vancouver, Canada, and co-pilot Chung Chan Kyu, 36, of South Korea.

Captain Barry Edwards was given a temporary release from custody, and I heard through mutual friends that he managed to get back to Canada. Sometime later, I was told that the Korean government wanted to extradite Edwards back to Korea; however, the Koreans were not successful in the extradition.

In the United States, nearly all aircraft accidents are treated as accidents, and I cannot recall an instance when pilots were jailed on suspicion that they caused an accident. This is a very sobering illustration of a serious difference between the Federal Air Regulations in the United States and those in South Korea. It seriously concerned me as an expatriate captain for Korean Airlines. The last thing I wanted was to end up in a Korean jail eating *institutional kimchi* for the rest of my life. That was the stuff that real nightmares were made of!

Fixation

On a bright sunny morning while coming back from Guam on KAL flight 7315, I was letting a co-pilot fly the ILS approach into Seoul's Kimpo Airport. He was flying a great approach, but I noticed that he seemed fixated on the instruments. In the meantime, a Korean Airlines MD-80 series airplane that was landing about three miles ahead of us touched down about thirty degrees off the runway heading, and the plane's wingtip struck the ground. I could see a lot of smoke and quite a few parts coming off the MD-80.

I asked my Korean co-pilot if he was planning to continue the approach to a landing. He looked at me with a quizzical expression; he didn't know what I was talking about. I directed him to look at the airplane that had just landed. Finally, he got it and called for a missed approach.

Going Down the Primrose Path—Not

My last memorable experience in Korea was with a check airman who gave me a special check ride to Cheju Airport. Cheju is notorious for gusty cross-winds and its short runway, and landing there required a special check ride.

My approach and landing into Cheju Airport on KAL flight 7314 went exactly by the book. The Korean check airman was in the co-pilot's seat. This was going to be a quick turn-around.

We were served our lunch, which consisted of barbeque beef and spicy seaweed (quite yummy) while the passengers boarded. After that, we got all instruments and radios set for departure and then I called for the before-start checklist. The cabin door was closed, and I was waiting for confirmation from the cabin staff that the cabin was ready.

In the meantime, the check airman started speaking Korean with the ground crew, and before I knew what they were about to do, the ground crew started pushing the airplane back. Luckily, I got the parking brakes off almost instantly, when I felt the ground tug (tractor) pushing the plane—fortunately, *before* the tug had a chance to break the nose wheel of the airplane. I proceeded to loudly chew out the check airman for arranging to have the aircraft pushed back (speaking in Korean) without telling me. I was extremely angry, and he knew it.

We finally got underway, and the takeoff and departure went exactly as expected and by the book.

When we were about eighty miles out of Seoul at twenty-five thousand feet, I asked the check pilot to request lower altitude. He didn't respond. When I asked him again, he said that we "had a lot of time." I disagreed and told him to request lower altitude. I could see that he was attempting some kind of a payback for my chewing him out. He was trying to get me into a *situation*, but I wasn't falling for it.

Air traffic control finally recognized that we needed a lower altitude, but by then, we were too close and too high for a safe, stabilized, straight-in approach. We were about six miles out at four thousand feet when we should have been at about two thousand feet altitude at that close distance to the airport. After pulling all power off and using speed brakes, we still weren't going to get down in time. When I told the check pilot that we were too high to land he said, "No, it's okay to land."

"No, it's not safe," I said, "missed approach, max power, flaps fifteen, gear up." During the missed approach, ATC gave us a vector around the airport and positioned us for a visual approach from which we landed smoothly.

I wasn't sure what the check pilot was thinking, though my guess was that he wanted to get me into an embarrassing situation because he had lost face when I'd chewed him out earlier. This was a dangerous game to be playing, and who knows what a less experienced captain might have done if he'd allowed this character to intimidate him. This situation that the check airman created could have started a chain of events that led to an accident. The key to prevention of an accident is to break this chain of events.

As I became more aware of the risks associated with South Korean air traffic control and factored in Korean civil air regulations, as applied in the case of my Canadian friend, I could see another dimension of risk associated with flying in Korea.

I began to think about finishing the rest of my flying career in the United States. In addition, when my dad became sick and had to be admitted to a nursing home in Lake Tahoe, I wanted to be closer so I could visit him as often as possible. It was time to go back home to the West Coast.

CHAPTER 13

1996

Last Great Cowboys

✱

Bruce, a pharmacist friend who was an aspiring airline pilot, told me that Great American Airways was hiring MD-87 captains. Great American Airways was owned by a successful Nevada casino chain, with bases in Reno, Nevada, and Wendover, Utah. With dad in Lake Tahoe, this was perfect. I applied and was hired.

We were flying out of the old Wendover Air Base, about two hours driving distance from Salt Lake City. Wendover was famous for its role as a B-29 bomber training base in World War II, which led to the success in the dropping of the two atomic bombs that ended the war. The base was activated in April 1942, and a city of salt was built on the Bonneville Salt Flats. All told, twenty-one bomber groups and over a thousand aircrews were given bombardment training on the Salt Flats range.

The 393rd bombardment group moved to Wendover in September 1944. The 393rd was to become the core of the project to deliver the bombs. Between October 1944 and August 1945, 155 inert bombs in the shapes of "Little Boy" and "Fat

Man," the nicknames given the real bombs, were dropped by air-crews from Wendover on the Salt Flats to obtain information on detonators, release mechanisms, electrical fusing of the bombs, and flying characteristics of the aircraft. On June 14, 1945, the *Enola Gay* left Wendover airbase for Guam. You know the rest of the story only too well.

Three weeks of ground school training were held in Reno at Great American's corporate offices, followed by twenty hours of training in the MD-87 simulator at the McDonnell Douglas plant in Long beach, California. The ground school instructor did the simulator training as well, and the training was very professional.

When the time came for the FAA-rating check ride, Great American didn't have an available MD-87 on the ramp that day. So instead of rescheduling the check ride, the airline requested that I do the check ride in a DC-9-10, which was parked outside. The only problem was that I had never flown a DC-9-10 or even a DC-9-10 simulator in my life.

I wish I had a picture of the FAA inspector's face when he asked me how many hours I had in a DC-9-10 and I told him none. He reluctantly gave me the check ride anyway, and fortu-nately, it went well. A week later, I was scheduled for an initial line check, this time in an MD-87, with the same FAA inspector. He was in the jump seat, with Great American's director of flight operations in the right seat.

We flew from Reno to Bellingham, Washington, with pas-sengers, and then to Las Vegas. When we landed in Vegas, the director of flight operations told a company co-pilot, who was in the passenger cabin of the airplane, to take his place. He said he didn't need to see any more line checks from me; he was going to the terminal to catch a flight back to Reno. The aston-ished FAA inspector protested that the FAA would decide when the line check ended, especially as I had no previous operating experience in the MD-87 aircraft.

The director of operations left the plane, and I got another flight segment back to Bellingham and then on to Reno, with a co-pilot in the right seat and the FAA inspector in the jump seat, grumbling all the way. After we got back to Reno, the inspector said he was satisfied with the check rides and signed me off.

Flying for Great American out of Wendover was a lot of fun—kind of like being a member of the world's best flying club. There was even a parking space with a sign next to the ramp where the MD-87 was parked that said, RESERVED, MD-87 CAPTAIN. In thirty-five years of airline flying, I'd never seen that before.

Great American Airways Douglas MD-87, circa 1996.
Photo courtesy of Mike Mc Laughlin and Airliners.net

With Great American, if you were an experienced captain and a maverick—were safety-conscious, used reasonably good judgment, and could conduct flights efficiently—they loved you. When you took off in the morning, you were on your own. About the only contact with the company that you had during the day was when you called in departure and arrival times. The company never second-guessed the captain on fuel loads or most other decisions. It was like aviation had been in the 70s or 80s, except that we were flying nearly new jet planes with glass cockpits.

(In 1987, Douglas came out with the MD-87, which used modern glass electronic gauges to replace the old "steam gauge" mechanical instrumentation. These were a precursor to the current state-of-the-art electronic cockpits. The A-320 Airbus and Boeing 757 and 747-400 would be considered state-of-the-art until the arrival of the Boeing 777. In 2012 the 787 is set to surpass the 777 technology.)

Great American MD-87 cockpit, circa 1996.

Great American had an excellent safety record. The only incident I ever heard of was that of a very experienced senior MD-87 captain catching a wing tip during an extremely windy approach into Columbus, Ohio, on a day that most of the scheduled airlines were diverting to their alternates. Fortunately, the only damage to the airplane was to the retractable landing light, which was extended; when it scraped the runway concrete, it was ground down to a nub. My co-pilot, Tyler Beal, told me that the captain wrote in the incident report that he'd had a bird strike! He was a maverick and got things done, and management laughed about it. These folks were the *last great cowboys*.

Our flight schedule was to fly ten days on with twenty days off. What could have been better than that? Flights were scheduled to cities such as San Antonio, Texas; Madison, Wisconsin; and Columbus, Ohio, to pick up folks who liked to gamble and to bring them back to the casino in Wendover. Passengers were always in a great mood coming to Wendover, and on the return trip, after being served unlimited *refreshments*, they were even in a good mood going home.

Most of the flights' destinations were large and medium-sized airports, although we occasionally flew into fairly small airports without a control tower. When we flew into these airports, we always made numerous radio transmissions to announce our approach and landing before entering the airport traffic pattern. With a traffic pattern speed of 180 knots, the last thing we wanted was to be breathing down the tail feathers of a Cessna 150 doing 70 knots. When we announced on the common traffic advisory frequency (CTAF) that we were a Douglas MD-87 turbojet arriving, it wasn't unusual to see all of the light planes scatter and leave the traffic pattern. Actually, I probably would have done the same if I were flying a small aircraft. The vortex turbulence generated at the MD-87 wing tips was often much more than a light plane could handle, if it was landing close behind us.

The MD-87 was a reliable aircraft that experienced very few chronic maintenance problems. One thing worth noting was that the MD-87 didn't have the creature comforts of a DC-10. The MD-87 cockpit was much smaller, and the pilot seats weren't nearly as comfortable as those of the DC-10, but otherwise, from a pilot's perspective, the aircraft flew very well. It was quiet in the cockpit, and the plane had very gentle flying characteristics.

We practiced stalls, single-engine approaches, and missed approaches in initial flight training and every six months during recurrent training. The plane had predictable stall characteristics and was easy to fly on a single engine.

Aside from the lower level of comfort, the only issue I had with the MD-80–series aircraft was that the wings did not perform that well at high altitudes with high gross weights. With the MD-80s, it was usually better to burn off some fuel before climbing above thirty-one thousand feet, especially early in the flight.

The Pushy Flight Attendant

Since the mid-eighties, I have witnessed a very disturbing trend in the airlines: the occasional pushy flight attendant who not only wants to be in charge in the cabin but also tries to intimidate the flight crew. While some captains might tolerate this behavior for the sake of accommodation, this captain had a low tolerance for it. I recall one flight with Great American when we were just about to taxi from the gate. The lead flight attendant came up to the cockpit to report an *unruly* passenger whom she stated either would be put off the airplane or she wouldn't fly the flight. I asked her what the problem was, and she said that the passenger wouldn't obey her order to return to his seat from the lavatory. I shut the engines down on the MD-87 and asked her to take me to the passenger. She directed me to a middle-aged passenger, the only passenger on the airplane who was nicely dressed with a jacket and tie. I asked the passenger what the problem was, and he apologized and said he was sick to his stomach and had to make it to the lavatory to prevent an embarrassing accident. I looked at the flight attendant and asked her if she would accept the apology that the passenger gave her. She said she wouldn't and refused to fly with the passenger. I took her aside and told her to please be a little understanding of the passenger's gastric distress. She refused, so I told her that there was an extra flight attendant on this flight, and that if she didn't want to fly with this passenger, she would not be needed for this trip. Bottom line: she decided to fly the flight, and the passenger was fine and well behaved for the remainder of the flight.

It seems to me that since about 1985, there has been the occasional incident of a flight attendant acting as though the captain's responsibility ends at the cockpit door. I am of the old school mentality and believe that the captain is ultimately responsible for the safety of the entire airplane, including passengers and crew. Think about it: in an emergency, should the lead flight attendant have the *final* say about when to evacuate an airplane? For that matter, who should be in charge of the passengers in life rafts in the event of a ditching at sea, the lead flight attendant or the airplane's captain? Unfortunately, these lines are blurring, and the airlines love it. Divide and conquer is the corporate mentality. Unfortunately, it results in the breakdown of the hierarchy of aircraft command.

Interception

Late one night, flying back into Wendover, we were cleared to descend to eighteen thousand feet. A moment later, the traffic alert and collision avoidance system (TCAS) sounded an alarm in the cockpit called a resolution advisory. We were over the Great Salt Lake, and it was pitch black outside. I looked at the TCAS indicator and saw two targets approaching us from the rear. We were traveling about 570 miles per hour, but these aircraft were coming so fast that it seemed as though we were standing still.

As I watched, TCAS indicated one target passing on our left wingtip and one on our right wingtip, both mighty damn close. We couldn't see anything. The *targets*, were most likely military fighters planes. The pilots of those planes must have turned off their position lights, and strobe lights.

When you consider that we had 130 passengers plus six crew onboard, you can appreciate how disturbing this was to us. I called Salt Lake Center, and they said they hadn't seen anything on their radar screens. I could hardly believe that. I've never experienced anything like it before or since. A friend of mine who used to be an ATC supervisor suggested that it could have been two military aircraft practicing an intercept maneuver on a civilian airliner, although he said that wasn't supposed to be done.

Unfortunately, in 1997, due to flight time limitation disputes with the FAA, Great American filed bankruptcy and ceased operations. Had the company remained in business, I probably would have flown with them until retirement. They were a great company to work for. They were true cowboys who made flying fun again.

1998
Back to the DC-10

I had two more years to fly before mandatory FAA retirement (age sixty). (Due to a change in the regulations, mandatory retirement age is now sixty-five.) Financially, I was comfortable. I was more interested in an enjoyable flying position than a high-paying job. I applied for and was hired by Ryan International Airlines to be a DC-10 captain and check airman.

The ground school and simulator were given by American Airlines. I was quickly checked out as captain and shortly after that was designated a company check airman by the FAA. The flying was good, although I was flying so many trips, without much rest in between, that my back was starting to give me a lot of discomfort on longer flights.

Also, it seemed to me that in the late nineties, many airlines started to treat employees poorly. Loyalty wasn't valued, and hard work and exceptional performance were simply expected; they were neither appreciated nor properly compensated. This was probably the same thing that was happening in every other industry.

I'd had a wonderful career as an airline pilot. I had accumulated such varied flying experience in so many types of airplanes that finding a flying job was easy, and flying for a new airline was fun and exciting. Many of my friends who'd retired from large, scheduled airlines were amazed by the variety of experiences I could recount; none experienced the same kind of adventure with the scheduled airlines. By the middle of 1999, I decided to retire. I wanted to finish my career on a very happy note.

I celebrated my approaching retirement by buying a high performance Cessna 185 on amphibian floats. For the previous fifteen years, I had been renting float-planes from Kenmore Air on Lake Washington as well as from my friend Lane Older, the owner of Float Haven sea plane base on Lake Whatcom in Bellingham, Washington. Floatplanes combined my love of flying, the water, and fishing all into one, but flying them required extremely good judgment and a lot of caution.

It is said that a floatplane's position of greatest stability is upside down, on its back. While that may be true, it is not a position in which a floatplane pilot wants to find himself. Problem is, it's fairly easy to get there in a float plane. I think floatplane flying is one of the most challenging types of flying there is. Although my floatplane was an amphibian, meaning that it could also land on airport runways, its floatplane capability was what made it so fun. Before you could land on a runway, it was necessary to lower the landing gear. Conversely, when you landed on water, it was absolutely necessary that the landing gear be *up*. Landing on water with the landing gear *mistakenly in the down position* has resulted in many tragic, fatal accidents. It is also the reason amphibian floatplane hull insurance is so expensive.

While pilots landing on airport runways seldom have to worry about hitting other vehicles or people on the runway (because common sense normally keeps people and their cars off runways), the same cannot be said about landing a float-plane in the water. When a pilot lands a float-plane in a lake or river, he must constantly be on the alert for boats, kayaks, Jet Skis, and the waves that some of these craft produce. Hit a big wave on takeoff or landing with a floatplane, and it can have disastrous consequences.

Having said all this, floatplane flying is probably the most fun type of flying that exists. You can fly into many lakes and rivers that you might not otherwise be able to access. If you combine floatplane flying with camping and fishing, you have a combination that can't be beat. I have flown into many rivers and lakes in Washington, British Columbia, Canada, and Alaska where the fly-fishing was fantastic. Remember, the fish always seem to hang out where fewer people fish. The float-plane can get you to that seldom-fished spot better than almost any other form of transportation. I don't know of any way to fish for larger and more plentiful steelhead trout and salmon or to view and photograph more incredible wildlife than by floatplane.

In the thirty years I have been flying floatplanes I have had only three bad experiences—and they actually weren't all that bad.

*Landing the floatplane on a high altitude
mountain lake in Washington State, circa 1999.*

In the late sixties, I landed on the south shore of Long Island and taxied over to a sandy island for a nice picnic. After the picnic, Elke (my wife at the time) and I took a little swim, dried off, and then decided to fly back. I got on one of the floats and paddled the plane out away from the sandy island. This floatplane did not have an electric starter; it was a two-seat Luscumbe 8E on straight floats. To start the engine, you would stand on the float behind the wing strut and hand-prop the engine. I instructed Elke to retard the throttle to idle when the engine started. On the second attempt, the engine started, but instead of Elke retarding the throttle, she went to maximum power. It was quite a sight. I grabbed the wing strut with a death grip while my legs went out straight behind me. I shouted, "Pull the throttle back." Elke finally got the message and brought the power to idle, and my feet came back down to the top of the float. We should have filmed it. I am sure it looked pretty funny.

During the summer of 1968, I was living in Oakland, California, and a friend, Ed Golden, and I rented a floatplane in Sausalito to fly from there to Lake Pillsbury in northern California. It was beautiful weather, and we had some terrific fly-fishing that day on the south end of the lake near the dam. When we got ready to go, the air temperature on the lake had really heated up. I attempted a takeoff but could not lift off the water. It was too hot, and the airplane simply didn't have the performance capability on that high altitude lake at that temperature. I decided to try some special techniques. I attempted the takeoff in the normal manner, and after nearly achieving takeoff speed, I lifted one float out of the water. The plane almost lifted off, at which time I moved the stick in a quick circular movement to help the floatplane stagger into the air. The airplane touched down again after gaining a little more speed, so I did the maneuver again. This time, when we staggered into the air again, we slowly gained flying speed. I stayed in ground effect, close to the water surface until we had attained normal climb speed and then climbed up to our cruise altitude to fly back to the Bay Area. When we got back to the Bay Area, the weather had gotten bad; a low fog bank now obscured the bay and was blanketing the top of the Golden Gate Bridge. I descended down to about 150 feet above the water at the edge of the fog bank and could see that there was good visibility underneath the fog; I could clearly see the lower sections of Golden Gate Bridge. I turned toward the bridge, flew under it, and turned in toward Sausalito Bay and landed. The turbulence above the water, due to the adiabatic fog, was so extreme that it made the little floatplane nearly uncontrollable until right before touchdown, when the plane entered ground effect. Not the most fun I ever had in a float-plane.

The final, somewhat bad floatplane experience was on a fishing trip from the land runway at Smithers in British Columbia, Canada, to a beautiful lake about one hundred miles away. I was with Bill, a friend who was also a floatplane pilot and fellow fly fisherman. It was a beautiful summer day with clear skies and one hundred miles of visibility. I landed on Lake Morrisey and taxied toward an old cabin and dock on the east side of the lake near where a crystal-clear river flowed into the lake. I had caught huge steelhead trout there in years past, and I had great expectations on this trip. We taxied slowly up to the old dock and cut the engine once I knew I could sail to the dock without it. The left float came up against the dock, and I stepped onto it. I wasn't on the dock more than about five seconds, when the entire dock collapsed, trapping my leg under large pieces of dry-rotted dock lumber. It took some time to get the rotted lumber off my leg and to scramble on top of what was left of the dock. Luckily, my leg was not hurt, and more importantly, I was not trapped underwater.

That's the way it is flying floatplanes up into wilderness lakes and rivers; it often entails being on your own, and preventing mishaps before they happen. In fact, Canada used to recommend that floatplane pilots carry rifles or shotguns when going into wilderness areas with floatplanes. (Note: It is forbidden to carry pistols into Canada. Also, check on the current Canadian firearm regulations before you go.) I always carried a portable satellite telephone when I flew a plane into Canada, as that is the surest way to get help if you are injured or your plane is down. Of course, it is required to have an emergency locator beacon onboard as well. In addition, the more good training a floatplane pilot can get from an experienced bush pilot, the better. The only caveat I would make is that first, you should have some good solid training and experience in normal floatplane flying. Then, you can develop your personal limits and comfort zone before you start your bush pilot training. Bush flying is risky, and you have to recognize when you are crossing the invisible boundary between normal floatplane flying and bush flying.

A refreshing swim in a beautiful high mountain lake in
Washington State, circa 1999.

For the remainder of the summer and fall of 1999, I operated my floatplane into and out of the pristine lakes and rivers of British Columbia as well as many of western Washington's high-altitude lakes that were largely inaccessible except by air. One cannot imagine the beauty and seclusion!

The fishing was excellent, with abundant steelhead from six to twenty pounds. It was a particularly nice fall, with a long Indian summer. I put many hours on the Cessna 185 and celebrated my well-earned retirement by flying all over the northwest with fellow fly-fishing friends until the frost came. Winter was around the corner, and I was dreaming about spending it some place warm and sunny.

CHAPTER 14

1999

Approaching Retirement

✶

The name I gave my 1982 Morgan Out Island 416 was *Jet Lag*. Charlie Morgan designed the 416, and he always remarked what a great boat it was for the Caribbean. I felt that it was the boating equivalent of the Douglas DC-3. The DC-3 was already seventy years old and one of the most successful airplanes ever designed, and that plane is still in service. So it was with the Morgan 416. This was a boat built like a battleship with an incredibly heavy and thick fiberglass hull. As old as these boats are, they are still much revered. My 416 was a Ketch, a sailboat with two masts. The auxiliary engine was the indestructible Perkins 4-154, a four-cylinder diesel engine that burned an economical three-quarters of a gallon per hour. My boat, *Jet Lag*, was equipped with a bow thruster, which is essentially a powerful reversible electric motor with a propeller attached to it. It was located in a tunnel cut into the bow area below the water line. By powering the electric motor in one direction or the other, I could move the bow of the boat left or right. This was indispensable when backing into a slip with a long-keeled boat. With a bow thruster installed, the captain of the boat looked like the most qualified skipper you had ever seen, as he effortlessly docked the boat. There is no doubt in my mind that bow thrusters have saved enumerable marriages. (Think, no screaming at the first mate while docking.)

My boat was docked on the east end of St. Thomas in an area called Red Hook. St. Thomas is the largest and most populated island in the U.S. Virgin Island chain. The most wonderful aspects of the Virgin Islands are the idyllic air and water temperature. The average year-round temperature is the mid-eighties, with relatively low humidity. The water temperature is equally perfect; it hovers between seventy-nine and eighty-two degrees Fahrenheit. Even with a population of fifty-three thousand, the surrounding waters of St. Thomas are crystal clear and unpolluted. The only caveat about St. Thomas is that one cannot go out at night *alone* in certain parts of the island. Period! Unfortunately, it has been like that since the mid-eighties.

Relaxing aboard Jet Lag, in the U.S. Virgin Islands, circa 1999. .

Red Hook on St. Thomas had everything one could want: boat chandleries, gourmet food markets, transportation, and mail forwarding services. Best of all, it was only a half-hour sail to beautiful St. John, one of the nicest of the Virgin Islands, with delightful white sandy beaches and peaceful anchorages. I would provision for a two-week sail and cruise from island to island, anchoring off dreamy beaches for several days at a time before moving on to explore the next lovely island. I kept four scuba tanks aboard and enjoyed scuba diving and exploring shipwreck sites that I found by researching old books about shipwrecks. Often, I would team up with a friend, Dave De Beers, who was a charter skipper on a sailing vessel based in Red Hook. Dave looked like an old pirate himself. He was a short, burly, powerful man with deep, flashing blue eyes. Dave loved the sea. I met Dave many years ago in Francis Bay on St. John. My ship's batteries had run down, and Dave, whom I had only just met, volunteered a significant amount of his time to get my batteries jumpstarted and my boat back in service. We've been good friends ever since.

Dave had spent a great deal of time exploring Norman Island in the British Virgin Islands. Robert Louis Stevenson had used Norman Island as the basis for many of his pirate novels. Stevenson knew what he was talking about; Dave and I uncovered numerous valuable items over the years on Norman Island, which confirmed that there had indeed been pirates on the island. With metal detectors, we found flintlock pistol and musket actions with decayed wood from the stocks, cutlass swords, silver and copper coins, and many boarding hooks.

Diving in the Virgin Islands was relatively safe. There's a fairly small tidal change from high to low tide, usually averaging only about a foot. As a result, there are no particularly strong currents in the majority of the locations one would likely dive.

Most people think about sharks. Shark attacks have occurred in the Virgin Islands but are not nearly as frequent there as they are in California, Florida, Australia, or South Africa.

I am aware of only two confirmed fatal shark attacks in the Virgin Islands: one occurred in Magens Bay, on the north side of St. Thomas in April 1963. Lt. John Gibson, who was a U.S. Navy underwater diver, was killed by a Galapagos shark while swimming in the bay; this shark is somewhat rare to those waters. When he was attacked, his girlfriend, Donna Waugh, swam to him despite his warning that she should get out of the water. Luckily, Donna Waugh was not bitten during her rescue attempt. Unfortunately, Gibson's femoral artery was severed by the shark attack, and he bled to death. For Ms. Waugh's bravery, the U.S. Treasury awarded her the Gold Lifesaving medal.

Another fatal shark attack that I heard about numerous times while sailing in the Virgin Islands, although I could not find documentation of it in the National Shark Attack Files, concerned two brothers who were attacked while spear fishing off Carrot Rock in the British Virgin Islands in the 1960s. The story was that one of the brothers was fatally bitten by a hammerhead shark and the other died of a heart attack.

This brings up another issue I would like to point out. I have long noticed that many incidents involving sharks are often mischaracterized or *swept under the rug*. In most cases, it appears that this is done to protect tourism. The very people in charge of deciding whether a shark attack took place are the people and organizations that depend on tourism for their funding. This kind of conflict of interest may have a detrimental effect on water safety. This is especially true if real shark attacks go unreported, as this conveys to swimmers a false sense of security. I cannot count the number of times I have seen partying bareboat charter guests and skippers jump into Caribbean waters at night, especially after consuming alcohol. This is not something a sane person should do.

Here is a distressing case to illustrate my point as reported in numerous Caribbean newspapers: A fifty-three-year-old, experienced diver from Florida disappeared on December 19, 2007, while scuba diving off Green Cay, near Jost Van Dyke. Jost is a small, cozy little island with a local population of 297. The diver and his two sons were diving at about 10:00 a.m. After the dive, he was snorkeling on the surface with his sons (the sons were unharmed), when he simply vanished. The death was ruled a *drowning*. However, there was testimony from the three sea rescue volunteers of Virgin Island Search and Rescue Service (VISAR) that tiger sharks were eating the diver when VISAR found the body. Need I say more? Again, the death was ruled a drowning. Sharks are everywhere. Most of the time, they see you before you see them.

Best shark avoidance tips are the following: dive with other experienced divers, always dive in good light and good visibility, and don't spearfish when you snorkel or dive. A speared, injured fish and the fish blood will attract sharks from many miles away.

I'm especially interested in shark attacks because of my own encounter in 1989. I was snorkeling off a reef near Cam Bay in the British Virgin Islands when two seven-to eight-foot reef sharks and a barracuda suddenly appeared from deep water next to the reef. The two sharks headed straight for me, dorsal fins down and shaking their heads, displaying very aggressive behavior. Fortunately, I was only a few feet from the reef and I scrambled onto it, cutting and abrading myself on the coral. The sharks sped past the reef and then turned back into the deep water, not to be seen by me again. I considered that a close call and somewhat of an unusual occurrence for the Virgin Islands. The coral cuts and abrasions took months to heal, but they served to remind me of what might have happened.

In all the years I've been swimming and diving in the U.S and British Virgin Islands, I've had only four encounters with sharks. In one of these, a good friend of mine, Dr. Peter Murray, was spending a week aboard my boat and asked if we could snorkel where he might see a shark. I agreed reluctantly, and Barbara, (with whom I have lived since my retirement and who became my life partner), Peter, and I headed for Money Bay on Norman Island.

Barbara was wading off a small beach on the southeast side of Money Bay while Peter and I snorkeled along the most seaward part of the rocky shore, when I heard Peter shout "Shark!" I looked toward Barbara and saw a large eight-to-nine-foot bull shark (Zambezi shark), swim within a length of her; then it continued past me and Peter, not acting the slightest bit aggressive. It swam past us out into the Caribbean Sea and faded into the blue depths. Needless to say, Peter was very happy to have had a chance to snorkel with a shark—Barbara, not so much.

One afternoon on Norman Island, Dave De Beers and I decided to explore a ballast pile that we had spotted in Money Bay from the top of a hill we'd hiked to the day before. When you find a pile of river rock on the ocean bottom, the wreckage and contents of an old ship are frequently nearby. This was a remote part of the south coast that was treacherous to enter from the seaward side in all but the calmest of weather. Once inside the bay, you had to carefully pick your way through coral heads to the one spot in the northeast corner of the bay where you could anchor.

After anchoring, Dave and I put on our tanks and snorkeled over to the pile of river rock we'd discovered. We opened each other's tank valves, checked our air gauges, and descended fifty-five feet below the water's surface. As we approached the ballast pile, we became distracted by a tremendous lobster weighing over twenty pounds. Dave swam in front of it, and

I approached from behind. The lobster swam backwards, as they do when being chased, and ended up in my open goody bag.

We were giving each other big grins and thumbs-up when something even bigger caught our eye. Two nine-foot bull sharks, apparently sensing the commotion with the lobster, had come to investigate. They didn't look at all friendly; their dorsal fins were pointing straight down, and they were moving their huge toothy heads from side to side, indicating a very aggressive mood.

Dave and I instinctively moved toward each other, positioning ourselves back to back. We started moving in a circle, standing on the sandy ocean bottom in about fifty-five feet of water, focusing our eyes on the circling, hungry-looking sharks. If there was anything fortunate about our situation, it was that we both had nearly full tanks of air—one less thing to worry about. The circle the sharks were swimming in got smaller. Suddenly, one swam toward us and bumped very hard against Dave's shoulder and light-weight wetsuit. Dave pushed against the shark, and I could see the eerie-looking shark's membrane (eyelid) close to protect its big black eye. This was starting to get serious.

I grabbed the nylon pouch attached to my goody bag and began to assemble the aluminum four-piece spear I carried. No, I wasn't about to spear the shark; I was going to poke it, if I needed to—if things got any nastier.

This standoff lasted a very tense six to eight minutes. Gradually, the sharks were either losing interest or had begun to figure out that we were not going to be an easy meal. Slowly, the circle they were swimming around us became less defined. Then, abruptly, the male swam toward the open sea, followed by his female friend. We both felt a great sense of relief, and we would have a lobster dinner after all.

Money Bay, Norman Island, British Virgin Islands.
Keeping a close watch on these two toothy critters, circa 2000.

Dave and I explored the wreck at Money Bay the rest of that day, and I continued to dive it on other occasions. Although we have both found numerous artifacts and some coins there, neither of us has found anything of extraordinary value.

I was beginning to come to terms with my retirement, planning the rest of my life (as much as anyone ever dares to do) while aboard *Jet Lag.* I needed to find activities that were intellectually stimulating while providing the excitement and adventure I enjoyed as an airline pilot. It seemed to me that continuing to fly my floatplane in search of large steelhead trout in the U.S. Northwest, Canada, and Alaska in the summer would fulfill half the requirement for adventure. During the winter; sailing, diving, and fly-fishing for bonefish and tarpon in the Caribbean would likely fulfill the rest of my cravings.

Trophy Fly-fishing in the Virgin Islands

While anchored near Hurricane Hole off St. John in the U.S. Virgin Islands, I noticed some flashes on a shallow coral flat, which was a couple of hundred yards from my sailboat. I was already interested in tarpon fishing and had done some in the Florida Keys, but I had no idea what kind of fish would have these bright reflections off their fins. I called my friend Allen Brock, who worked for World Wide Sportsman in Islamorada. Allen was pretty sure that what I was seeing were bonefish. He was correct, and after he sent me a selection of Crazy Charlie flies and a couple of fly lines, I was off and running. Thus began my twenty-plus years of fly-fishing in the Caribbean.

One day while fishing the west side of Leinster Bay, St. John, wading in the eighty-two degree water in my swimsuit and reef walker shoes, I spotted a large school of bonefish tailing along the shoreline near the mangroves. I cast a pink Crazy Charlie about three feet in front of the first bonefish. After pausing a second, I began slowly stripping the line. The moment the Crazy Charlie moved along the bottom, the bonefish pounced on it. I set the hook with a strip strike, and the bonefish took off across the flat at high speed. Within a minute, the bonefish had taken all of my fly line and was way into my backing. I took off running as fast I could after the bonefish to get some of the line backing onto my reel again. The fish wasn't finished with me yet, as he took off across the flat in the other direction. By the time I had finally fought the bonefish to the point where he was ready to give up, I was ready to give up as well and was out of breath from chasing him. He was a twelve-pound fish that was just shy of a world record on six-pound test tippet. That was a good day's fishing!

A twelve pound bonefish on a six pound test leader.
Just short of a world record.

A few months later, *Jet Lag* was anchored off Guana Bay, one morning, on the north side of Tortola in the British Virgin Islands. The bay was flat calm when I saw a pair of tarpon roll, about 200 feet away. I climbed into my 8 foot Avon inflatable dingy and rowed out to where I thought the fish might pass by.

I waited patiently until I saw the tarpon swim in my direction, about ninety feet ahead. I stripped out some line and then false casted until I had about sixty feet of fly-line in the air. I released the cast, and when my 1/0 purple fly was two feet above the water, the huge tarpon came crashing out of the water like a missile and swallowed the fly. When the tarpon took the fly, he sounded (dove), and I did a strip strike of the hook five or six times. The big tarpon took off at high speed in the direction of some coral heads. Thing was, he was pulling me and my dingy with him. I wasn't sure how big he was, but he looked as if he was at least 110 pounds. He made a fast run and then jumped clear of the water. I bowed to the fish so that he wouldn't fall on a taut line and break the fly line tippet. As he neared the coral heads, he switched direction and headed seaward. I had now been fighting this fish for about twenty minutes, and he had jumped clear of the water four times and did not seem to be getting tired. We were about a quarter-mile from shore, and I was wondering how far he would pull me out to sea before he got tired and gave up. He had a fair amount of my backing now, as he would occasionally go deep. I started putting as much pressure as I could on the fish without breaking the sixteen-pound tippet. At the forty-five minute mark, we were both getting tired. In addition, we were about a mile offshore on the north side of Tortola, and I began to think that it was too far and too choppy to be out there in that fragile little dingy without an engine. After fighting the tarpon for an hour, I had him fairly close to the boat and took some photographs of this beautiful fish. I decided not to try to release him along-side the dingy. If he thrashed around and the large 1/0 hook punctured the inflatable, I would certainly regret the decision to bring the fish so close. I took up the slack in the fly line and pulled hard, snapping the sixteen-pound test tippet. The tarpon happily swam away.

Big tarpon on the fly line off the north coast of Tortola, BVI.

My problem now was that I was more than a mile offshore and had a long row ahead of me. Luckily, the trade wind was behind me, although I could see that I wouldn't be able to make landfall in Guana Bay. I could probably make landfall closer to Cane Garden Bay, about four miles to the west. When I was about a quarter-mile off Cane Garden Bay, I was able to catch the attention of a skipper from Connecticut who was on a Moorings charter boat. We tied my dingy to the back of his boat and, after he heard my story, agreed to take me back to Guana Bay. I invited him and his wife to join me for dinner that evening, and we all happily celebrated another memorable day in the beautiful Virgin Islands.

Since those days, bone fishing in St. John in the U.S. Virgin Islands and on Tortola and Virgin Gorda in the British Virgin Islands has declined a bit due to increased fishing pressure. I still fish for tarpon and bonefish on the Island of Anegada in the British Virgin Islands, where many schools of hundreds of bonefish are seen every day. The bone fishing on Anegada is still excellent due to the remoteness of the island and the color of the bottom of the flats. These fish are very hard to see in this location because they blend in with the bottom color perfectly and seldom, if ever, tail. To see and catch bonefish in Anegada, I recommend hiring a local guide. They will see the fish even when you don't. It is an island thing, I guess. It is amazing how they are able to get you into schools of bonefish as long as it is a day with little or no cloud cover. With the mild temperatures, beautiful water colors, and pleasant trade-wind breezes, fly-fishing the Virgin Islands was an absolute delight.

Sailing into Retirement

As time went on, it became apparent that some aspects of sailing in the Virgin Islands were changing—and not always for the better.

From the mid '70s through the early '80s, it was common to encounter other boaters in the anchorages, and pleasant conversations would invariably lead to invitations for drinks and conversation before or after dinner. Seldom did such social events result in long-term friendships, but that wasn't the point. It was the friendship and camaraderie while sharing a common experience that mattered. Unfortunately, I have to report that this has changed. Now people seldom wave at one another from boat to boat. If you do, your wave may be returned with a look from the other party that seems to say, "Does that person think he knows me?"

There are now moorings (that you pay for) at most anchorages in the British Virgin Islands. Although this makes cruising in the islands simpler, as you don't have to worry about anchoring techniques, it has led to a dumbing down of the skills of the average person skippering there and has eliminated some of the adventure. The British Virgin Islands have become more and more built up as they have become better known. Now there's a noisy bar and restaurant in almost every major anchorage there. If one wants peace and quiet, I would recommend the anchorages around St. John.

Jet Lag anchored off a dreamy beach in the British Virgin Islands, circa 1999.

One day in May 1999, I was anchored off a lovely beach in beautiful Hawknest Bay on St. John. It was a pretty morning, and Barbara and I were sitting in *Jet Lag*'s cockpit sipping some chocolate-blended coffee when my cell phone woke me out of my daydream. I recognized the caller immediately. "Jay, we could use you for some trips to the Middle East. Can you get your tail up to Dover, Delaware, in the next few days?"

"Sorry, Bud, I can't. I'm done, retired. Fini."

"Listen, we really need you to do this for us, and you can't say no."

"Bud, I said no before, and I'm saying no again!" I hated the implied threat in the bureaucrat's voice.

"Wait a minute—"

"No, Bud, you wait a minute—remember Moscow? I nearly got my tit in the proverbial ringer over that one, and how did you guys help me? You pulled the sat phone line (Discrete Satellite telephone contact number for the project) when I needed help. Talk about throwing someone under the bus!"

"Well, we knew you could handle it. That's why we need you now."

"Tell you what, Bud, I'll give it some thought."

I walked toward the bow and stepped on the rubber-covered anchor windlass switch. The chain started rolling smoothly into the hawse pipe. (Hawse pipe is the pipe that guides the chain into the chain locker.) The caller asked what the noise was, and I pressed the end call button and switched off the phone. A moment later, the stainless steel plow anchor ran over the bowsprit with a metallic bang. "Who was that?" asked Barbara. My answer was a hug and a kiss on her forehead. It was a beautiful day to begin a sail to Barbuda (a very beautiful island near Antigua).

As we sailed, I was thinking about my dad. He had passed away unexpectedly in 1996. He was a kind, hardworking man who for relaxation loved spending a little time betting on the horses. He didn't seem to lose much and, on occasion, had some good wins. He always said that he would know *when to quit.*

I thought about when to quit, as many pilots do, especially if they have experienced some *dangerous lessons* or have had a few close calls. I'd had more than my share of both. I wondered if for me, *when to quit* was now.

I held my course southeast as I cleared the Horse Shoe Reef and entered the Anegada Passage. The next hundred miles of open-ocean could be very rough at times. A weather front had gone through the previous day, and in a stroke of luck, we would have the wind on our back and thus smooth seas all the way to St. Martin. Barbara brought me a cup of her special hot chocolate. We were watching the sun set behind us, hoping to see that Holy Grail of sailor sunsets that is known as the *green flash*.

Suddenly, it dawned on me that the *green flash* is a perfect way to describe one's life.

AFTERWORD

For Those Interested in an Airline Pilot Career

B ob Bartho, a friend of mine who retired from United
Airlines, once said, "Flying is a hard way to earn an easy
living." In this chapter, I'm going to tell it like it is—the
good, the bad, and the ugly.

In general, I believe a career as an airline pilot is one of the
most satisfying careers a person can have. However, it is not the
easiest profession to succeed in. There are typically two ways
to obtain the training and flight experience necessary to be successful in obtaining a position as an airline pilot. You can train
in the military, or in a civilian flight school. I will discuss both
approaches in detail. Regardless of the method, the pilot-to-be
must be highly motivated; a half-hearted approach won't cut it.

Keep in mind that as an airline pilot, you will spend long periods of time away from home. You will also be subject to alcohol
and drug screening on a regular basis. So, if you have a history
of drug use, don't even consider this profession. Likewise, if
you've had a felony conviction or a history of moving traffic
violations, I suggest that you choose another career.

You will be required to have training, or check rides (usually in an aircraft simulator with the airlines check pilot), every six months, as well as periodic line check evaluations (with either the airlines check pilot or an FAA inspector). I don't know of any other career that has such stringent requirements.

Other aspects of a person's suitability to become an airline pilot are more subjective. I believe that among the important personal characteristics are the following:

- An ability to stay focused.
- Ability to concentrate.
- Excellent decision-making abilities.
- Ability to remain "cool" under pressure.
- Natural curiosity and a desire to continually learn new skills and acquire knowledge.
- Good physical health and vision.
- Good interpersonal skills.
- Good character and ethical behavior.

Generally speaking, it is of significant benefit for an aspiring airline pilot to have a Bachelor of Science degree, possibly in aviation or engineering. That said, there are many airline pilots with all types of academic degrees.

I would recommend that the applicant have an airline transport pilot's license with two thousand hours of flight time, of which at least five hundred hours is as pilot in command, and five hundred hours of multi-engine time, with at least two hundred hours of that with turbine engines. How one obtains these ratings and this flight experience depends on the approach one takes.

The Military Approach

The military approach may be the least expensive route but may also be the most competitive approach, not to mention the requirement of a military commitment. All three branches of service train pilots, but there are differences in the type of flying and types of airplanes used by the army, navy, and air force. The air force typically trains more transport pilots than the other two services do.

To become a military pilot, you must first become a commissioned officer. To become a commissioned officer in the air force, for example, you can go to the air force academy, attend ROTC at your university, or join the air national guard or the air force reserves. The competition is great, so you will need to keep a high grade-point average in college (3.5 or above) and be a well-rounded type of student. Involvement in sports and civic activities is considered a plus.

After being commissioned, you will need to find a flight training vacancy. It is imperative that you score high in all flying tests and all along the way in flight training. The military will not guarantee your completion of flight training, and a failure in the program usually means that you will finish your tour of duty at a desk job. If you earn a flying slot, you may have up to a ten-year service commitment.

On the other hand, after being commissioned as an officer, the flight training the military provides will cost you nothing. Then, when you get a flying assignment, the flying hours you accumulate will help to build up your airline resume while you are being paid to accumulate that valuable logbook time and experience.

Be sure to check with an experienced military recruiter and your local reserve unit for the latest requirements! The military flying experience and the military ratings you receive are usually transferable to civilian licensing.

The Civilian Approach

It has been said that the medical profession is the natural enemy of the aviation profession. While I think that may be an exaggeration, I strongly suggest that you find an FAA medical examiner and take the first-class medical examination. Obviously, if you have a medical condition that prevents you from being an airline pilot, it would be better to find out long before you invest a great deal of time and money in training.

Look for a well-respected flight school or flying club that has a number of good training aircraft and enough professional flight instructors to ensure not just the availability but the continuity of training.

Another possible alternative is to buy your own instrument flight rules (IFR)-equipped airplane; you would still have to find well-qualified flight instructors to train you in your own aircraft. In some cases, this may be a cost-effective approach, but be aware that it is expensive to maintain an aircraft in accordance with Federal Air Regulations. On top of that, there's the cost of insurance, fuel, and tie-down, or hangar fees.

Either way, work first on obtaining your private license, for which you will need a *minimum* of forty hours of flight time (the national average is more than sixty hours). The forty hours minimum flight time will be a combination of dual instruction, local solo flying, and cross-country dual and solo flying, plus your flight test in the airplane.

Choosing a Flight Instructor

Without any doubt, one of the biggest challenges in learning to fly is finding a really good flight instructor. There are several factors that make it somewhat complex. For example, the personal characteristics and the flying experience of an instructor who is teaching you to be a private pilot should be different from those of the instructor training you for the airline transport pilot rating. You would want a competent instructor in both cases, but your first flight instructor should be an especially patient instructor who instills your confidence in his or her flying experience, as you don't have any flying experience at this point. The instructor should not be overly critical of your performance; he should be striving for you to learn to fly safely rather than expecting you to fly with high precision. It is not uncommon for a flight instructor who is very experienced and trains pilots for the commercial pilot's license, instrument rating, or airline transport pilot rating to tend toward being too critical when teaching a brand new pilot. It would be an exceptional instructor who could teach both the student pilot and the airline transport pilot equally well. Thus, I would highly recommend that the beginning student pilot find a relatively new flight instructor who has two to three years of experience as an instructor and is very enthusiastic. You want to try to find an instructor who is interested in seeing you succeed. Of course, in training for your commercial pilot's license and instrument rating, you will look for an instructor with more experience who will expect far higher standards of precision.

Another thing to keep in mind is that if the flight instructor you have chosen is not working out satisfactorily, or if there are personality conflicts, you have every right to change instructors. After all, it is your money, and you have to be sure you are getting good value for your money and that your instructor has your best interest at heart. If you decide to learn to fly in a flight school, be sure to speak with the chief flight instructor or the assistant chief flight instructor before selecting your instructor. Discuss your goals and detail your concerns, and ask them to suggest a few flight instructors that you could meet with to discuss your flight training. Then, when you have selected a flight instructor, schedule an introductory lesson with him or her to see if you are a good match.

As a general rule, good flight instructors are enthusiastic about instructing. You will quickly see how knowledgeable they are by asking a few thoughtful and appropriate questions. Good instructors will often ask you questions about the topics covered in the previous lesson—questions that require answers that demonstrate how well you have understood the lesson you have just received. Each lesson will often have a critique section in which the instructor and you should honestly evaluate your progress and outline any difficulties you may seem to be having. A good instructor will demonstrate every maneuver you are being taught so that you can see what it is that you are supposed to learn during the lesson. However, *you* should be doing most of the flying. Your instructor should make sure you are keeping a good lookout for other aircraft, and you should observe that your instructor is keeping a good lookout for air traffic as well. This is an important habit to learn early in your training because *you* will need to do this every time you fly, especially in non-instrument conditions.

A good instructor is always punctual. Your instructor should give you confidence and cause you to feel safe. The instructor should never exhibit poor judgment that might put you or the airplane at risk.

I would recommend that you choose a flight school that has standardized training aircraft (aircraft of the same make and model, as well as similar instrument panels). Also, hopefully all training aircraft have moving map GPS units like the Garmin 430.

It is important that you fully understand the financial costs of training. Know how the aircraft flight time is charged; by engine running time, or from the time that the *aircraft master electrical switch* is turned on. You should know the cost of the flight instructor and how you are being charged for the flight instruction time. Find out the details of the flight school's aircraft insurance program and what you could be liable for in the event of a mishap.

Ground school for your private pilot's license is a very important part of your training. You will have to learn quite a bit of technical information to be a safe private pilot. You will also have to pass an FAA private pilot written test. The ground school will not only teach you a great deal of what you need to know to pass the written test but also will provide you with information on many important flying subjects that you will continually use during all of your subsequent flying. Consider taking the ground school in the beginning of your training and again toward the end of your private pilot training course. This will be good reinforcement and will help you to retain important information; it will also act as a good review prior to your written test. It is worthwhile noting that ground school is an integral part of flight training that continues through every level of aviation right up to and including the time when you are a successful airline pilot and are transitioning from one type of aircraft to another. It is very important that you take ground school very seriously and always come to class well rested and prepared to learn.

The principles of good flight instruction have changed quite a bit over the last twenty years. The FAA has invested a great deal of effort in promoting improvements in teaching techniques that parallel those of professional teaching standards. When I first became a flight instructor in the mid-sixties, there was much less emphasis on the principles of established teaching techniques. There have been other changes as well; computer programs and modeling have allowed for far more detailed knowledge of aerodynamics, which is now taught during ground school instruction. It is also worth noting that now, a flight instructor must either take a refresher course every two years or have a recent history of successful recommendations of pilot applicants that have *passed* their practical tests. All of this helps to ensure that every student pilot is taught by a flight instructor who is up-to-date on the latest FAA requirements and training techniques.

After you have passed your private pilot's license test and begin flying on your own is when the learning process *really* begins. The learning does not stop with passing a test. Consider your private pilot's license as a license to learn.

After passing your private pilot's test, you will begin training toward becoming a commercial pilot. You will most likely also want to become a certified flight instructor. An advantage of obtaining an instructor's license is that you can build flight time while instructing and be paid for it. Further, I have always thought that I learned the most about flying while teaching others to fly.

You will need two hundred hours of flying experience to qualify for the practical test for a commercial pilot's license. In general, the commercial pilot's license requires learning additional technical subjects. Also, you will be required to demonstrate more sophisticated maneuvers with a higher degree of precision than were necessary for the private pilot's license.

Next on your agenda will be to become an instrument-rated pilot. No single rating is more fundamental to an airline pilot than the instrument rating. It is imperative that the instrument pilot candidate understand the principles of instrument flying and become proficient in all phases of instrument flying. It is relatively easy to learn to fly solely on instruments at three thousand feet above a cloud deck in smooth air. Obviously, flying in weather (in clouds) with turbulence and possibly icing conditions is much more demanding and difficult but must also be learned and practiced. It is a significant challenge to fly an instrument approach to *published minimums* (the minimum altitude to which a pilot may descend without having the runway in sight) in bad weather, turbulence, and possibly icing while communicating with approach control—and then, if necessary, execute a safe and properly performed *missed approach* (the published procedure to be flown if the runway is not visible at published minimums). Besides a pilot having to demonstrate that he is sufficiently proficient and knowledgeable to pass the FAA instrument practical test, each instrument-rated pilot must maintain instrument proficiency/currency by practicing actual or simulated instrument approaches regularly, as prescribed by the Federal Air Regulations. It is easy to lose proficiency if a pilot doesn't practice instrument flying. There is, unfortunately, a significant amount of statistical evidence of instrument-rated pilots who did not maintain their proficiency and got into serious trouble while attempting instrument approaches in bad weather.

As an airline pilot, you are required to take regularly scheduled simulator checks. These simulator checks are flown under simulated instrument conditions and may include various simulated emergency situations. A pilot's ability to fly under instrument conditions and to handle simulated emergencies is soon revealed. Any pilot who is not a proficient instrument pilot will have a difficult time becoming an airline pilot. Take your instrument training very seriously. Work very diligently at becoming an expert instrument pilot, and maintain your proficiency at a level greater than *the minimum standards* required by Federal Air Regulations.

When you have accumulated a minimum of 1,500 hours, which includes at least 500 hours of cross-country flight time, 100 hours of night flight time, and 75 hours of instrument flight time in actual or simulated conditions, you will have the experience requirements for the airline transport pilot's license. Basically, the airline transport pilot's practical license test is used to demonstrate to the Federal Aviation Agency that you have achieved the minimum knowledge and proficiency required to fly an airplane carrying passengers or cargo in airline transport category aircraft. To be the pilot-in-command of an aircraft weighing over 12,500 pounds takeoff weight, you would also need a type rating in that airplane. That is a separate practical test that every airline pilot takes to qualify as pilot-in-command.

College Requirements

If you don't have a four-year degree, you'll need to work on completing that. While there are some airline pilots hired without a four-year college degree, they are a rare breed today. Do not limit your chances of getting hired by not having a college degree. Keep in mind that there are some good colleges with aviation programs that include training for all of your required pilot's licenses. Embry Riddle in Florida, the University of North Dakota, and Purdue University in Indiana might be among the choices to consider.

The Delta Connection Academy in Atlanta, Georgia, and the Mesa Airlines Pilot Development Program in Phoenix, Arizona, would be other options. Often these programs lead to a position as first officer for a regional carrier. Contact these airlines for the latest details on their current programs, which change to meet forecasted hiring requirements.

Although the civilian approach to becoming an airline pilot has the advantage of you being able to progress at your own speed, it is generally a much more expensive approach than the military approach and in some ways will require more initiative and commitment on your part. With the hourly rate of training aircraft in flight schools well over $100 per hour, plus the hourly cost of a flight instructor, one could invest $50,000 to $150,000 to obtain an airline transport rating. That said, a significant portion of this cost could be met by becoming a flight instructor for a good flight school and doing multi-engine and instrument instruction or by obtaining a first officer position for a regional airline and building up multi-engine time in turbine aircraft.

The airline industry has always gone through cycles of hiring and furloughs. The industry is healthiest and most stable during good financial times. I have recently spoken with the owner of a large flight academy in the northwest. As a result of this discussion, as well as from my own analysis, I believe there will be a significant pilot shortage in the next five to seven years. If becoming an airline pilot is what you really want to do, then obtain your college degree and work on getting all of your ratings, up to and including your airline transport pilot's license. Then you'll be ready for the hiring boom that will come as large numbers of older pilots begin to retire.

The key to a successful airline pilot career is to be young enough to weather the furloughs that you may be subjected to while building up airline seniority, which will then minimize the furloughs you have to endure once you are older and have established a family.

One unfortunate aspect of being an airline pilot is that if your airline goes bankrupt or is acquired by another carrier, you may lose seniority and could wind up starting at the bottom of another airline's seniority list. It is imperative that you join the most stable and financially successful airline that will hire you. Seniority determines your position on the flight deck and your choice of flight schedules, bases, airplane type, routes, and days off, as well as the likelihood of being furloughed if there is a reduction in business.

I strongly recommend that you *network* with as many airline pilots as you can. Many airline pilots got their airline job interview through a recommendation by a pilot they knew. You will also glean a great deal of information on the current state of the industry and will get to see how airline pilots think. Also, getting to know airline pilots will give you the opportunity to observe their demeanor, which in most cases you probably would want to emulate. I have found that experienced airline pilots are quite often very helpful to a motivated young person just starting out to become a pilot.

Important General Information

Another topic I want to emphasize, which you aren't likely to read about in any other book on becoming an airline pilot, is that of developing your ***demeanor***: your outward manner and bearing. There is a time to have lots of fun in life, but remember that much of life is serious. Take your work and your school studies seriously, and let this show. If you are in college, put maximum effort into your studies and learn all you can. Take your homework assignments to heart. Always exceed the minimum requirements by a wide margin.

In whatever job you accept, no matter how menial, be sure to always do your best. You want your **work ethic** to stand out. Don't complain; if your boss seems hard on you, work harder. You'll find that this kind of attitude and behavior will serve you your entire life. Do your job to the highest standards, and I guarantee that you will eventually be successful.

Try to keep a *positive* frame of mind no matter what comes your way. Try to see the glass as half full rather than as half empty. Even unpleasant situations or experiences often have a beneficial side; try to find that benefit. You may be pleasantly surprised.

Be ethical in your dealings with others. Be fair with people you deal with, and try to treat them as you would want to be treated. This will help you not only in your career but also in your personal life.

Be responsible, and accept responsibility. Try to *always* do the right thing to set a good example for others to follow.

Be Persistent. There will always be setbacks in life, and these setbacks are teachable moments. Don't give up; try harder. Eventually you *will* succeed.

Do your best to ensure that your *personal grooming* is maintained to the highest standards. Keep your hair neatly groomed, shoes shined, and your clothes clean and pressed. Avoid earrings, tattoos, and body piercings if you want to be an airline pilot. You may think those things look "cool," but believe me, the people in charge of hiring will not! Be sure your personal hygiene is always impeccable.

One last point that is very important: In the last few years, the FAA has begun to track and document the results of every FAA infraction and incident, and this information is now made available to potential employers. More than ever, it is of paramount importance that you be very well prepared for every FAA test and check ride and that you pass every test with high scores, completing every check ride to a high standard.

If you are fortunate enough to be hired by an airline, take your job extremely seriously and always perform to the very best of your ability during each and every flight. After each flight, critique yourself and try to figure out what you could have done better. Strive to fly the perfect flight every time. Hold yourself to the highest standards. Be helpful to your fellow crew members, and be *non-judgmental* in the cockpit as far as personalities are concerned. Don't speak badly of others. Keep gossip out of the cockpit.

Try to be cheerful, to see the positive side of things; this will serve you well your entire career. Speak less, and listen more! You'll never learn anything while you're talking—remember that! These final three pages may be the most important in this book if you're a young person still building and shaping your character. Refer to them often. Remember, this information will serve you well regardless of the career you choose.

One very important thing I have learned as I have matured is that nearly all of life's most worthwhile endeavors require a *large effort* in order to succeed in them. Also, they are usually more complicated to accomplish than less worthwhile goals. Think about any well-respected profession, especially those in which there are good financial rewards, and you will find this to be true. If becoming an airline pilot were easy, tens of millions of people would be attempting to enter this profession. The airline pilot profession will require a sustained, long-term, methodical effort to achieve success.

Finally, if you decide on an airline pilot career, prepare yourself to be *patient*. It will take years to land that airline job, but when you do, you will find yourself in a great fraternity of professionals admired for their skills, intelligence, demonstrated responsibility, and, yes, earning power.

PJS

Glossary

ADF: Automatic direction finder—indicator needle points toward ground-based transmitter

ATC: Air traffic control

BACK COURSE: The reciprocal of the localizer (front) course of an instrument landing system

BARBER POLE: An instrument in a jet aircraft that is often marked with red-and-white stripes, which indicates the never-exceed speed. Exceeding that speed will cause transonic shock waves to build up on the aircraft wing.

BASE LEG: A short descending flight path at right angles to the approach and extended centerline of the runway.

BIPLANE: Airplanes with two sets of wings

BOX: Nickname for aircraft simulator

COAST OUT: Geographical position from where the aircraft begins the overwater portion of the flight.

DIRECTIONAL GYRO: Indicator that displays magnetic heading

DOPPLER RADAR: Dead reckoning performed automatically by a device that gives a continuous indication of position by integrating the speed and the crab angle of the aircraft as derived from measurement of the Doppler effect of echoes from directed beams of radiant energy transmitted from the aircraft.

DOWN WIND LEG: A long level flight path parallel to but in the opposite direction of the landing runway (the landing runway direction is nearly always into the wind, to reduce aircraft ground speed).

ELEVATOR: Flight control surface on the aircraft tail section that causes the aircraft to climb or descend

EPR: Engine pressure ratio—shows engine power output

FAA: Federal Aviation Administration

FLAPS: Control surface attached to aircraft wing to add lift and drag

FLY AWAY KIT: Aircraft spare parts; tires, brakes, oil, etc.

IFR: Instrument flight rules

ILS: Instrument landing system: usually consists of ground-based glideslope and localizer transmitter.

INS: Inertial navigation system consisting of accelerometers, gyros, computers, and indicator control unit.

JATO: Jet- assisted takeoff

LANDING BRIEFING: The briefing that the flying pilot gives prior to landing explaining all procedures to be used on the approach and landing. Usually very specific and thoroughly detailed.

LINK TRAINER: Old-style aircraft simulator

LORAN C: Long-range navigation system consisting of the receiver in the aircraft and pairs of low-frequency ground-based transmitters

MINIMUMS: The minimum altitude to which the aircraft may legally descend to unless the runway environment is identified. If the runway environment is not seen, a missed approached is performed.

MULTIMETER: Voltmeter and ohmmeter used to service electronic equipment

NDB: Non-directional beacon: Used to locate a geographical position over the ground. Consists of a ground-based transmitter and antenna system.

PINS (GEAR PINS): Metal pins inserted in the main and nose-landing gear to prevent accidental retraction of the landing gear when a/c is parked.

RIME ICE: Rough,milky,opaque ice formed by the instantaneous freezing of small supercooled water droplets.

ROTATE: The point in the takeoff roll when the nose is raised to increase (wing) lift for takeoff.

SPERRY FLIGHT DIRECTOR: Instrument made by Sperry Corp. that combines an artificial horizon and computer-integrated glide slope and localizer signals.

SAINT ELMOS FIRE: A weather phenomenon in which luminous plasma is created by a coronal discharge. Often appears as a static discharge on aircraft windshields.

STABILIZER: The tail horizontal aerodynamic wing surfaces that provide aircraft stability, as well as pitch up and down trim.

THRUST REVERSERS: Bucket doors on a jet engine that, when opened, deflect thrust forward, reducing aircraft speed.

V-1: Decision speed. At speeds less than V-1 the aircraft takeoff can be aborted and stopped on the runway remaining. At speeds equal to or greater than V-1 aircraft must continue takeoff.

V-2: Takeoff safety speed. The minimum speed required to continue flight with an engine failure.

VOR: Very high-frequency, omni-directional range—A ground-based electronic navigation aid transmitting very high-frequency navigational signals. These signals radiate out completely around 360 degrees in azimuth, oriented from magnetic north.

VOR RADIAL: A magnetic course tracking out from a VOR transmitter ground station.

YAW DAMPER: Component of the auto-pilot system that provides an equal and opposite input to the aircraft rudder to dampen out yaw.

Appendix

Index To Appendices

SUPER CONSTELLATION   236
CONSTELLATION Accidents   239
DOUGLAS DC-4   243
CURTIS COMMANDO C-46   245
C-46 Accidents   248
BEECH D-18 / C-45   249
DOUGLAS DC-9 / MD-87   251
Douglas DC-9 ACCIDENTS   254
Alaska Flt 261 Accident   257
DOUGLAS DC-8   269
DC-8 Accidents   272
Douglas DC-10   275
DC-10 Accidents   278

Notes:
1) The airplanes in this appendix are the airplane types written about in the stories in this book.
2) The accidents listed in the appendix are a partial list.

Lockheed Super Constellation ("Connie")

The Lockheed Super Constellation is considered by many to be one of the prettiest airliners ever built. This unusual and beautiful appearance is due to the continuously variable shape of the fuselage. No two bulkheads were the same shape or size.

The major operators of the "Connie" were Pan American, TWA, Eastern Airlines, KLM, Lufthansa, and Air France. Approximately 850 Lockheed Super Constellations were built. Designed by Hal Hibbard, Kelly Johnson, and Willis Hawkins, the aircraft was produced at the Lockheed Burbank plant from 1943 to 1958. The first Connie entered airline service with TWA in 1945.

The Connie was powered by four supercharged eighteen-cylinder Wright R-3350 engines. Each engine produced 3250 horsepower. Initially, these engines proved less than reliable, resulting in a fair amount of engine failures.

Several unusual features set the Constellation apart from other aircraft of that time. The flight controls were hydraulically boosted, which made the aircraft lighter on the controls, particularly during an engine failure procedure. Also, the wings could be thermally heated to de-ice instead of using rubber de-icing boots. This feature alone put the Connie way ahead of its day. Another distinctive feature was its triple tail, which enabled the Connie to be maintained in existing aircraft hangars of lower height.

General

At the end of World War II, the Super Constellation became a popular civilian airliner. In fact, it was one of the first pressurized airliners in widespread use. The "Connie" was a flight engineer's airplane; the flight engineer was charged with fuel management, pressurization, de-icing, cabin/cockpit temperature control, and monitoring the four eighteen-cylinder Wright supercharged engines with an onboard cathode ray tube display. The "Connie" was a very nice airplane to fly: docile during stalls and slow flight but with a lot of power. Control pressures were moderate. Lockheed built an L-649, L-749, L-1049, and L-1649. A model L-1149 was proposed using Allison turbine engines but was never built.

When jet airliners such as the Douglas DC-8 were introduced in 1958, Lockheed realized that the Super Constellation's days were numbered and shut down the airliner's production. As of February 2011, there were six known Super Constellations still flying.

Records

A TWA Lockheed Super Constellation holds the record for the longest-duration flight with passengers: a 1957 flight of twenty-three hours and nineteen minutes from London, England, to San Francisco, California.

Military

A military version of the Super Constellation called the C-69 was intended as a troop transport aircraft, and the United States Army Air Force ordered approximately two hundred of them. Twenty-two aircraft were delivered before the end of World War II, at which time the remainder of the order was cancelled.

Lockheed Super Constellation

Specifications and Performance

LENGTH: 116 feet
WINGSPAN: 126 feet
HEIGHT: 25 feet
WING AREA: 1660 square feet
EMPTY WEIGHT: 80,000 pounds
USEFUL LOAD: 57,000 pounds passengers,
cargo, and fuel.
MAX TAKEOFF WEIGHT: 137,000 pounds
ENGINES: Four WRIGHT R-3350 super-charged
18-cylinder radial engines
CRUISING SPEED: 290 knots
MAXIMUM SPEED: 327 knots
STALL SPEED: 90 knots
CRUISING RANGE: 5300 SM
NUMBER OF PASSENGERS 60–105,
PRODUCTION: 1943–58

Constellation

Accidents and Incidents

L-049 AND C-69

- September 18, 1945: A USAF C-69, *42-94551*, was damaged beyond repair after a wheels-up landing following engine problems at Topeka, Kansas, United States.
- December 28, 1946: TWA Flight 6963 crashed attempting to land at Shannon Airport, Ireland.
- May 11, 1947: TWA *NC86508*, crashed near the Brandywine Shoal lighthouse, Cape May, New Jersey at 8:45 a.m. EST while conducting practice emergency landing procedures, killing all four crew onboard.
- April 15, 1948: Pan Am Flight 1-10 (NC88858) crashed attempting to land at Shannon Airport, Ireland.
- July 28, 1950: Panair do Brasil aircraft registration NC88862, tail number PP-PCG crashed on the Chapel Hill (29°50□12.25□S 51°6□18.03□W29.8367361°S 51.1050083°W) after an aborted landing, killing 46 passengers and 10 crew.
- May 1, 1959: Capital Airlines Flight 983 (N2735A), c/o 1978, ground looped and caught fire after landing at Kanawha Airport in Charleston, West Virginia, United States; one passenger and one crew member died.
- November 8, 1961: Imperial Airlines Flight 201/8 (N2737A), was destroyed following an attempted emergency landing at Byrd Airport in Richmond, Virginia, United States; 74 passengers and two crew died.

- March 1, 1964: Paradise Airlines Flight 901A crashed during controlled flight into terrain following an abandoned approach to Tahoe Valley Airport in California, United States; all 85 onboard killed.

L-649 Constellation
L-749 Constellation

- June 23, 1949: A KLM L-749, registration *PH-TER*, crashed near Bari, Italy, killing all 33 passengers and crew onboard.
- July 12, 1949: A KLM L-749, registration *PH-TDF*, crashed near Bombay, India, killing all 45 passengers and crew onboard.
- October 28, 1949: An Air France Lockheed L-749 Constellation, F-BAZN, crashed into the Monte Redondo (São Miguel Island, Azores) while approaching the intermediate stop airport at Santa Maria. All 11 crew members and 37 passengers onboard died, including French boxer Marcel Cerdan and the famous French violinist Ginette Neveu.
- July 19, 1951: Eastern Airlines Flight 601, a Lockheed L-749A Constellation N119A, suffered severe buffeting after an access door opened in flight. A flapless wheels-up landing was made at Curles Neck Farm, Virginia. The aircraft was later repaired and returned to service.
- March 23, 1952: A KLM L-749, registration *PH-TFF*, crashed during landing at Don Muang, Thailand; all 33 passengers and crew onboard survived.
- October 19, 1953: An Eastern Airlines flight from Idlewild International Airport to San Juan, Puerto Rico, a Lockheed L-749A Constellation N119A, crashed on takeoff. Two passengers were killed.

- July 28, 1969: L-749A, 5N85H, crashed in Mount Toubkal, Atlas Mountains, Morocco, 60 miles south of Marrakesh; 8 onboard died. The Constellation, which was carrying weapons to Biafra, was discovered about a year later on July 18, 1970, by mountaineers.

L-1049 Super Connie

- October 30, 1954: United States Navy Flight 57 crashed into the Atlantic Ocean, killing all 42 passengers and crew.
- July 16, 1957: KLM Flight 844 crashed near Biak, New Guinea (now Indonesia), killing 58 passengers and crew onboard; 10 passengers survived.
- January 11, 1959: Lufthansa Flight 502, a Lockheed L-1049G Super Constellation registration D-ALAK flying from Hamburg to Rio de Janeiro-Galeão via Frankfurt, Paris-Orly, and Dakar, crashed during approach under heavy rain at Rio de Janeiro. From the 39 passengers and crew aboard, 3 survived. This was the first accident of Lufthansa after it was reestablished.
- January 21, 1960: Avianca Flight 671, an L-1049E, crashed and burned on landing at Montego Bay International Airport in Jamaica, resulting in the deaths of 37 aboard.
- August 24, 1960: A Qantas L-1049G, VH-EAC crashed during takeoff from runway 13 at Plaisance International Airport Mauritius. The Super Constellation bounced over a low embankment, crashed into a gulley, and caught fire. Of the 38 passengers and 12 crew, all survived the crash.
- December 16, 1960: TWA Flight 266 was struck by United Airlines Flight 826 (a Douglas DC-8) over Staten Island, New York. It broke apart and crashed, with 44

onboard dying. Flight 826 soon crashed in Brooklyn, New York; 84 people onboard and 6 on the ground were killed.

• August 5, 1973: A Happy Hours Air Travel Club L-1049, N6202C, lost power on all four engines due to fuel starvation and made a forced landing in Tamarac, Florida, on approach to Fort Lauderdale. The aircraft was damaged beyond repair.

L-1649 Starliner

• May 10, 1961: An Air France L-1649A, F-BHBM, nicknamed "De Grasse" suffered an explosion in flight and crashed in the Algerian Sahara. All 9 crew and 69 passengers were killed.

Douglas DC-4

Skymaster

The Douglas DC-4 was intended as a replacement for the two-engine Douglas DC-3. United Airlines had a requirement for a longer-range four-engine aircraft, and the Douglas DC-4 was designed to fulfill United's requirement. Although Douglas offered the option of pressurization, all civilian DC-4s were built unpressurized.

The most significant change from the Douglas DC-3, other than it's being a four-engine airplane, was the tri-cycle landing gear: it had a nose wheel instead of a tail wheel. This afforded pilots much better visibility while taxiing on the ground and virtually eliminated the chance of a ground loop occurring while landing or taking off. In addition to allowing improved ground handling, the DC-4 set the stage for extending a fuselage of nearly constant cross section into the later DC-6 and Douglas DC-7 versions.

There were a total of 580 C-54/DC-4s built. Many of the military C-54s and R5-Ds were converted for use with civilian charter airlines after the war.

Douglas DC-4

Specifications and Performance

LENGTH: 94 feet
WINGSPAN: 117 feet
HEIGHT: 27 feet
WING AREA: 1460 square feet
EMPTY WEIGHT: 43,000 pounds
USEFUL LOAD: 20,000 pounds
MAXIMUM TAKEOFF WEIGHT:
73,000 pounds
ENGINES: Four PRATT & WHITNEY
2000 Radial Engines 1450 HP
CRUISING SPEED: 227 MPH
MAXIMUM SPEED: 280 MPH
MAX CRUISING ALTITUDE: 22,300
STALL SPEED: 89 MPH
MAX CRUISING RANGE: 4250 miles
NUMBER OF PASSENGERS: 86
PRODUCTION: 1938–47

Curtis Wright C-46

Curtis Commando

The C-46 was an interesting transport-category aircraft with an exceptional service history. The airplane was designed as a pressurized, high-altitude airliner by George Page of Curtis-Wright. Although a number of American airlines expressed interest in the plane, no firm orders were received, and the first airplane built was sold to the United States Army Air Force. During testing, General "Hap" Arnold saw the potential of the C-46, and thus began a long history of orders from the military for this plane.

Many changes and modifications were made throughout the production years. For example, the R-2600-1600 HP Wright-Cyclone engines were replaced with the Pratt & Whitney R-2800-2000 HP engines. Among other changes and modifications were enlarged cargo doors, strengthened floors, and fuel system modifications, the latter of which resolved a problem that had caused several in-flight explosions. None of the more than 3,000 aircraft purchased by the military were pressurized.

The C-46 was one of the largest retractable tail-wheel airplanes ever built, with a gross takeoff weight twice that of the Douglas DC-3. The C-46 has a distinctive appearance due to its patented fuselage design, often referred to as the "Double-Bubble." The design provided for additional strength and load-carrying ability.

The C-46 played a very important role during World War II in China, Burma, and India. A huge portion of the cargo flown over the Himalayas, "The Hump" as they were nicknamed, was flown by the tough C-46 Curtis Commando. The amount of cargo it could lift and the altitude it could fly exceeded the capabilities of any other twin-engine aircraft at that time. By every measure, the C-46 was also very successful in the Pacific theater.

The airplane had somewhat more limited use and success in Europe as a troop transport and for paratroop drop operations. Because the C-46 wasn't retrofitted with self-sealing fuel tanks like the Douglas DC-3 was, a number of the planes were lost due to heavy anti-aircraft fire in the European theater.

Author's notes: The C-46 was not an easy aircraft to fly. Its large rudder surface made the airplane difficult to manage in a crosswind, especially on a wet or icy runway. The rudder pedals in a strong crosswind could require full displacement and, at slow speeds, the aileron controls could likewise require full input in the opposite direction. For a pilot of less than 5'9" in height, this would be difficult because of the large rudder pedal throw required.

Another unsettling aspect of the C-46 was the gas cockpit heater. It was not unusual for it to backfire loudly at unexpected times, which was fairly startling, given the history of wing explosions that had plagued the C-46 early on.

In my opinion, if you could fly the C-46, you could fly any other piston propeller airplane.

Curtis Wright C-46

Specifications and Performance

LENGTH: 76 feet
WINGSPAN: 108 feet
Height: 22 feet
WING AREA: 1360 square feet
EMPTY WEIGHT: 32,400 pounds
USEFUL LOAD: 13,000 pounds
MAXIMUM TAKEOFF WEIGHT: 48,000 pounds
ENGINES: two PRATT&WHITNEY R-2800 engines
2000 HP each
CRUISING SPEED: 173 MPH
MAXIMUM SPEED: 269 MPH
STALL SPEED: 78 MPH
CRUISING RANGE: 2950 miles
SERVICE CEILING: 27000 feet
NUMBER OF PASSENGERS: 60
PRODUCTION: 1940–45

C-46

Accidents and Incidents

- October 12, 1945: While trying to navigate their approach to Beijing Nanyuan Airport, a USAAF C-46 (carrying 4 U.S. crew members and 55 Chinese soldiers) struck a radio antenna and crashed, killing all onboard.
- January 16, 1959: Austral Líneas Aéreas Flight 205 crashed on approach to Mar del Plata, killing 51 occupants: five crew members and 46 passengers. The cause of the crash was determined as pilot error.
- June 1, 1959: An *Aerolíneas Nacionales* C-46 was shot down by the Nicaraguan Air Force over Nicaragua, killing all 50 people onboard.
- October 29, 1960: A chartered C-46 carrying the Cal Poly football team crashed on takeoff in Toledo, Ohio, killing 22 of the 48 people onboard.
- April 16, 1969: Shortly after takeoff, a CIA-chartered C-46 crashed into the Congo River, killing all 45 people onboard. The pilot had reported a landing gear malfunction and was trying to return to Kinshasa International Airport.

Beech D-18/C-45: Twin Beech

The twin-engine Beech D-18 is a low-wing, tail-wheel, twin-tail aircraft capable of carrying up to eleven passengers and crew. The military version of the aircraft was designated the C-45. Designed by Walter Beech, the Beech D-18/C-45, with Pratt & Whitney R-985 radial engines, was amazingly successful by any standards. More than nine thousand of these aircraft were built in the production run of thirty-three years.

During World War II, the C-45 was extensively used by our armed forces, primarily as liaison aircraft and trainers. There have been over thirty versions of the aircraft and nearly two hundred modifications. In 1952, a new Beech D-18 cost $79,000 dollars.

Probably the most serious shortcoming of the aircraft has been corrosion of the main wing spar. This prompted the FAA to issue an airworthiness directive requiring the installation of a spar strap plus regular inspections and X-ray. Still, despite their age, a significant number of Beech 18s are flying today. Though they're not fuel efficient considering today's aviation fuel prices, they are a beautifully designed airplane and very much fun to fly.

Author's notes: Flying a Beech 18 feels like flying a large twin-engine piston airliner that actually weighs only 8,700 pounds. They are great airplanes with lots of nostalgia surrounding them. But don't underestimate them in a cross wind. The combination of tail wheel and twin tails can turn around and bite you!

Beech D-18/C-45

Specifications and Performance

LENGTH: 34 feet
WINGSPAN: 47 feet
HEIGHT: 9 feet 7 inches
WING AREA: 350 square feet
EMPTY WEIGHT: 6200 pounds
USEFUL LOAD: 2500 pounds
MAXIMUM TAKEOFF WEIGHT: 8730 pounds
ENGINES: Two PRATT & WHITNEY R-985 radial engines 450 HP each
CRUISING SPEED: 210 MPH
MAXIMUM SPEED: 225 MPH
STALL SPEED: 77 MPH
CRUISING RANGE 1200 miles
SERVICE CEILING: 26,000 feet
NUMBER OF PASSENGERS: 11
PRODUCTION: 1937–70

Douglas DC-9-30s
and MD-80 Series

The McDonnell Douglas DC-9 made its debut in 1965. A total of 2,400 aircraft, all variations of the original DC-9 have been produced. The DC-9-10 series, 20 series, 30 series, 40 series, and 50 series were all similar in design with extensions of the fuselage and wings as well as upgraded engine thrust. In 1980 Douglas came out with the MD-80 series. A glass cockpit was introduced with the MD-87 series. The DC-9/30 series is also in use by the military. It is designated the C-9A Nightingale for the USAF.

Without a doubt, the DC-9/MD-80 airplane was a considerable success. It fulfilled the role of a short-to medium-range twin jet airliner that was relatively easy to maintain and provided a good level of reliability.

As of 2011, a total of 160 DC-9/MD-80s were still in commercial service. However, despite unsuccessful attempts to improve their fuel efficiency through wing and engine modifications, it's likely that these remaining aircraft will be replaced by newer and more fuel-efficient aircraft models as time goes on.

Author's Notes: The DC-9/MD-80 series were a pleasure to fly. First, they were very quiet in the cockpit due to the rear-mounted engines. Another advantage of the engine mounting was its nearly centerline thrust. Engine failures were easy to manage, requiring only small rudder inputs when flying on a single engine.

Probably the single most bothersome tendency of the MD-80 series was that the longer fuselage models had a tendency to pitch up when the pilot applied relatively large amounts of reverse thrust after touchdown. A few incidents have occurred because of this. But overall, these were great airplanes, greatly admired by those who flew them.

Douglas
DC-9/MD-80 Series

Specifications and Performance

LENGTH: 119 feet
WINGSPAN: 93 feet
WING AREA: 1209 square feet (MD-87)
TAIL HEIGHT: 28 feet
MAXIMUM TAKEOFF WEIGHT: 110,000 pounds
ENGINES: Two JT8D-9, 14,000 pounds of thrust each
CRUISING SPEED: 570 MPH
STALL SPEED: 100MPH (varies with landing weight)
CRUISING RANGE: 1881 miles
NUMBER OF PASSENGERS: 115
PRODUCTION: 1965–92

Douglas DC-9

Accidents and Incidents

- March 9, 1967: TWA Flight 553 fell to earth in a field in Concord Township, near Urbana, Ohio, following a mid-air collision with a Beechcraft Baron, an accident that triggered substantial changes in air traffic control procedures.
- March 17, 1969: Viasa Flight 742 crashed into the La Trinidad neighborhood of Maracaibo during a failed takeoff. All 84 people onboard the aircraft as well as 71 people on the ground were killed.
- June 27, 1969: Douglas DC-9-31 N906H of Hawaiian Airlines collided on the ground with Vickers Viscount N7410 of Aloha Airlines at Honolulu International Airport. The Viscount was damaged beyond repair.
- September 9, 1969: Allegheny Airlines Flight 853, a McDonnell Douglas DC-9-30, collided in mid-air with a Piper PA-28 Cherokee near Fairland, Indiana. The DC-9 carried 78 passengers and 4 crew members, the Piper had one pilot onboard. The occupants of both aircraft were killed in the accident, and the aircraft were destroyed.
- February 15, 1970: a Dominicana de Aviación DC-9 crashed after taking off from Santo Domingo. The crash, possibly caused by contaminated fuel, killed all 102 passengers and crew, including champion boxer Teo Cruz.
- May 2, 1970: an Overseas National Airways DC-9, wet-leased to ALM Dutch Antilles Airlines and operating as ALM Flight 980, ditched in the Caribbean Sea on a flight from New York's John F. Kennedy International Airport to Princess Juliana International Airport on Saint Maarten. After three landing attempts in poor weather at

Saint Maarten, the pilots began to divert to their alternate of Saint Croix, U.S. Virgin Islands, but ran out of fuel 30 miles (48 km) short of the island. After about 10 minutes, the aircraft sank in 5,000 ft. (1524 m) of water and was never recovered. Forty people survived the ditching; 23 perished.

- April 4, 1977: Southern Airways Flight 242, a DC-9-31, crash-landed onto what was then a highway in New Hope, Georgia. The crash and fire resulted in the deaths of both flight crew and 61 passengers. Nine people on the ground also died. Both flight attendants and 20 passengers survived.
- June 26, 1978: Air Canada Flight 189, a DC-9, overran the runway in Toronto after aborting the takeoff due to a blown tire. Two of the 107 passengers and crew were killed.
- September 14, 1979: Aero Trasporti Italiani Flight 12, a DC-9-32, crashed in the mountains near Cagliari, Italy, while approaching Cagliari-Elmas Airport. All 27 passengers and 4 crew members died in the crash and ensuing fire.
- December 3, 1990: Northwest Airlines Flight 1482, a DC-9-14, went on the wrong taxiway in dense fog at Detroit-Metropolitan Wayne County Airport, Michigan (DTW). It entered the active runway instead of the taxiway instructed by air traffic controllers and collided with a departing Northwest Boeing 727. Nine people were killed.
- November 9, 1999: TAESA Flight 725 crashed a few minutes after leaving the Uruapan Airport en route to Mexico City. Eighteen people were killed in the accident.
- October 6, 2000: Aeroméxico Flight 250 en route from Mexico City to Reynosa, Mexico, overran the runway during landing. The 83 passengers and 5 crew members

aboard the airplane were killed. The cause of the crash was poor visibility during a storm.

- April 15, 2008: a Hewa Bora Airways DC-9 crashed into a residential neighborhood, in Goma, Democratic Republic, of the Congo, resulting in the deaths of at least 44 people.

This **unedited** accident summary is included to illustrate the similarity with the incident described in chapter 10 of this book.

The following is an NTSB accident summary involving a Douglas MD-83 aircraft:

Alaska 261

NTSB Identification: **DCA00MA023**.
The docket is stored in the Docket Management System (DMS). Please contact Records Management Division
Scheduled 14 CFR operation of ALASKA AIRLINES INC
Accident occurred Monday, January 31, 2000 in Port Hueneme, CA
Probable Cause Approval Date: 5/29/2003
Aircraft: Douglas MD-83, registration: N963AS
Injuries: 88 Fatal.

The Board's full report is available at http://www.ntsb. gov/publictn/publictn.htm.

On January 31, 2000, about 1621 Pacific standard time, Alaska Airlines, Inc., flight 261, a McDonnell Douglas MD-83, N963AS, crashed into the Pacific Ocean about 2.7 miles north of Anacapa Island, California. The 2 pilots, 3 cabin crew members, and 83 passengers on board were killed, and the airplane was destroyed by impact forces. Flight 261 was operating as a scheduled international passenger flight under the provisions of 14 Code of Federal Regulations Part 121 from Lic Gustavo Diaz Ordaz International Airport, Puerto Vallarta, Mexico, to Seattle Tacoma International Airport, Seattle, Washington, with an intermediate stop planned at San Francisco International Airport, San Francisco, California. Visual meteorological conditions prevailed for the flight, which operated on an instrument flight rules flight plan.

The National Transportation Safety Board determines the probable cause(s) of this accident as follows:

A loss of airplane pitch control resulting from the in-flight failure of the horizontal stabilizer trim system jackscrew assembly's acme nut threads. The thread failure was caused by excessive wear resulting from Alaska Airlines' insufficient lubrication of the jackscrew assembly. Contributing to the accident were Alaska Airlines' extended lubrication interval and the Federal Aviation Administration's (FAA) approval of that extension, which increased the likelihood that a missed or inadequate lubrication would result in excessive wear of the acme nut threads, and Alaska Airlines' extended end play check interval and the FAA's approval of that extension, which allowed the excessive wear of the acme nut threads to progress to failure without the opportunity for detection. Also contributing to the accident was the absence on the McDonnell Douglas MD-80 of a fail-safe mechanism to prevent the catastrophic effects of total acme nut thread loss.

The Safety Board's full report is available at www.ntsb. gov/publictn/publictn.htm.

On January 31, 2000, about 1621 Pacific standard time, Alaska Airlines, Inc., flight 261, a McDonnell Douglas MD-83 (MD-83), N963AS, crashed into the Pacific Ocean about 2.7 miles north of Anacapa Island, California. The 2 pilots, 3 cabin crew members, and 83 passengers on board were killed, and the airplane was destroyed by impact forces. Flight 261 was operating as a scheduled international passenger flight under the provisions of 14 Code of Federal Regulations Part 121 from Lic Gustavo Diaz Ordaz International Airport (PVR), Puerto Vallarta, Mexico, to Seattle-Tacoma International Airport (SEA), Seattle, Washington, with an intermediate stop planned at San Francisco

International Airport (SFO), San Francisco, California. Visual meteorological conditions prevailed for the flight, which operated on an instrument flight rules flight plan.

The accident airplane arrived at PVR about 1239 on the day of the accident. The inbound pilots stated that they met the accident pilots outside the airplane and briefly discussed its status.

Flight data recorder (FDR) information from the accident flight indicated that during taxi for takeoff, when the FDR started recording, the horizontal stabilizer was at the 7° airplane-nose-up position, which was the takeoff pitch trim setting. About 1337, the accident airplane departed PVR as flight 261. A National Transportation Safety Board review of FAA air traffic control (ATC) tapes and FDR data from the accident flight indicated that the first officer was the pilot flying immediately after the airplane's departure. The flight plan indicated that flight 261's cruising altitude would be flight level (FL) 310.

FDR data indicated that during the initial portion of the climb, the horizontal stabilizer moved at the primary trim motor rate of 1/3° per second from 7° to 2° airplane nose up. According to FDR data, the autopilot was engaged at 1340:12, as the airplane climbed through an altitude of approximately 6,200 feet. Thereafter, the FDR recorded horizontal stabilizer movement at the alternate trim motor rate of 1/10° per second from 2° airplane nose up to 0.4° airplane nose down. At 1349:51, as the airplane continued to climb through approximately 23,400 feet at 331 knots indicated airspeed (KIAS), the cockpit voice recorder (CVR) recorded the horizontal stabilizer move from 0.25° to 0.4° airplane nose down. This was the last horizontal stabilizer movement recorded until the airplane's initial dive about 2 hours and 20 minutes later. At 1353:12, when the airplane was climbing through 28,557 feet at 296 KIAS, the autopilot disengaged.

FDR information and airplane performance calculations indicated that, during the next 7 minutes, the airplane continued to climb at a much slower rate. During this part of the ascent, the elevators were deflected between -1° and ?3°, and the airplane was flown manually using up to as much as 50 pounds of control column pulling force. After reaching level flight, the airplane was flown for about 24 minutes using approximately 30 pounds of pulling force at approximately 31,050 feet and 280 KIAS. The airspeed was then increased to 301 KIAS, and the airplane was flown for almost another 1 hour 22 minutes using about 10 pounds of pulling force. At 1546:59, the autopilot was re-engaged.

According to Alaska Airlines documents, ATC and CVR information, and post accident interviews with Alaska Airlines dispatch and maintenance personnel, the flight crew contacted the airline's dispatch and maintenance control facilities in SEA some time before the beginning of the CVR transcript at 1549:49 to discuss a jammed horizontal stabilizer and a possible diversion to Los Angeles International Airport (LAX), Los Angeles, California. These discussions were conducted on a shared company radio frequency between Alaska Airlines' dispatch and maintenance facilities at SEA and its operations and maintenance facilities at LAX.

At 1549:56, the autopilot was disengaged; it was re-engaged at 1550:15. According to the CVR transcript, at 1550:44, SEA maintenance asked the flight crew, "understand you're requesting...diversion to LA...is there a specific reason you prefer LA over San Francisco?" The captain replied, "well a lotta times its windy and rainy and wet in San Francisco and uh, it seemed to me that a dry runway...where the wind is usually right down the runway seemed a little more reasonable."

At 1552:02, an SEA dispatcher provided the flight crew with the current SFO weather (wind was 180° at 6 knots; visibility was 9 miles). The SEA dispatcher added, "if uh you want to land at LA of course for safety reasons we will do that... we'll...tell you though that if we land in LA...we'll be looking at probably an hour to an hour and a half we have a major flow program going right now." At 1552:41, the captain replied,

"I really didn't want to hear about the flow being the reason you're calling us cause I'm concerned about overflying suitable airports." At 1553:28, the captain discussed with the first officer potential landing runways at SFO, stating, "one eight zero at six...so that's runway one six what we need is runway one nine, and they're not landing runway one nine." The first officer replied, "I don't think so." At 1553:46, the captain asked SEA dispatch if they could "get some support" or "any ideas" from an instructor to troubleshoot the problem; he received no response. At 1555:00, the captain commented, "it just blows me away they think we're gonna land, they're gonna fix it, now they're worried about the flow, I'm sorry this airplane's [not] gonna go anywhere for a while...so you know." A flight attendant replied, "so they're trying to put the pressure on you," the captain stated, "well, no, yea."

At 1556:08, the SEA dispatcher informed the flight crew that, according to the SFO automatic terminal information service, the landing runways in use at SFO were 28R and 28L and that "it hasn't rained there in hours so I'm looking at...probably a dry runway." At 1556:26, the captain stated that he was waiting for a requested center of gravity (CG) update (for landing), and then he requested information on wind conditions at LAX. At 1556:50, the SEA dispatcher replied that the wind at LAX was 260° at 9 knots.

Nine seconds later, the captain, comparing SFO and LAX wind conditions, told the SEA dispatcher, "versus a direct crosswind which is effectively no change in groundspeed...I gotta tell you, when I look at it from a safety point I think that something that lowers my groundspeed makes sense." The SEA dispatcher replied, "that'll mean LAX then for you." He then asked the captain to provide LAX operations with the information needed to recompute the airplane's CG because "they can probably whip out that CG for you real quick." At 1558:15, the captain told the SEA dispatcher, "we're goin to LAX we're gonna stay up here and burn a little more gas get all our ducks in a row, and then we'll uh be talking to LAX when we start down to go in there." At 1558:45, the captain asked LAX operations if it could "compute [the airplane's] current CG based on the information we had at takeoff."

At 1602:33, the captain asked LAX operations for wind information at SFO. LAX operations replied that the winds at SFO were 170° at 6 knots. The captain replied, "that's what I needed. We are comin in to see you." At 1603:56, the first officer began giving LAX operations the information it needed to recompute the airplane's CG for landing.

At 1607:54, a mechanic at Alaska Airlines' LAX maintenance facility contacted the flight crew on the company radio frequency and asked, "are you [the] guys with the uh, horizontal [stabilizer] situation?" The captain replied, "affirmative," and the mechanic, referring to the stabilizer's primary trim system, asked, "did you try the suitcase handles and the pickle switches?" At 1608:03, the captain replied, "yea we tried everything together." At 1608:08, the captain added, "we've run just about everything if you've got any hidden circuit breakers we'd love to know about 'em." The mechanic stated that he would "look at the uh circuit breaker uh guide just as a double check." The LAX mechanic then asked the flight crew about the status of the alternate trim system, and, at 1608:35, the captain replied that "it appears to be jammed...the whole thing, it [the AC load meter] spikes out when we use the primary, we get AC [electrical] load that tells me the motor's tryin to run but the brake won't move it. when we use the alternate, nothing happens."

At 1608:50, the LAX mechanic asked, "you say you get a spike...on the meter up there in the cockpit when you uh try to move it with the...primary right?" According to the CVR transcript, at 1608:59, the captain addressed the first officer before responding to the mechanic, stating, "I'm gonna click it off you got it." One second later, the first officer replied, "ok." At 1609:01, the captain reiterated to the LAX mechanic that the spike occurred "when we do the primary trim but there's no appreciable uh change in the uh electrical uh when we do the alternate." The LAX mechanic replied that he would see them when they arrived at the LAX maintenance facility.

At 1609:13, the captain stated, "lets do that." At 1609:14.8, the CVR recorded the sound of a click and, at the same time, the captain stating, "this'll click it off." According to FDR data, the autopilot was disengaged at 1609:16. At the same time, the CVR recorded the sound of a clunk, followed by two faint thumps in short succession at 1609:16.9. The CVR recorded a sound similar to the horizontal stabilizer-in-motion tone at 1609:17. At 1609:19.6, the CVR again recorded a sound similar to the horizontal stabilizer-in-motion tone, followed by the captain's comment, "you got it?" (FDR data indicated that during the 3 to 4 seconds after the autopilot was disengaged, the horizontal stabilizer moved from 0.4° to a recorded position of 2.5° airplane nose down, and the airplane began to pitch nose down, starting a dive that lasted about 80 seconds as the airplane went from about 31,050 to between 23,000 and 24,000 feet.)

At 1609:26, the captain stated, "it got worse," and, 5 seconds later, he stated "you're stalled." One second later, the CVR recorded a sound similar to airframe vibration getting louder. At 1609:33, the captain stated, "no no you gotta release it ya gotta release it." This statement was followed by the sound of a click 1 second later. At 1609:52, the captain stated, "help me back help me back." Two seconds later, the first officer responded, "ok."

One second later, at 1609:55, the captain contacted the Los Angeles Air Route Traffic Control Center (ARTCC) and stated, "center Alaska two sixty one we are uh in a dive here." At 1610:01.6, the captain added, "and I've lost control, vertical pitch." At 1610:01.9, the CVR recorded the sound of the overspeed warning (which continued for the next 33 seconds). At 1610:05, the controller asked flight 261 to repeat the transmission, and, at 1610:06, the captain responded, "yea we're out of twenty six thousand feet, we are in a vertical dive...not a dive yet...but uh we've lost vertical control of our airplane." At 1610:20, the captain stated, "just help me."

At 1610:28.2, the captain informed the Los Angeles ARTCC controller, "we're at twenty three seven request uh." At 1610:33, the captain added, "yea we got it back under control here." One second later, the first officer transmitted, "no we don't." At 1610:45, the first officer stated, "let's take the speedbrakes off." One second later, the captain responded, "no no leave them there. it seems to be helping." At 1610:55, the captain stated, "ok it really wants to pitch down." At 1611:06.6, the captain stated that they were at "twenty four thousand feet, kinda stabilized." Three seconds later he added, "we're slowin' here, and uh, we're gonna uh do a little troubleshooting, can you gimme a block [altitude] between uh, twenty and twenty five?" FDR data indicated that, by 1611:13, the airplane's airspeed had decreased to 262 KIAS, and the airplane was maintaining an altitude of approximately 24,400 feet with a pitch angle of 4.4°. At 1611:21, the controller assigned flight 261 a block altitude of between FL 200 and 250. Airplane performance calculations indicated that between about 130 and 140 pounds of pulling force was required to recover from the dive.

At 1611:43, the first officer stated, "whatever we did is no good, don't do that again." One second later, the captain responded, "yea, no it went down it went to full nose down." Four seconds later, the first officer asked, "uh it's a lot worse than it was?" At 1611:50, the captain replied, "yea yea we're in much worse shape now," adding, at 1611:59, "I think it's at the stop, full stop...and I'm thinking...can it go any worse...but it probably can...but when we slowed down, lets slow it lets get down to two hundred knots and see what happens."

At 1612:33, the captain told LAX maintenance, "we did both the pickle switch and the suitcase handles and it ran away full nose trim down." At 1612:42, the captain added, "and now we're in a pinch so we're holding uh we're worse than we were." At 1613:04, the captain indicated to LAX maintenance that he was reluctant to try troubleshooting the trim system again because the trim might "go in the other direction." At 1613:10, the LAX mechanic responded, "ok well your discretion uh if you want to try it, that's ok with me if not that's fine. um we'll see you at the gate." At 1613:22, the captain stated, "I went tab down...right, and it should have come back instead it went the other way." At 1613:32, the captain asked the first officer, "you wanna try it or not?" The first officer replied, "uhh no. boy I don't know." Airplane performance calculations indicated that about 120 pounds of pulling force was being applied to the pilots' control columns at this point.

At 1614:54, the Los Angeles ARTCC controller instructed the flight crew to contact another ARTCC controller on frequency 126.52, which the flight crew acknowledged. At 1615:19, the first officer contacted another ARTCC controller on 126.52 and stated, "we're with you we're at twenty two five, we have a jammed stabilizer and we're maintaining altitude with difficulty. uh but uh we can maintain altitude we think...our intention is to land at Los Angeles." The controller cleared the airplane direct to LAX and then asked, "you want lower [altitude] now or what do you want to do sir?" At 1615:56, the captain replied, "I need to get down about ten, change my configuration, make sure I can control the jet and I'd like to do that out here over the bay if I may."

At 1616:32, the Los Angeles ARTCC controller issued flight 261 a heading of 280° and cleared the flight to descend to 17,000 feet. At 1616:39, the captain acknowledged, "two eight zero and one seven seventeen thousand Alaska two sixty one. and we generally need a block altitude." At 1616:45, the controller responded, "ok and just um I tell you what do that for now sir, and contact LA center on one three five point five they'll have further uh instructions for you sir." At 1616:56.9, the first officer acknowledged, "ok thirty five five say the altimeter setting." The controller responded, "the LA altimeter is three zero one eight." At 1617:02, the first officer responded, "thank you."

According to the CVR and ATC recordings, this was the last radio transmission made from flight 261.

After the radio transmission, the captain told a flight attendant that he needed "everything picked up" and "everybody strapped down." At 1617:04, the captain added, "I'm gonna unload the airplane and see if we can...we can regain control of it that way." At 1617:09, the flight attendant stated, "ok we had like a big bang back there," and, the captain replied, "yea I heard it." At 1617:15, the captain stated, "I think the stab trim thing is broke." At 1617:21, the captain again told the flight attendant to make sure the passengers were "strapped in now," adding 3 seconds later, "cause I'm gonna I'm going to release the back pressure and see if I can get it...back."

At 1617:54, the captain stated, "gimme slats extend," and, at 1617:56.6, a sound similar to slat/flap handle movement was recorded by the CVR. At 1617:58, the captain added, "I'm test flyin now." At 1618:05, the captain commanded an 11° flap deployment, and, at 1618:07, a sound similar to slat/flap handle movement was recorded. At 1618:17, the captain stated, "its pretty stable right here...see but we got to get down to a hundred an[d] eighty [knots]." At 1618:26, the captain stated, "OK...bring bring the flaps and slats back up for me," and, at 1618:36.8, sounds similar to slat/flap handle movement were recorded. At 1618:47, the captain stated, "what I wanna do...is get the nose up...and then let the nose fall through and see if we can stab it when it's unloaded."

At 1618:56, the first officer responded, "you mean use this again? I don't think we should...if it can fly." At 1619:01, the captain replied, "it's on the stop now, it's on the stop." At 1619:04, the first officer replied, "well not according to that it's not." At this time, FDR data indicated a horizontal stabilizer angle of 2.5° airplane nose down. Three seconds later, the first officer added, "the trim might be, and then it might be uh, if something's popped back there...it might be mechanical damage too." At 1619:14, the first officer stated, "I think if it's controllable, we oughta just try to land it." Two seconds later, the captain replied, "you think so? ok lets head for LA."

About 5 seconds later, the CVR recorded the sound of a series of at least four distinct "thumps." At 1619:24, the first officer asked, "you feel that?" and the captain replied, "yea." At 1619:29, the captain stated, "ok gimme sl—." At 1619:32.8, the CVR recorded the sound of two clicks similar to the sound of slat/flap movement. At 1619:36.6, the CVR recorded the sound of an "extremely loud noise" and the sound of background noise increasing, which continued until the end of the recording. At the same time, the CVR also recorded sounds similar to loose articles moving around the cockpit. FDR data indicated that at 1619:36.6, the flaps were extending and the slats were moving to the mid position. The next few seconds of FDR data indicated a maximum airplane nose-down pitch rate of nearly 25° per second. The FDR recorded a significant decrease in vertical acceleration values (negative Gs), a nose-down pitch angle, and a significant decrease in lateral acceleration values. By 1619:40, the airplane was rolling left wing down, and the rudder was deflected 3° to the right.

FDR data indicated that, by 1619:42, the airplane had reached its maximum valid recorded airplane-nose down pitch angle of -70°. At this time, the roll angle was passing through -76° left wing down. At 1619:43, the first officer stated, "mayday," but did not make a radio transmission. Six seconds later, the captain stated, "push and roll, push and roll." FDR data indicated that, by 1619:45, the pitch angle had increased to ?28°, and the airplane had rolled to -180° (inverted). Further, the airplane had descended to 16,420 feet, and the indicated airspeed had decreased to 208 knots.

At 1619:54, the captain stated, "ok, we are inverted...and now we gotta get it." FDR data indicated that at this time, the left aileron moved to more than 16° (to command right wing down), then, during the next 6 seconds, it moved in the opposite direction to ?13° (to command left wing down). At 1619:57, the rudder returned to the near 0° position, the flaps were retracted, and the airplane was rolling through -150° with an airplane-nose down pitch angle of -9°. After 1619:57, the airplane remained near inverted and its pitch oscillated in the nose-down position.

At 1620:04, the captain stated, "push push push...push the blue side up." At 1620:16, the captain stated, "ok now lets kick rudder...left rudder left rudder." Two seconds later, the first officer replied, "I can't reach it." At 1620:20, the captain replied, "ok right rudder...right rudder." At 1620:38, the captain stated, "gotta get it over again...at least upside down we're flyin." At 1620:49, the CVR recorded sounds similar to engine compressor stalls and engine spool down. At 1620:54, the captain commanded deployment of the speed brakes, and, about 1 second later, the first officer replied, "got it." At 1620:56.2, the captain stated, "ah here we go." The FDR recording ended at 1620:56.3, and the CVR recording ended at 1620:57.1.

The airplane impacted the Pacific Ocean near Port Hueneme, California. Pieces of the airplane wreckage were found floating on and beneath the surface of the ocean. The main wreckage was found at 34° 03.5' north latitude and 119° 20.8' west longitude.

Douglas DC-8 Series

The Douglas DC-8 series aircraft was a very successful four-engine jetliner that remained in production from 1958 to 1972. Over 555 of these aircraft were built and flown by many airlines in the United States and other countries around the world. As of 2010, an estimated 85 DC-8s of all series were still in airline service.

A 70 series DC-8 was developed by Douglas in the late 1970s. This aircraft model used the larger, quieter, and more fuel-efficient CFM-56 engine. The 70 series proved very successful, and many of these planes made their way into cargo airline fleets such as UPS.

Records

In 1962, a Douglas DC-8-40 series aircraft was the first commercial civilian airliner to break the sound barrier during a dive through 40,000 feet while testing a new leading-edge wing design. By any measure, this was proof of just how strong the DC-8 aircraft was.

The Douglas DC-8 lived up to its reputation of being relatively easy to maintain while simultaneously providing good reliability. Both the 60 and 70 series had excellent lift capability plus good range and performance.

Author's notes: Most pilots who flew the DC-8 liked it. I certainly thought it was a very "honest" airplane with very few quirks. The landing gear system was strong but fairly *stiff*. To make soft landings, a technique called "rolling it on," was sometimes used. Just prior to touchdown, the pilot would gently release a *slight* amount of control wheel back pressure. This had to be done with care, however, to avoid the possibility of landing on the nose gear.

The cockpit was somewhat noisy due to the four cabin turbo compressors (CTCs) used for pressurization. To alleviate the noise, some engineers flew with one or two CTCs off.

In the mid-70s, I had to land a DC-8 with both engines shut down on one wing and less than full power available in the remaining two engines on the other wing. The emergency landing was successful, which I think speaks volumes for this airplane.

Originally, the DC-8 was flown over water with a navigator as the fourth cockpit crew member. In the early 1970s, Doppler computers and Loran C replaced the navigators and their bubble sextants. In the late 70s, Doppler and Loran C were replaced by an inertial navigation system (INS), which proved extremely reliable and accurate—a great improvement.

Douglas DC-8-63

Specifications and Performance

LENGTH: 187 feet
WINGSPAN: 148 feet
HEIGHT: 43 feet
WING AREA: 2930 square feet
EMPTY WEIGHT: 146,400 pounds
MAXIMUM TAKEOFF WEIGHT: 355,000 pounds
ENGINES: PRATT & WHITNEY JT3D-7
TURBO FAN 19,000 pounds of thrust each.
CRUISING SPEED: 596 MPH
SERVICE CEILING: 42,000 feet
CRUISING RANGE: 4480 miles
NUMBER OF PASSENGERS: 260
PRODUCTION: 1958–72 (70 series program 'til 1988)

Douglas DC-8

Accidents and Incidents

- December 16, 1960: United Airlines Flight 826, a DC-8, collided with a TWA Lockheed Constellation (as Flight 266) in mid-air over Staten Island, New York, United States, resulting in a total of 134 fatalities.
- May 30, 1961: Viasa Flight 897, a DC-8, crashed into the Atlantic Ocean shortly after takeoff from Lisbon, Portela Airport. All 61 passengers and crew onboard were killed.
- August 20, 1962: a Panair do Brasil DC-8-33, registration PP-PDT flying from Rio de Janeiro—Galeão to Lisbon, overran the runway into the ocean during an aborted takeoff. Of the 105 passengers and crew aboard, 15 died.
- November 29, 1963: Trans-Canada Air Lines Flight 831, a DC-8, crashed shortly after takeoff from Montréal/ Dorval Airport, killing all 118 people onboard.
- February 25, 1964: Eastern Air Lines Flight 304, a DC-8 flying from New Orleans International Airport to Washington National Airport, crashed into Lake Pontchartrain, killing all 51 passengers and 7 crew aboard. The cause was determined to be related to an abnormal trim setting and a stabilizer trim system failure.
- March 4, 1966: Canadian Pacific Airlines Flight 402 (CP402), a DC-8-43, crashed on landing at Tokyo International Airport in Japan, killing 64 passengers and crew; 8 passengers survived.
- March 5, 1967: Varig Airlines Flight 837, a DC-8-33, hit buildings while on the approach to Monrovia Airport, Liberia. Of the 71 passengers and 19 crew onboard, 66 passengers and 1 crew member (the flight engineer)

were killed. The DC-8-33 was on a scheduled flight from Beirut to Rio de Janeiro via Rome and Monrovia. Five persons on the ground were also killed.

- July 1, 1968: Seaboard World Airlines Flight 253, a DC-8, was forced to land in the Soviet Union. Onboard were over 200 American troops bound for Vietnam.
- January 13, 1969: Scandinavian Airlines Flight 933, a DC-8, crashed into the Pacific Ocean west of Los Angeles International Airport. Of the 36 passengers and 9 crew aboard, 15 were killed in the crash.
- July 5, 1970: Air Canada Flight 621, a DC-8-63, exploded near Toronto Pearson International Airport, with 109 fatalities, when premature deployment of the wing spoilers caused an engine to detach, igniting onboard fuel during the subsequent go around.
- May 5, 1972: Alitalia Flight 112, a DC-8-43, crashed into a mountain in the outskirts of Palermo and disintegrated, killing all 115 people onboard (108 passengers and 7 crew).
- September 24, 1972: Japan Airlines Flight 472, a DC-8, overran the runway after landing in the wrong airport. There were 108 passengers and 14 crew onboard; 11 were injured, and there were no fatalities. The aircraft was destroyed.
- November 27, 1972: Japan Airlines Flight 446, a DC-8-62, crashed while in an initial climb en route from Sheremetyevo International Airport, Moscow to Haneda Airport of Tokyo. Nine of 14 crew members and 52 of 62 passengers died, with a total of 61 of 76 occupants dead.
- December 4, 1974: Martinair Flight 138 flew into the side of a mountain while on landing approach in Colombo, Sri Lanka. All 191 passengers and crew onboard were killed.
- October 6, 1976: Cubana Flight 455, a DC-8, was bombed by anti-Castro terrorists and crashed near Bridgetown, Barbados, killing all 73 people onboard.

- September 27, 1977: Japan Airlines Flight 715, a DC-8, crashed into a hill as the aircraft was on approach into Sultan Abdul Aziz Shah Airport, Malaysia. The accident killed 34 out of 79 passengers and crew onboard.
- September 28, 1977: Japan Airlines Flight 472, a DC-8, was hijacked by Japanese Red Army (JRA) terrorists after taking off from Mumbai, India. The terrorists forced the airplane to land in Dhaka, Bangladesh, where they demanded US$6 million and the release of 9 imprisoned JRA members being held in Japan. The Japanese government complied, and all of the hostages were eventually released.
- December 28, 1978: United Airlines Flight 173, a DC-8, ran out of fuel while circling near Portland, Oregon, while the crew investigated a light indicating a problem with the landing gear. The airplane crashed in a wooded area, killing 10 and injuring 24 of the 181 onboard.
- February 9, 1982: Japan Airlines Flight 350, a DC-8-61, crashed on approach to Tokyo International Airport (Haneda). Among the 166 passengers and 8 crew, 24 passengers were killed.
- December 12, 1985: Arrow Air Flight 1285, a DC-8, crashed after takeoff in Gander, Newfoundland, killing all 256 passengers and crew onboard, making it the worst air disaster to occur in Canada; the cause was determined to be a stall most likely due to wing icing.
- June 7, 1989: Surinam Airways Flight PY764, a DC-8, crashed while attempting to land in heavy fog at Paramaribo, Suriname. The plane hit trees and flipped upside down, killing 176 of 187 people onboard.
- July 11, 1991: Nigeria Airways Flight 2120, a Nation Air DC-8-61, chartered by Nigeria Airways to transport Nigerian pilgrims to Mecca, crashed shortly after takeoff from Jeddah, Saudi Arabia, due to a fire caused by tire failure. All 261 onboard died, including 14 Canadian crew members.

Douglas DC-10

One of the world's great airliners, the Douglas DC-10, is universally loved by nearly every pilot who has flown it. Almost 450 of these planes were built at the Long Beach plant, and it's estimated that more than 50 are still flying as military in-flight tankers, with another 150 in service with airlines in the United States and around the world, as of January 2010.

The DC-10 is a three-engine, wide-body aircraft capable of heavy lift and long range. Variations of the DC-10 are the 10, 15, 20, 30, and 40 series. The DC-10-30 and 40 series have a significant visible difference from other aircraft in the series in that they have a third (additional) set of main gear wheels. This allows for operating the aircraft at higher gross weights and provides improved braking and stopping.

A modernized version of the DC-10 is known as the MD-10. The MD-10 is a DC-10 that has been retrofitted with a glass cockpit. The MD-10 is certified for a two man crew, which eliminates the requirement for a flight engineer. The KC-10 is a DC-10-30 that was built for aerial refueling for the military.

The DC-10 was very successful, although a series of tragic accidents damaged its reputation. Rather than being designed as a plug-type door, the cargo doors of the DC-10 were designed to open outward, necessitating reliance on a very heavy-duty locking mechanism. Unfortunately, either improper operation of the locking mechanism by ground personnel or a failure of the cargo door visual locking indicator caused two tragic fatal accidents. After the second one, the FAA issued mandatory cargo door modification requirements, and no further accidents relating to the cargo doors have occurred.

Another accident resulted from an air carrier's maintenance department using a shortcut to save man hours; there was structural damage to the aircraft, which resulted in engine separation in flight. During the separation, hydraulic lines were damaged, causing the slats on one wing to retract and rendering the aircraft uncontrollable. The lack of a slat locking mechanism was a design flaw that required modifications to all the DC-10s in service.

In 1989, a United DC-10 crashed during an emergency landing in Sioux City, Iowa. Due to the skill of the captain (Al Haynes) and crew aboard the flight, an emergency landing was executed despite the loss of control of the elevators, ailerons, spoilers, horizontal stabilizer, rudder, flaps, and slats. Miraculously, as a result of the crew's heroic efforts, 185 of the 296 people onboard the aircraft survived. The cause of the accident was fan disk failure of the Number-two (tail) engine, resulting in damage to all three hydraulic system lines.

A DC-10 fleet-wide modification, requiring hydraulic fuses to be installed on all DC-10s, has been made to preclude the loss of hydraulic fluid to all flight controls simultaneously in the event of damage in the tail area.

Author's notes: I have flown more than 6,000 hours as DC-10 captain all over the world. What other jet airliner can you *hand fly* at 40,000 feet at .83 percent of the speed of sound and still maintain your assigned altitude within 50 feet? At that altitude, the DC-10 handles like a DC-3 at 3,000 feet. The DC-10 is a real pleasure to fly.

Landing the DC-10 is a piece of cake. Just observe several landings using the auto-land function of the airplane's autopilot in a coupled ILS approach, and copy that technique. If you imitate the autopilot, you'll make beautiful landings every time.

Finally, the DC-10 cockpit is incredible. It's large and has very comfortable seats with six-way power adjustments; very large windows affording tremendous visibility; and best of all, it's extremely quiet.

Douglas DC-10-30

Specifications and Performance

LENGTH: 171 feet
WINGSPAN: 165 feet
WING Area: 3958 square feet
HEIGHT: 58 feet
EMPTY WEIGHT: 266,200 pounds
MAXIMUM TAKEOFF WEIGHT: 572,000 pounds
ENGINES: GE CF6-50, 50,000 pounds thrust each
NORMAL CRUISE SPEED: 565 MPH mach .82
MAX CRUISING SPEED: 610 MPH mach .88
MAXIMUM RANGE LOADED: 6225 miles
MAXIMUM OPERATING ALTITUDE: 42,000 feet
NUMBER OF PASSENGERS: 380
PRODUCTION: 1968–88

Douglas DC-10

Accidents and Incidents

- November 3, 1973: National Airlines Flight 27, a DC-10-10, experienced an uncontained failure of the right (#3) engine. The cabin was penetrated by shrapnel from the engine and lost pressure. One passenger was killed. The crew initiated an emergency descent, and landed the aircraft safely.
- November 28, 1979: Air New Zealand Flight 901, DC-10-30 ZK-NZP, crashed into Mount Erebus on Ross Island, Antarctica, during a sightseeing flight over the continent, killing all 257 onboard. The accident was caused by the flight coordinates having been altered without the flight crew's knowledge, combined with unique Antarctic weather conditions.
- January 23, 1982: World Airways Flight 30, a DC-10-30CF, registration N113WA, overran the runway at Boston Logan International Airport. All 12 crew survived, but 2 of the 200 passengers were reported missing.
- September 13, 1982: Spantax Flight BX995, DC-10-30CF EC-DEG, was destroyed by fire after an aborted takeoff at Málaga, Spain. Fifty passengers were killed, and 110 passengers were injured by the flames.
- December 23, 1983: Korean Air Cargo Flight 084, DC-10-30CF HL7339, was destroyed after colliding head-on with a Piper PA-31 Navajo while taxiing at Anchorage, Alaska. All onboard both aircraft survived.
- July 27, 1989: Korean Air Flight 803, DC-10-30, registration HL7328 crashed short of the runway in bad weather while trying to land at Tripoli, Libya. A total of 75 of the 199 onboard were killed.

- September 19, 1989: Union des Transports Aériens Flight 772, DC-10-30 N54629, crashed in the Ténéré Desert following an in-flight bomb explosion, claiming the lives of all onboard.
- December 21, 1992: Martinair Flight 495, DC-10-30CF PH-MBN, crashed while landing in bad weather at Faro, Portugal.
- April 7, 1994: FedEx Flight 705, DC-10-30 N306FE, experienced an attempted hijacking. FedEx employee Auburn Calloway tried to hijack the plane, but the crew fought him off and returned to Memphis.
- June 13, 1996: Garuda Indonesia Flight 865, DC-10-30 PK-GIE, had just taken off from Fukuoka Airport, Japan, when a high-pressure blade from engine #3 separated. The aircraft was just a few feet above the runway, and the pilot decided to abort the takeoff. Consequently, the DC-10 skidded off the runway and came to a halt 1,600 ft. (490 m) past the end of it, losing one of its engines and its landing gear.
- January 31, 2001: Japan Airlines Flight 958, bound for Narita International Airport from Gimhae International Airport, nearly collided with another Japan Airlines aircraft. The other aircraft, a Boeing 747, suddenly dove and avoided the Narita-bound DC-10.
- March 26, 2009: an Arrow Air DC-10 en route from Manaus, Brazil, to Bogotá, Colombia, sustained engine failure during flight. Large pieces from the engine fell onto the town of Manaus, damaging 12 houses but causing no injuries. The aircraft managed to land safely in Colombia.

Super Constellation References

"Accident description: Lockheed Constellation N2735A." *aviation-safety.net*, Aviation Safety Network, July 18, 2009. Accessed July 18, 2009.

"Accident description: Lockheed Constellation N3737A." *aviation-safety.net*, Aviation Safety Network, November 1, 2008. Accessed July 18, 2009.

"Accident description: Lockheed Constellation N86504." *aviation-safety.net*, Aviation Safety Network, November 10, 2008. Accessed July 18, 2009.

"Accident description: Lockheed Constellation PH-TER." *Aviation Safety Network*. Accessed January 10, 2011.

"Accident description: Lockheed Constellation PH-TDF." *Aviation Safety Network*. Accessed January 10, 2011.

"Accident description: Lockheed Constellation F-BAZN." *Aviation Safety Network*. Accessed January 10, 2011.

"Accident description: Eastern Airlines Flight 601." *Aviation Safety Network*. Accessed March 11, 2010.

"Accident description: Lockheed Constellation PH-TFF." *Aviation Safety Network*. Accessed January 10, 2011.

"Accident description: Eastern Airlines." *Aviation Safety Network*. Accessed March 11, 2010.

"L-749A 5N85H." *Air Britain Archive,* Issue 2, 2008. Accessed March 25, 2010.

"Accident description: Lockheed R7V-1 Constellation." *Aviation Safety Network*. Accessed January 10, 2011.

"Accident description: Lockheed Super Constellation PH-LKT." *Aviation Safety Network*. Accessed January 10, 2011.

"Accident description: Lockheed Constellation D-ALAK." *Aviation Safety Network*. Accessed January 10, 2011.

"From Avianca to CanJet: MoBay Airport at Centre of J'can Aviation History." *Jamaica Observer*, April 22, 2009. Accessed April 25, 2009.

"Qantas L-1049G Lockheed Constellation." *Aviation Safety Network.* Accessed September 1, 2010.

Wilson, Michael." Slope Plane Crash: Covering the Story." *New York Times,* December 15, 2010. Accessed December 15, 2010.

"Happy Hours Air Travel Club L-1049." *zoggavia.com.* Accessed September 1, 2010.

"Accident description: Lockheed Starliner F-BHBM." *Aviation Safety Network.* Accessed January 10, 2011.

DC-9/MD-80's References

National Transportation Safety Board (1967-12-11). "Aircraft Accident Report. West Coast Airlines, Inc DC-9 N9101.NearWemme,Oregon." http://libraryonline.erau.edu/online-full-text/ntsb/aircraft-accident-reports/AAR67-AF.pdf. Accessed March 22, 2009.

National Transportation Safety Board (1968-06-19). "Aircraft Accident Report. Trans World Airlines, Inc., Douglas DC-9, Tann Company Beechcraft Baron B-55 In-flight Collision near Urbana, Ohio, March 9, 1967." *AirDisaster.Com.* http://www.airdisaster.com/reports/ntsb/AAR68-AI.pdf. Accessed November 23, 2008.

D. Gero (2005-05-21). "ASN Aircraft accident McDonnell Douglas DC-9-32 HI-177 Santo Domingo." *Aviation Safety Network.* Flight Safety Foundation. http://aviation-Safety.net/database/record.php?id=19700215-0. Accessed November 23, 2008

"Former Champ Teo Cruz Dies in Plane Crash." *Modesto Bee.* Associated Press (Modesto, California): p. A-6. 1970-02-16. http://www.newspaperarchive.com/freepdfviewer.aspx?img=43102954. Accessed November 23, 2008

National Transportation Safety Board (1971-03-31). "Aircraft Accident Report: Overseas National Airways, Inc., operating as Antilliaanse Luchtvaart Maatschappij Flight 980, near St. Croix, Virgin Islands, May 2, 1970. DC-9 N935F.". *AirDisaster.Com.* http://www.airdisaster.com/reports/ntsb/AAR71-08.pdf. Accessed November 23, 2008.

National Transportation Safety Board (1978-01-26). "Aircraft Accident Report: Southern Airways, Inc. DC-9-31, N1335U. New Hope, Georgia. April 4, 1977." *AirDisaster. Com.* http://www.airdisaster.com/reports/ntsb/AAR78-03.pdf. Accessed November 23, 2008.

Vanderbilt, Tom (2010-03-12). "When Planes Land on Highways: The ins and outs of a surprisingly frequent phenomenon."

Slate. http://www.slate.com/id/2247545/. Accessed November, 12, 2011

Priest, Lisa; Rick Cash (2005-03-08). "Takeoffs and landings always pose risk of calamity, as history shows" (Fee required.). *Globe & Mail* (Toronto, Ontario, Canada). http://www.theglobeandmail.com/servlet/ArticleNews/TPStory/LAC/20050803/PLANELASTIME03/TPNational/Canada. Accessed November 23, *2008 "The last time an aircraft* skidded off the runway in Toronto, seriously injuring passengers, was more than a quarter-century ago. On June 26, 1978, an Air Canada DC-9 skidded off a taxi strip at Toronto International Airport (what is today Pearson International Airport) during an aborted takeoff, then belly-flopped into a swampy ravine, killing two passengers and injuring more than a hundred others." "ASN Aircraft Accident description of the 14 SEP 1979 accident of a McDonnell Douglas DC-9-32 I-ATJC at Sarroch." *Aviation Safety Network.* Flight Safety Foundation. February 21, 2006. http://aviation-safety.net/database/record.php?id=19790914-1. Accessed November 23, 2008

"ASN Aircraft accident Douglas DC-9-14 N3313L Detroit-Metropolitan Wayne County Airport, Michigan (DTW)." *Aviation Safety Network.* Flight Safety Foundation. November 23, 2008. http://aviation-safety.net/database/record.php?id=19901203-1. Accessed November 23, 2008.

National Transportation Safety Board (1991-06-25). "Aircraft Accident Report: Northwest Airlines Inc. Flights 1482 & 299, Runway Incursion and Collision, Detroit Metropolitan/Wayne County Airport, Romulus, Michigan, December 3, 1990." *AirDisaster.Com.* http://www.airdisaster.com/reports/ntsb/AAR91-05.pdf. Accessed November 23, 2008

"ASN Aircraft accident McDonnell Douglas DC-9-31F XA-TKN Uruapan." Aviation Safety Network. Accessed July 4, 2010.

"Plane crashes into African marketplace." CNN. April 15, 2008. "Toll from Congo plane crash rises to 44." Associated *Press*, Accessed November 20, 2011

DC-8 References

Whittle, John A. (1972). *The McDonnell Douglas DC-8*. Peterborough, Kent: Air-Britain. p. 5. ISBN 0-8513-0024-

"Douglas Passenger Jet Breaks Sound Barrier" DC8.org. August21,1961. http://www.dc8.org/library/supersonic/index. php. Accessed November 10, 2011

"Final UPS DC-8 flight lands at Louisville International Airport". *Business First of Louisville*. May 11, 2009. http://louisville.bizjournals.com/louisville/stories/2009/05/11/daily33. html. Accessed May 13, 2009.

Norris, Guy and Wagner, Mark (1999). *Douglas Jetliners*. MBI Publishing. ISBN 0-7603-0676-1.

"World Airliner Census" (PDF). *Flight International*: 26–49.2010-08-24. http://www.flightglobal.com/assets/getAsset.aspx?ItemID=35827. Accessed November 12, 2011

"Directory: World Air Forces" (PDF). *Flight International*: 52–76. November 11–17, 2008. http://www.flightglobal.com/assets/getasset.aspx?ItemID=26061.

Douglas DC-8 Aviation Safety Network. August 26, 2008. Aviation Safety Network.

Douglas DC-8 Aviation Safety Network. December 3, 2007.

DC-10 References

"DC-10 Family." Boeing Commercial Airplanes. http://www.boeing.com/commercial/dc-10/index.html. Accessed January 4, 2011.

"McDonnell Douglas DC-10/KC-10 Transport." *Boeing.* Accessed February 28, 2006.

Roach, John and Anthony Eastwood. "Jet Airliner Production List, Volume 2." *The Aviation Hobby Shop* online, July 2006. Accessed September 19, 2010.

"Omega Air Refuelling FAQs." *Omega Air Refueling.* Accessed January 11, 2010.

"KC-10 Air Refueling Tanker Aircraft." *Global Airtanker Service.* Accessed January 11, 2010.

"McDonnell Douglas and Federal Express to Launch MD-10 Program." *McDonnell Douglas,* September 16, 1996. Accessed February 9, 2007.

"DC-10 list." *Planelist.net.* Accessed January 11, 2010.

"Biman Bangladesh Airlines Details and Fleet History." *Planespotters.net.* Accessed June 21, 2009.

Sarsfield, Kate. "Firefighting DC-10 available to lease." *Flight International,* March 30, 2009.

Kaminski-Morrow, David. "Orbis to convert ex-United DC-10-30 into new airborne eye hospital." *Flight International,* April 8, 2008.

"ORBIS Flying Eye Hospital Visits Los Angeles to Collaborate with MD-10 Project Supporters." *Orbis.org.* Accessed July 11, 2010.

"The ORBIS MD-10 Project." *Orbis.org.* Accessed September 19, 2010.

"ORBIS Launches MD-10 Flying Eye Hospital Project." *slideshare.net.* Accessed September 19, 2010.

"World Airliner Census" *Flight International,* August 18–24, 2009.

"McDonnell Douglas DC-10 incidents." *Aviation-Safety.net.* Accessed August 27, 2009.

"McDonnell Douglas DC-10 hull-losses." *Aviation-Safety. net.* Accessed August 27, 2009.

"McDonnell Douglas DC-10 Statistics." *Aviation-Safety.net.* Accessed January 11, 2010.

Hopfinger, Tony. "I Will Survive: Laurence Gonzales: 'Who Lives, Who Dies, and Why." *Anchorage Press,* October 23–29, 2003. Accessed August 27, 2009.

"Statistical Summary of Commercial Jet Airplane Accidents (1959–2008)." *Boeing.* Accessed January 11, 2010.

NTSB-AAR-73-02 Report, "Aircraft Accident Report: American Airlines, Inc. McDonnell Douglas DC-10-10, N103AA. Near Windsor, Ontario, Canada. June 12, 1972." Washington DC: National Transportation Safety Board. February 28, 1973.

"Behind Closed Doors." *Air Crash Investigation, Mayday (TV series)* National Geographic Channel, Season 5, Number 2.

"Turkish Airlines DC-10, TC-JAV. Report on the accident in the Ermenonville Forest, France on March 3, 1974." *UK Air Accidents Investigation Branch (AAIB),* February 1976.

"American Airlines 191." *airdisaster.com.* Accessed January 11, 2010.

"Aircraft Accident report, DC-10-10, N110A, NTSB, 1979." *libraryonline.erau.edu.* Accessed September 19, 2010.

"Flight 191 accident description." *Aviation-Safety.net.* Accessed January 11, 2010.

"NTSB/AAR-90/06, Aircraft Accident Report United Airlines Flight 232, McDonnell Douglas DC-10-40, Sioux Gateway Airport, Sioux City, Iowa, July 19, 1989." *NTSB,* November 1, 1990.

"NTSB/Safety Recommendation to FAA" NTSB, August 21, 2003.

"DC-10 accident entry: July 27, 1989." *Aviation Safety Network.* Accessed July 11, 2010.

Kaminski-Morrow, David. "Arrow Cargo DC-10 sheds large engine parts over Manaus." *Flight International.* Accessed March 27, 2009.

"DC-10 history page." *Boeing.* Accessed January 11, 2010.

"The McDonnell Douglas DC-10 & Boeing MD-10." *Airliners.net.* Accessed September 19, 2010.

"McDonnell Douglas DC-10-10F." *Flight International.* Accessed January 11, 2010.

Super Constellation Bibliography

Boyne, Walter J. *Beyond the Horizons: The Lockheed Story.* New York: St. Martin's Press, 1998. ISBN 0-31224-438-X.

- Cacutt, Len, ed. "Lockheed Constellation." *Great Aircraft of the World.* London: Marshall Cavendish, 1989. ISBN 1-85435-250-4.
- Germain, Scott E. Lockheed Constellation *and Super Constellation.* North Branch, Minnesota: Specialty Press, 1998. ISBN 1-58007-000-0.
- Marson, Peter J. *The Lockheed Constellation Series.* Tonbridge, Kent, UK: Air-Britain (Historians), 1982. ISBN 0-85130-100-2.

C-46 Bibliography

- Bowers, Peter M. *Curtiss Aircraft, 1907-1947.* London: Putnam & Company Ltd., 1979. ISBN 0-370-10029-8.
- Davis, John M., Harold G. Martin and John A. Whittle. *The Curtiss C-46 Commando.* Tonbridge, Kent, UK: Air-Britain (Historians) Ltd., 1978. ISBN 0-85130-065-0.
- Johnson, E.R. "The Airliner that Went to War." *Aviation History* Vol. 18, no. 1, September 2007.
- Love, Terry. C-46 *Commando in Action.* Carrollton, Texas: Squadron/Signal Publications, 2003. ISBN 0-89747-452-X.

DC-10 Bibliography

- Endres, Günter. *McDonnell Douglas DC-10*. Osceola, WI: MBI Publishing Company, 1998. ISBN 0-7603-0617-6.
- Fielder, J.H. and D. Birsch. *The DC-10 Case: A study in Applied Ethics, Technology, and Society*. Albany, NY: SUNY Press, 1992. ISBN 0-79141-087-0.

Index

Accra, 92
Aerolineas Latinas, 140
AFN Verdun, 10
Air France F-BELI, 25
Alaska, 196
Alaska flight-261, 257
Appendix, 235
Argentina, 109
At the Right Place at the
    Right Time, 59
Atomic Bomb, 187
A-320, 167
Back in the Saddle
    Again, 140
ballast rock, 206
ball lightning, 32
barber pole, 144
Bartho, Bob, 217
Bates, Al, 28
Beech D-18, 47
Berko, Antal (Tony), 31
Berlin Corridor, 24
Biafra, 16
Bioren, Bob, 28
Board of Directors
    ALPA, 120
Bogata, Approach
    in fog, 149

Boredom and Terror, 145
bomb proof, 63
Brock,Allen, 209
BVI's, 203
Capitol C-46, 22
captain's meal, 69
Cessna-185, 195
Challenge of my Career. 75
Chimehuin River, 111
chairmen of the -
    negotiating committee, 120
civilian approach to flight
    training, 219
Happy birthday shave, 120
C-46, 245
C-46 specifications, 247
C-46 accidents, 248
DC-4, 243
DC-4 specifications, 244
DC-8, 269
DC-8; specifications, 271
DC-8 accidents, 272
DC-9, 251
DC-9 specifications, 253
DC-9 accidents, 254
DC-10, 275
DC-10 performance, 277
DC-10 accidents, 278

deicing Moscow,157
demeanor, 227
diving, treasure, 70
drug testing, 77, 217
drug use, 217
Down the primrose path, 184
Eagan, Fred, 109
East Meets West, 171
Ecuador, 142
Escobar, Pablo,143
ethical, 218, 228
Expect the Unexpected, 180
FAA designated
    check pilot, 163
ferry, 3-engine, Accra–
    Madrid, 93
ferry JFK–Boston, 85
first transatlantic
    Jet flight, 89
Fishman, Marty, 49
Fismer, Carl, 70
flight instructor-
    license, 12, 223
Flying the Line, 89
Forbes, Scotty, 45
French Foreign legion, 97
French Red Cross, 20
French Secret Service, 18
Fuel Burn Chart, 175
Gander, 82
Glossary, 231
Graber, Julius, 18
Grand Bazaar, 160
Great American, 187
Gourmets, 138

Guardian angel, 79, 82, 148
Hairpiece, 61
Ham radio-Greenland, 9
Harpole, John, 79-84, 142
Hassi Massoud, 21
Hawknest Bay, 214
Honeymooners, 138
honeytrap, 161
Hosteria Chimehuin, 113
How to become an airline
    pilot, 217
Hydraulic motor-
    jack screw, 147
IG Farben, 42
In and Out of Africa, 92
INS, 124, 127
Islamorada, 209
Istanbul, 159
Jamaica, New York, 1
JATO, 51
Jet Lag, 201
Johnson, Sam, 64
Junin de Los Andes, 111
Keeping a Sharp-Lookout, 176
Kimchee, 174
Korean Airlines, 171
Korean Aviation Law, 182
Kugler, Jim, 32
Lago Huechulaufquen, 114
Lane Older, 195
Leisure Air, 162
Lockheed Super constellation-
    1049, 15, 236
Malaga Spain, 69
Mantle, Mickey, 46

Mapuche language, 111
Marks, Robert, 72
Martin, Auggie, 21
MIG-19 Jet fighter, 25
McNichols, Mac, 153,171
McNulty, Dick, 26
Milan Malpensa, 37
military training-
     approach, 218
Mom, 3-4
Money Bay, 206, 208
Morgan, Sally and
     Charlie, 201
Mortenson, Frank, 10
Moscow, 155
Murphy's Law, 32
Negotiating with-
     Korean Air, 178
Niamey Niger, 97
Nigerian Civil War, 16
Norman Island, 206
Overseas National-
     Airlines, 50
ONA ditching, 52, 254
Pan Am N-317PA, 25
Parents, (my) 4, 7
Pate, Billy, 115
Persistence, 14, 228
personal characteristics of
     airline pilots, 218
personal grooming, 228
Pickett, Lucien, 15, 21
Piper Cub J-3, 5
pitot heat inop, 67
Port Harcourt, 16

Prince Radziwill, Charles, 113
Project Dew Drop, 7
PTC, 146
Qualifications to become
     airline pilot, 217-229
Red Hook, 203
Respass, John, 94
Ritz, Charles, 114
Rome Airport, 82
Russian ATC, 156
Ryan Airlines, 194
San Carlos de Bariloche, 110
SAT- missions, 156
Savacool, Bob, 140
Scene of the Crash, 1
Sebastion Inlet, 71
Sembach military aeroclub, 5
Serranilla Banks
     Sharks, 72
Seasoning of an Airline-
     Pilot, 31
snorkel and dive with-
     sharks, 204-208
Southern Air Transport, 155
Sperry Flight Director, 83
Spies, 161
St. John, 203
St. Croix ditching-
     ONA, 52, 254
Stacy, Harry, 5, 13
Stampe-biplane, 11
Swiss Hotel, 160
TCAS resolution-
     advisory, 193
The Jet Age Arrives, 45

The most exciting flight of
    my life, 85
The Last Great Cowboys, 187
The Perfect Co-pilot, 124
The Wine Tasters, 137
The 2¾ Engine Ferry, 93
Transtar Airlines, 153
troopship, 6
UAL flight-232, 276

UFO, 117
ULI Nigeria, 22
US Airways Frankfurt
    Germany, 15
Wendover AAF base, 187
Wharton, Hank, aka-
    Heinrich Wartski, 19
Wine tasters, 137
work ethic, 228

About the Author

PJ Spivack continues to enjoy flying, fly-fishing, sailing, amateur radio and flight instructing. He lives in Seattle.

Still boring holes in the sky, well into retirement circa 2010.

13547465R00182

Made in the USA
Charleston, SC
16 July 2012